PENGUIN BOOKS

BLACK LIVINGSTONE

Pagan Kennedy is the author of seven books, including her most recent novel, *The Exes*. She is the recipient of a grant from the National Endowment of the Arts, and was shortlisted for the Orange Prize for Fiction, Britain's prestigious literary award. She lives outside of Boston.

Praise for *Black Livingstone*

"This is a gripping tale. Pagan Kennedy takes us through William Sheppard's extraordinary adventures and eventful life with humor, insight and elegance."
—Michela Wrong, author of *In the Footsteps of Mr. Kurtz*

"The connection Kennedy establishes with her subject has little to do with race, creed, or region. It's a kinship of the imagination, and it's in this respect that *Black Livingstone* is most fun."
—*The New York Times Book Review*

"Kennedy resists the temptation to inflict a politically correct paradigm on her story and simply lets it tell itself—which it does, compellingly. The result is a page-turner that illuminates while it breaks the heart."
—*The Philadelphia Enquirer*

"[Pagan Kennedy] restores a forgotten life, crafting an enticing portrait of a man whose accomplishments defied the narrow and racist limitations of his times."
—*The Boston Globe*

"Long forgotten and ignored, Sheppard's story has been rescued from obscurity by Pagan Kennedy's lively and engaging narrative."
—*Boston Herald*

"Kennedy offers a smoothly written tale of Sheppard's life and is to be commended for bringing his extraordinary story to greater prominence."
—*The Washington Post*

"Kennedy has managed to piece together an admiring biography of a charismatic pioneer who circumvented racism, slew hippos, outwitted cannibals, and helped liberate Africans from the worst of colonialism."
—*Pages*

"The author's enthusiasm for her subject is infections and makes the book an engaging, quick read."
—*Houston Chronicle*

Black Livingstone

A True Tale of Adventure in the Nineteenth-Century Congo

PAGAN KENNEDY

PENGUIN BOOKS

PENGUIN BOOKS
Published by the Penguin Group
Penguin Putnam Inc., 375 Hudson Street, New York, New York 10014, U.S.A.
Penguin Books Ltd, 80 Strand, London WC2R 0RL, England
Penguin Books Australia Ltd, 250 Camberwell Road, Camberwell, Victoria 3124, Australia
Penguin Books Canada Ltd, 10 Alcorn Avenue, Toronto, Ontario, Canada M4V 3B2
Penguin Books India (P) Ltd, 11 Community Centre,
Panchsheel Park, New Delhi – 110 017, India
Penguin Books (N.Z.) Ltd, Cnr Rosedale and Airborne Roads,
Albany, Auckland, New Zealand
Penguin Books (South Africa) (Pty) Ltd, 24 Sturdee Avenue,
Rosebank, Johannesburg 2196, South Africa

Penguin Books Ltd, Registered Offices:
Harmondsworth, Middlesex, England

First published in the United States of America by Viking Penguin,
a member of Penguin Putnam Inc. 2002
Published in Penguin Books 2003

1 3 5 7 9 10 8 6 4 2

THE LIBRARY OF CONGRESS HAS CATALOGED THE HARDCOVER EDITION AS FOLLOWS:
Kennedy, Pagan, date.
Black Livingstone : a true tale of adventure in
the nineteenth-century Congo / Pagan Kennedy.
p.   cm.
Includes bibliographical references (p.) and index.
ISBN 0-670-03036-8 (hc.)
ISBN 0 14 20.0176 7 (pbk.)
1. Sheppard, William H. (William Henry), 1865–1927.   2. African American
missionaries—Congo (Democratic Republic)—Biography.   3. Missionaries—Congo
(Democratic Republic)—Biography.   4. African American Presbyterians—Congo
(Democratic Republic)—Biography.   5. Presbyterians—Congo (Democratic Republic)—
Biography.   6. African American missionaries—Biography.   7. Missionaries—United
States—Biography.   8. African American Presbyterians—Biography.   9. Presbyterians—
United States—Biography.   10. Presbyterian Church in the U.S.—Missions—
Congo (Democratic Republic)—History.   I. Title.
BV3625.C63 S544 2002
266'.51'092—dc21
[B]   ·   2001026096

Printed in the United States of America
Set in Adobe Caslon
Designed by Nancy Resnick

To my sister,
who worked to prevent famine in Angola,
stayed as the country collapsed,
and evacuated only when bombs began to fall

An engraving shows Luebo as it would have appeared to Sheppard and Lapsley when they first arrived in 1891.

Engraving by C. S. Latrobe Bateman

THE CROSS

God laid upon my back a grievous load,
A heavy cross to bear along the road;
I staggered on, till lo! One weary day,
An angry lion leaped across my way.
I prayed to God, and swift at His command
The cross became a weapon in my hand;
It slew my raging enemy, and then
It leaped upon my back a cross again!
I faltered many a league, until at length,
Groaning, I fell and found no further strength.
I cried, "Oh God! I am so weak and lame,"
And swift the cross a winged staff became.
It swept me on until I retrieved my loss,
Then leaped upon my back again a cross.
I reached a desert; on its burning track
I still perceived the cross upon my back.
No shade was there, and in the burning sun
I sank me down and thought my day was done;
But God's grace works many a sweet surprise.
The cross became a tree before mine eyes.
I slept, awoke, and had the strength of ten,
Then felt the cross upon my back again.
And thus through all my days, from that to this,
The cross, my burden, has become my bliss;
Nor shall I ever lay my burden down,
For God shall one day make my cross a crown.

—*William Henry Sheppard*

CONTENTS

INTRODUCTION

I met William Henry Sheppard in a book. Though he'd been dead seventy years and now consisted of nothing but a few pages of text in a well-thumbed paperback, he swept into my life with all the urgency of a new lover. The book in question was *Ota Benga: The Pygmy in the Zoo* by Harvey Blume and Phillips Verner Bradford. Sheppard was only a minor character in the nonfiction epic, and truthfully, the authors could have left him out if they had wanted to—he was tangential to their story.

But what author could pass up a character like William Sheppard? At the turn of the century, he had traveled deep into the Congo jungle in search of the hidden kingdom. Once he found his way into the capital city—the first Westerner ever to do so—he was hailed as a reincarnated prince by its people.

The story had all the hallmarks of an MGM movie from the 1930s— an Afrocentric retelling of *Lost Horizon,* perhaps. And it was only the first episode in Sheppard's incredible life—the prelude to his trips to the White House, his one-man intervention in a massacre, his international fame as a witness against the atrocities of the Belgian regime. I had to know more about this astonishing, lost hero—this black American missionary. But when I searched him out, I discovered that little had been written about Sheppard. He appeared now and then in books about the Congo, but always as one character among many, like a blurry face in a group photo.

I kept thinking he should have his own book, and I assumed someone else would write it someday. The author would be an Africa specialist with a flair for embellishment, preferably a man, preferably an African American. He would work on the book during his sabbatical from Harvard, getting graduate students to help him with the extensive research; he'd travel to the Congo, retrace Sheppard's steps. I certainly was not equipped to take on the job; and as a white woman I wasn't sure that I had the insight to portray a black man during the Jim Crow period. Furthermore, I felt uncomfortable about intruding into African American history.

Eventually, I discovered that Sheppard *did* have his own book—an autobiography, of sorts. The copy of it that I managed to track down was a slim volume, rebound some years back to protect its decaying spine, little more than a tract, called *Presbyterian Pioneers in Congo*. It was put out by the church in 1917.

Here he was, the real Sheppard—in his own words. I read the whole book at a coffee shop next to the library, the chatter and clatter of the place drowned out by Sheppard's humorous, fanciful prose. The book had been adapted from the lectures he gave when he toured the country in the 1890s and again in the 1910s, when he billed himself as "Black Livingstone," an explorer returned from Africa. To understand what the book is like, you have to imagine him pacing on the stage before a meeting hall strung with newfangled electric lights, charming a crowd (the blacks up in the balcony, the whites down front). He coaxes them into laughter, and then suddenly swoops into tragedy, prompting more than a few ladies to pull out linen hankies. Sheppard knows himself to be a great entertainer and a great curiosity—a man who's survived Africa (few went, and one out of three did not make it home). He's returned with anecdotes about crocodile attacks and bronze-colored queens, tattooed faces and filed teeth. It is the era of Horatio Alger and Booker T.

Washington, of snake oil and Chautauqua, of steam and coal and vast, humming machines, of magical exhibitions and the miracle of new wealth. It is also the era of Jim Crow.

In his book, Sheppard tiptoes around race issues, and who can blame him? In the first year he went on the speaking circuit, more than a hundred blacks were recorded as lynched. So Sheppard's account of his childhood in America is, above all, polite. But when he describes Africa, his prose changes; he suddenly shifts into high gear, becoming fable-ist, fabulist, and picaresque hero. He tells how eating eggs helped him to navigate the secret trails of Africa. He displays the African executioner's knife that was nearly used on his own neck. He seduces his audience with exotica: "We saw a rain-maker . . . dressed up in leopard skins and his hair filled with hawk feathers, and in his hand were a buffalo tail and a sprig of a tree."

Indeed, Sheppard *was* a black Livingstone, a man caught between the nineteenth century and the twentieth, between white colonialism and black pride. Like Livingstone, the famous English missionary, he brought home an Africa scented with the perfume of palm wine—an exotic Beyond the Looking Glass, a mirror-image land. But unlike Livingstone, he often treated Congo culture as the equal of his own. He forced his audience to reckon with an idea that W. E. B. Du Bois would expand upon in 1946 when that leader wrote, "Here is a history of the world written from the African point of view." Sheppard had stepped through the looking glass, gazed back at his own country through African eyes, and begun to question which point of view was real.

I wondered who this marvelous man had been in private, and what made him die of paralysis and apparent heartbreak at the age of sixty-one. Such mysteries drove me to special-order books from obscure libraries, books that arrived swaddled in beautiful jackets with little notes inside them: "Very delicate condition. Use extreme care in handling."

I had to solve this puzzle. I had to understand him. For—and I couldn't say why—as I read Sheppard's writings, I began to believe that he held a key to my own history. Perhaps he could answer the riddle that had dogged me ever since I was a girl: When you stripped off the hoop skirts and crinoline of my father's illusions, who were we?

Like Sheppard's people, mine had been Presbyterians from Virginia. They had been senators, lawyers, doctors, poets, officers of the Confederate government—and slaveowners. In our family's history and letters, black people survived only as shadows. In the margins of our stories were hints of their story. A mammy who tended children all through the shuttered, sweltering nights of Civil War fever. A quadroon who insisted on having her fun in town, until the master threatened to sell her down river. Sis, the hunchback housemaid, much loved by the Virginia aristocrats. Who had these people been? And did anything remain of their stories now, besides the brief sketches in my family's history?

I was drawn to Sheppard partly because his voice sounded so much like the voices I'd been raised around, particularly my grandmother's. It was not just that he and she shared a certain antique Virginia accent; they both used the same trick of ladling humor over the painful truth, the way you'd pour gravy over rock-hard biscuits to soften them up.

My grandmother had been more or less abandoned as a child. When her own mother died, she was sent up to live with cousins she hardly knew on an impoverished plantation, where the elegant furniture rotted into dust. She survived by making up "family anecdotes"—tales that she constructed, memorized, and warehoused in her head. She could still reel them off at age ninety: How Ida Sissons baked a birthday cake covered with bugs. How Cousin Violet came to write an epic poem called "Sheep I Have Known." How her grandfather, a beetle-browed man with a beard like a prophet, told her God would smite her if she stole sugar from the pantry.

These are exactly the kind of tales Sheppard invented about his own life, stories that weave around like Brer Rabbit in the briar patch, through tragedy and comedy, always ending in a punch line. Also like my grandmother, he was obsessed with a very Presbyterian theme: the power of charm and social connections to overcome most any obstacle.

But alike as they were, Sheppard and my grandmother never could have met as equals. They never could have eaten at the same table, saying, "May I trouble you for the salt?" as they handed around the foods they both loved: day-old grits, sweet potatoes and ham crusted in brown sugar.

I wrote my grandmother about Sheppard. My letter flew between Boston and Virginia, where it would be sorted into a cubbyhole in the nursing home and carried up to her room—all that was the easy part of the message's journey. Because my grandmother was blind and nearly deaf, someone would have to shout every word of it into her ear, repeating syllables over and over again until she understood.

Soon after I sent the letter, I got a call from my mom. "Your grandmother seems very determined to tell you something," she said. "It's about your project."

Next time I visited, I found Grandma weaker than I remembered, but still elegant in her own particular way. Her coifed hair once curled in white waves around her forehead; now it was combined in a single poof. Her pale blue eyes seemed to be set like jewels into the folds of her face.

"Did you want to tell me something about the Congo?" I yelled into her ear.

"What?" she said, straining from the pillow. "Can you go?"

"No, the Congo," I tried again. It cracked my heart, this business of communicating. Many years ago, back when she could still hear perfectly, I'd tried to talk to her through a phone I made from Dixie cups and thread. My grandmother had hidden behind a door, connected to me only by a length of delicate thread. She'd patiently waited for my message.

Now, finally, I managed to make her understand. "Congo, oh yes," she said, squeezing her eyes, trying to imagine the rest of my sentence. "There was a Bedinger who was a missionary there." Bedinger had been my grandmother's maiden name. Someone in her family had once gone to the Congo. That was all she could tell me.

Back in Boston, I thought I might have found him: A man named Robert Dabney Bedinger, author of *Presbyterian Triumphs in the Congo*, had gone to the Congo one year after Sheppard left. He'd lived in the station founded by Sheppard, worked with many of the same colleagues, ministered to the Sheppards' beloved Kuba tribe. A call to my Great-aunt Rickie confirmed my suspicions: "Yes," she responded when I gave her the name. "Robert Dabney Bedinger was your grandmother's first cousin."

I was disinclined to like Robert Dabney Bedinger, suspicious as I was of all my ancestors, that confederacy of the dead whose behavior caused me no end of shame. But when I dug up Bedinger's privately published memoirs, I was pleasantly surprised. Written in a voice I knew, the lilting Virginia-smoked language of my grandparents, were words I thought I'd never hear from an ancestor. He admitted, at least in some small way, his own prejudice.

On his first trip to Africa in 1911, Bedinger had been treated with great kindness by a black couple named the Edmistons. These experienced missionaries had worked with the famous William Sheppard and would now labor alongside the young white man from Kentucky. On the ship to London, the Edmistons tried to make the newcomer feel welcome.

"Mr. Edmiston told me that they had arranged with the deck steward to place my chair alongside theirs and had also consulted the dining room steward to give me a place at their table," Bedinger wrote. "I thanked him and then did something which brought me shame and remorse even down to this day. I had my chair placed on the other side of the ship and had my place in the dining room changed to another table." Young Bedinger had never eaten at the same table as black people before.

He continued to wrestle with himself in London:

The Edmistons were warmly welcomed and I was shown every courtesy, but I did not feel at home. For one month the Edmistons and I walked the streets of London and purchased our tropical outfits in various shops. The merchants and clerks seemed to me unusually familiar with the Edmistons, but scarcely noticed me. I did not have the sense to realize that this was natural, because they had been there before and were meeting old friends. Every day we lunched together. I noticed that my Negro friends were served first.

A feeling of deep resentment began to well up within me. . . . I did not feel worthy to be a representative of Christ to the Africans. . . . In sheer desperation I . . . walked the streets of London for hours thinking and praying and trying to repent for my sin of racial prejudice. At last on a lonely street I stopped at a lamp post, knelt beside it and pleaded with God. . . . He heard my cry.

Bedinger lost his racism—or claimed to—after that walk through London. Thereafter, he devoted himself to publicizing the work of his black colleagues, hoping that people back home would finally appreciate their accomplishments. As he traveled through the Kasai region of the Congo, he gathered stories about the history of Presbyterians there, and of Sheppard. Victorian in sentiment, the texts are little better than Sunday school tracts. Still, Bedinger may have been the first person to write up a formal biography of Sheppard. And the Sheppard story was so important to him that he quoted from it at length in his own autobiography—as if the mystery of himself hinged on the black missionary who had gone before him.

Why were my ancestor and I both drawn to Sheppard's story? I can only speak for myself. I am fascinated—as I think most people will be, regardless of their background—with the way this man managed to mold his own identity. In America, Sheppard was considered black or mulatto; meanwhile, in Africa, he nearly lost his life several times because the Congolese had decided he was just another Caucasian invader. The hero himself, zigzagging between identities, grew so disoriented about race that he insisted African babies were born white—only after a few weeks of being pale did the youngster turn black. As for his own son, he gave the boy two names: Lapsley, for the white American who'd been one of his closest friends; and Maxamalinge, for an African prince. But it was Sheppard himself who had the double nature, existing in a nebulous no-man's-land where he acted according to some inner script, his own inimitable self.

Sheppard never fought American racism head-on. Instead, he challenged it the way a cross-dresser challenges gender. In drag as a colonial Brit—pith helmet, linens, and puttees—he roamed the outback with a rifle across his shoulder. During a time when American blacks were being exterminated by the thousands, were robbed of their rights to travel, were dissected in labs, brains weighed and analyzed to prove inferiority, Sheppard dared to be himself. It was the boldest and the bravest of his adventures.

PART I

Into the Forbidden Kingdom

CHAPTER 1

"When I Grow Up I Shall Go There"

In February 1890, on a New York pier, Sam Lapsley said his last good-byes to his parents. Then the wan young man with a dusting of blond hair climbed the gangway of the steamship *Adriatic*. "I felt as I never had in my life, when I saw you walk out of sight in the great shed," the twenty-three-year-old missionary wrote to his parents only hours after the vessel set sail. "I thought I saw you again on the Battery, and waved, and ran, and tried to see better, but lost you. I didn't know how much I loved you till today."

Lapsley's partner—another missionary, twenty-four years old—stood beside him at the rail of the ship, and the two watched the New York skyline recede into the distance. William Sheppard's coat appeared cheap and tattered next to his partner's; nonetheless, he was the more striking man—tall, with magnificent shoulders and a ready laugh. As the *Adriatic* pulled away, Lapsley's mother cried out, "Sheppard, take care of Sam." Almost thirty years later, Sheppard would remember her entreaty, and he would imagine what Lapsley's parents must have suffered after the steamship disappeared in the distance: "Judge Lapsley and his wife returned to their home in Alabama—that home had changed. There was a vacant chair and a voice that was not heard."

In typical Victorian fashion, both Sheppard and Lapsley recorded little of what happened on that day besides the parting between Sam and his parents, milking the scene for all the sentimental frisson it would have held for readers of the period.

Neither man remarked on what fascinates the modern observer: Lapsley was white; Sheppard, black. During one of the most cruelly racist periods in American history, when Jim Crow laws segregated everything from hotels to factory floors, the two men planned to travel through Africa as equal partners. Though it would have been illegal for them to ride together through some parts of the United States in the same train car, in the Congo they would sleep in the same tent, trade clothing, and nurse each other through fevers. The Southern Presbyterian Church, itself segregated into white and "colored" denominations, would pay each man the same salary. Whether they knew it or not, Sheppard and Lapsley would not only explore unmapped regions of the Congo, but also pioneer a new kind of relationship between the races.

That the men were traveling together at all was a miracle. A significant faction in the Presbyterian Church had opposed the hiring of a black missionary, arguing that blacks were morally unfit to live among "savages" and too slow to learn new languages. Even those kindly disposed to Sheppard did not expect much from him: Church leaders assumed it would be Lapsley who would oversee the American Presbyterian mission in the Congo, that it would be Lapsley who would perhaps achieve international fame. They were wrong.

William Henry Sheppard was born in Virginia near the end of the Civil War—March 8, 1865—a time and place in which black people might dare to be hopeful. One historian has called the period between 1867 and 1877 the "improbable years," when educated blacks became mayors, judges, and professors; schools were integrated; and some states recognized interracial marriages. What was the magic ingredient that allowed blacks to advance so quickly during that decade? Northern soldiers. In the decade after the Civil War, the federal government maintained a military presence in the territory it had defeated, intent on keeping the South from rising again. The North stripped former Confederates of their power and broke up old political machines. This allowed a coalition of educated blacks and progressive whites to enter state governments and reimagine what the South should and could be.

In Virginia during that miraculous decade, blacks had so much clout that even the Conservative Party could not hope to win elections without their votes. That is why, one summer day in 1869, the Conservatives sponsored a lavish barbecue for Richmond's elite blacks on a small island near the city. The picnic on Kitchen Island, with cicadas buzzing and the smell of cornbread on the grill, hardly ranks as one of the important historical events of Reconstruction; in fact, it is just one of the many forgettable moments of the era. And yet what happened that day tells us much about race relations at the end of the 1860s, about the swoop of hope and its quick collapse into tragedy.

That afternoon a crowd of three hundred—roughly half white and half black—gathered for the party. The island could only be reached by walking over a suspension bridge, and the lucky few with tickets presented them to a policeman and strolled across. Everyone else had to wait, swarming against a fence, for they were near enough to Kitchen Island to see what looked like an open bar, to smell the sizzling meats on the grill, and to hear the strains of a dance band that was just tuning up. They could see a banner unfurling between the tall trees; it showed a black man and a white man shaking hands, and it read, "United We Stand, Divided We Fall." The integrated crowd pressed closer together, straining toward that island of peace and plenty.

When the policeman finally opened the gate, sixty or so people swarmed onto the bridge at once. The wooden beams and steel chains swayed under their weight. Across the way, a white political candidate stood at the entrance to the island, waiting to greet them. "There's plenty for everyone," he called, "come across." Then, suddenly, one of the iron suspension chains broke free from its joist, whipping into the air. It flicked the politician into the water, where he drowned. Around him, people who'd fallen off the bridge flailed in the shallows, some of them trapped under broken beams.

A black barber who'd been watching from the shore plunged into the water and pulled several victims to safety. Another barber yelled at the onlookers to maintain proper decorum, to have some respect for the dead and the hurt.

Two bodies were carried to a bowling alley on the island, and the injured were helped back to town. For days afterward, Richmond mourned.

Reconstruction tends to be remembered as a time of race hatred and deep cynicism, a time when carpetbaggers descended from the North to buy up land and ragged ex-slaves sold their votes to shady politicians. This is only part of the truth.

Reconstruction was also like that picnic on Kitchen Island. For a moment, it had seemed possible for black and white people to march under a united banner, toward an enlightened future. In the late 1860s in Virginia, black delegates brought radical new ideas to the state's House of Delegates. Dr. Thomas Bayne, for instance, was an erudite dentist who wore elegant cutaway coats, and chided the Richmond newspapers for their racist comments. He and his colleagues envisioned a future of Jeffersonian dimensions, a democracy in which all men participated. The black delegates designed a public educational system and new way to vote—the secret ballot, which had never before been used in the United States.

But the bridge these visionaries planned to walk across was shaky indeed. They counted on the federal government to hold them up on their march to freedom, but by the mid-1870s Uncle Sam had other ideas. The Northern troops marched home, and with them went the firepower that had enforced equal rights. Almost immediately, the South slid into what it had been before the war. In 1876, Virginia instituted a poll tax that barred most blacks from voting. In the late '70s, the newly opened black schools began closing for lack of funds. In 1878, mixed marriages were proclaimed illegal. And by the end of the century, even the railroads—last bastion of integration—had been outfitted with Jim Crow cars.

Had William Henry Sheppard Sr. lived in Richmond rather than a hundred miles away, he might well have been among the men on Kitchen Island; instead, he was raising his family in Waynesboro, Virginia, a whistle-stop town on the railroad line. But though he didn't have much occasion to travel to Richmond, William Sr. was the kind of man who might have shown up at a Conservative Party fund-raiser. Like the two heroes of Kitchen Island, William Sr. worked as a barber. Most blacks had passed from slavery to sharecropping without much of a change in their fortunes, but a few had managed to rise out of poverty. Best off were undertakers, barbers, hairdressers, and others who rendered services to rich whites.

In a photo taken late in his life, William Sr. appears every inch the puritan, a biblical white beard flowing down over his stiff suit. He served in the town's First Presbyterian Church as a sexton, and was an imposing, strict man. "I was afraid of him and [his son William] was afraid of him, too," his grandnephew admitted in an interview many years later.

William Sr. ran his own shop; like so many barbers, he considered it part of his job to entertain his clients with conversation. While the men lay supine and swaddled under towels, the barber chatted with them about the latest news. It was an impressive performance. Because of his prodigious memory, William Sr. was able to rattle off the contents of the newspaper, which he had a literate friend read to him every morning. Few of his clients knew that their well-spoken barber could not read a word.

His wife, Fannie, appears to have been just as proper as her husband—in one photo, she wears delicate wire-framed glasses and an elaborate flounce at her collar. She worked an upscale job, tending ladies as a bath maid at Warm Springs Spa. As a mulatto freedwoman, she had never suffered the indignities of slavery. In the Augusta County Register of Free Blacks, Sarah Frances Martin is catalogued as "twenty-six years of age, . . . of dark mulatto complexion, has a long scar on the left elbow and was born free."

Had her husband also been free? A grandson, interviewed in 1980, could not say. A grandnephew also did not seem to know, though he kept Fannie's free papers in a safe as a memento. If William Sr. had suffered as a slave, he never spoke of it to the young people in his family. And the children were too afraid of the gruff old Presbyterian to press him for details.

According to American law, slavery was passed along from mother to children, and so it was not surprising that Fannie's status mattered more to the family than did her husband's. Because of her freedom, neither her daughter, Eva, nor her son, William, could have been made slaves—though since the boy was born just as the Confederacy collapsed, the question only applied for the first month of his life.

If the post–Civil War period can be said to have had a black lower middle class, the Sheppards were part of it. They fared better, at least materially, than even some of the whites in Waynesboro. "Mother never turned anyone from her door who came begging, whether white or colored," her son remembers in his autobiographical book, *Presbyterian Pioneers in Congo.*

Still, William had to become a tough little boy. Accounts from the late nineteenth century attest that black children suffered a moment of awakening when they realized the amount of hatred directed at them. Perhaps the most eloquent account of this terrible epiphany is W. E. B. Du Bois's:

> In a wee wooden schoolhouse, something put it into the boys' and girls' heads to buy gorgeous visiting-cards—ten cents a package—and exchange. The exchange was merry,

till one girl, a tall newcomer, refused my card—refused it peremptorily, with a glance. Then it dawned upon me with a certain suddenness that I was different from the others . . . shut out from their world by a vast veil.

Sheppard never alludes to this veil that must have descended over him when he was a boy; more than that, he denies its very existence. "The white people were always very kind to us—as they were to all the colored people," he writes of his childhood in Waynesboro.

It's important to remember that Sheppard could not speak as freely as Du Bois. Throughout his life, he was most passionate about helping the people of the Congo—by raising donations and encouraging others to volunteer as missionaries. Even when he sat down to write his life story, he had fund-raising in mind: In fact, one version of his autobiography was published as a kind of public relations pamphlet for the Presbyterian Foreign Mission. Outspoken when defending the rights of Africans, Sheppard never condemned American racism.

As a small boy, he had to bolster his parents' income with a variety of jobs: carrying water, hauling haycocks, fetching packages from the train station. At the age of eleven or twelve, William found himself a full-time job, as a stable boy to a dentist. Not yet a teenager, he left his hometown for Staunton, a town twelve miles away, and cast his lot with his new employer.

The Henkels regarded him as something between a servant and a foster son. William slept above the stables perhaps, in clothing cast off from the Henkel children; he learned to read from hand-me-down grammar books; and the eager-to-please boy learned other arts simply by watching the family that swirled around him. How to converse and joke in a way that set white people at ease. How to harden his face into a mask when they discussed the race question. He loved the Henkels— as many as thirty years later, he was still writing letters to the dentist. And yet, as close as he became to the family, he knew they'd never accept him as one of their own.

In his autobiography, Sheppard chose just one anecdote to tell about his two years with the Henkels, a story about his boyish fear of the dentist's lab. "In a back room of the doctor's office," he remembered, "was a box filled with teeth. It puzzled me much to think how in the world people on resurrection day were to get their own teeth back." What the adult Sheppard thought of as an amusing story would not have been funny at all to the boy of eleven or twelve. It is a nightmare vision: bodies of Christians rising from the grave and zombie-walking through the dentist's office to reclaim their lost teeth, only to be confounded by the box full of identical yellow molars. Men and women unable to recognize what was once part of their own bodies. Lost identity. Alienation. The image captures the dizzying sense of disconnection that young William must have suffered as he struggled to make himself into the boy the Henkels wanted him to be.

After two years with the dentist, Sheppard found a job as a waiter and by age fifteen managed to save up enough money to go to Hampton Institute (now Hampton University), far away from Waynesboro, in the southeastern corner of the state. Hampton was one of the few schools to offer advanced education to ex-slaves, Native Americans, and anyone else who could tough out its grueling work-study programs.

When Sheppard entered Hampton's innovative night school, it was run by a young teacher who would one day become the most famous black man in America: Booker T. Washington. He designed the school for students who were so poor that they couldn't pay for books or board. These students would work ten hours a day, attend classes for two hours a night, and study on top of that. Washington nicknamed his first graduates—Sheppard among them—"The Plucky Class."

Sheppard shrugged off the difficulties. "The first year I worked on the farm, and later worked in the bakery, going to school at night," he writes. "I loved to swim and fish, and every advantage was afforded to me. The Hampton creek was filled with fish, oysters and crabs, and the broad ocean beyond was at my disposal," he adds, making Hampton sound like a country club.

If Sheppard ignored his own hardship, it was perhaps because he'd been awakened to the suffering of others: The Hampton faculty, an idealistic lot, drummed social consciousness into their students. "One Sabbath afternoon [the school's chaplain] asked me to accompany him and some of the teachers to establish a mission Sunday school at Slabtown, a small village of poor colored people. . . . I felt from that afternoon that my future work was to carry the gospel to the poor, destitute and forgotten people."

The black educational system emphasized practical skills and public service, a hardscrabble education that made blacks highly effective missionaries. Meanwhile in white schools, students prepared for work in Africa by reading Greek and Latin, and by arguing theological doctrine—skills that did not serve them well when a hippo charged or a disgruntled African lobbed a spear.

After he graduated from Hampton in the mid-1880s, Sheppard moved to Alabama to study for the ministry at Tuscaloosa Theological Institute (later renamed Stillman Institute; now Stillman College). Again, the difficulties he faced prepared him, far more so than his white colleagues, for the rigors of Africa. When he traveled south from Virginia to his new school, he had to scramble to find a meal or a cot, since most restaurants and hotels refused service to blacks. It was a lonely trip. "I well remember how lost I felt when I stepped off the train in Tuscaloosa at two o'clock in the night," he wrote about his first day of graduate school. "No one was there to meet me. I made inquiries of a man who was driving a street car drawn by mules, and he told me that he could direct me to a place where I could spend the night. I got on his car and he drove me up Greensboro Avenue to the corner of Tenth Street, stopped and told me [that] if I would walk a block and a half east and knock on the door of a house that was occupied by a family named Jones that they would take me in for the night."

But such difficulties did not dim the young man's enthusiasm, most especially his ambition to be a hero, a swashbuckling Christian crusader. Sheppard, just entering his twenties, was beginning to recognize himself as an extraordinary person.

One day he was languishing in class when he heard screams from outside—somebody was yelling, "Fire!" Not content to use the door, Sheppard dove out the window and ran in the direction of the blaze. He found himself in front of a house that had roared up in flames, trapping its occupant on the second floor. Sheppard galloped up the fiery stairs, through clouds of smoke, to carry the person outside. He ended the rescue mission with yet another vault from a window: "He continued working, bringing down the household effects until the blasting blaze shut off his movements. He then threw the remaining things from the second story window and leaped, himself, for life."

This must have dazzled the faculty at Tuscaloosa Institute. When Sheppard graduated, one of his teachers asked him, "If you are called upon to go to Africa as a missionary, would you be willing to go?" And he answered, "With pleasure."

Charles Stillman, the white founder of the school for black ministers, believed his students would make excellent missionaries—if only their passionate natures could be kept under control. After all, it was hard enough to keep white missionaries from running amok, and Stillman, who believed black men had stronger libidos and weaker "mental balance," worried that his students would lose their self-control once they were tempted by topless African beauties.

So Stillman probably pressured Sheppard to find a fiancée. The Presbyterian Foreign Mission would be more open to hiring a black missionary if he had a sweetheart to write him letters, a Christian girl waiting at home to help distract him from the native women.

And so, just about the time he graduated in the late 1880s, Sheppard promised himself to a schoolteacher, Lucy Gantt, who happened to be passing through town on a visit to her mother. The couple did not marry until almost ten years later, after Sheppard had finally established a settlement in the Congo. During the agonizingly long courtship, he made it clear to her that Africa came first.

Photos show Lucy with her hair pulled back in a schoolmarmish bun, a ruffle of starched lace at her neck. Whatever makes a face look intelligent, Lucy has it: Her lips lift in a half smile and it's easy to imagine a sardonic remark coming from that mouth—though nothing *too* sardonic, for she was a devoted Christian. She taught sharecroppers' children in a one-room schoolhouse, lived on her own, sewed, prayed, and would one day tour with a singing troupe. She had only one living relative, her mother, to tie her to America. She would make the perfect missionary wife.

It's important to keep in mind how little anyone—Sheppard, his teachers, or Stillman himself—knew about Africa. In the 1880s, a map would have shown the continent's outline, a few port towns, some sketchy rivers that ended in dotted lines, and vast blank spaces. "I knew a few things which I had learned from geography, but it was all very vague," Sheppard says.

Not only vague, but glamorous. In 1871, when Sheppard was six years old, Henry Morton Stanley tramped into the mysterious African interior to find David Livingstone, the famous explorer-missionary rumored to be lost in the jungle. His objective achieved, Stanley uttered the words that became a favorite vaudeville punch line and a catch phrase for the rest of the century—"Dr. Livingstone, I presume?" Later, another naturalized American, Paul Belloni Du Chaillu, "discovered" the gorilla and the Pygmy. He wrote a slew of books in which Africa came to life as a hot hell and the gorilla as a demon with "evil gray eyes."

It was exactly the kind of place a boy would want to go. As Joseph Conrad remembered, "It was in 1868, when nine years old or thereabouts, that while looking at a map of Africa of the time and putting my finger on the blank space then representing the unsolved mystery of the continent, I said with absolute assurance and an amazing audacity which are no longer my character now: 'When I grow up I shall go *there*.'"

A hundred years ago, Africa was deadly to Westerners—fraught with the kind of danger that makes today's frontiers seem positively welcoming. These days, almost all of those who go up into space come back; even about seven in eight of those who climb Mount Everest manage to survive. In Sheppard's day one-third of all travelers to Africa died, usually of disease.

It was a place as unknown as Mars, a dark continent that contained veins of gold and magic spells and diseases that turned your blood to water. Africa was whatever you desired or feared. For Europeans it was a source of ivory and gold, a place to plunder. Americans, whose colonial ambitions lay elsewhere, decided that Africa would make an ideal ghetto.

White Southerners, eager to get rid of their former slaves, had long funded black emigration to Africa, particularly to Liberia. For instance, Senator John Tyler Morgan argued that blacks had to be shipped to their "fatherland" for their own good, otherwise, "we and they must . . . deal with their virtual extermination." Morgan believed that American blacks would either be killed off or shipped out.

So emigration was very much in the air during Sheppard's boyhood. In fact, before he knew what the word "Africa" meant, someone had already told him to go there. "One day [the young boy] was playing in the streets just after a heavy rain. He was bare-headed, bare-footed and bare-backed," Sheppard explains in his autobiographical pamphlet. "A good lady, Mrs. Anne Bruce, called to him and said, 'William, I pray for you and hope you will go to Africa someday as a missionary.' He had never heard of Africa." Thus did the good lady express both the best intentions and fears of Southern whites. She wished him a brilliant career—but only if he pursued it on another continent.

For all their enthusiasm about emigration, the Southern Presbyterians had nowhere to send Sheppard. Even as the faculty at Tuscaloosa quizzed him about missionary work, the church had yet to begin its mission to the Congo. So instead of the faraway continent, Sheppard found himself preaching at a black parish in Alabama, a job for which he'd never shown much enthusiasm. Three years later he was transferred to a Presbyterian church in Atlanta.

Sheppard, so at home in the out-of-doors, must have been ill at ease as he picked his way through the muddy streets of the city, surveying the skeletons of buildings immolated in the war. In the small towns where he'd lived, he'd been able to catch fish and oysters. But in Atlanta he could dine only at the dicey taverns reserved for black men without families. One of Sheppard's contemporaries, James Weldon Johnson, described such a tavern as

> smoky, the tables were covered with oil-cloth, the floor covered with sawdust, and from the kitchen came a rancid odor of fish fried over several times, which almost nauseated me. I asked my companion if this were the place where we were to eat. He informed me that it was the best place in town where a colored man could get a meal. I then wanted to know why somebody didn't open a place where respectable colored people who had money could be accommodated. He answered, "It wouldn't pay; all the respectable colored people eat at home."

Not only had Sheppard found himself in this ugly, violent city, but his church had stuck him in a job he must have hated. A colored minister for the Southern Presbyterian Church—it sounded like a joke. There *were* no colored Southern Presbyterians—or almost none. By 1892, many blacks had fled from segregated churches (like Sheppard's) to join congregations run by their own people.

Though he doesn't explicitly complain about his two years in Atlanta, Sheppard does tell us how vigorously he tried to escape the city. He repeatedly applied to the Presbyterian Foreign Missions Board in Baltimore, begging for a job in Africa. He received only polite refusals.

Finally, Sheppard acted in the bold way that would later characterize him. Traveling up to Baltimore, he presented himself to Matthew Houston, the man who'd been writing those evasive replies to his letters. Houston welcomed the young minister, sat him down, and then explained the difficult situation. The Foreign Mission would not think of sending a black man alone to Africa. Sheppard could go only if he were accompanied by a white partner—a situation that seemed unlikely to arise. It had been ten years since a white man had last dedicated his life to Africa. For all Houston knew, it could be ten more years before another volunteered.

Until then, Sheppard would be barred from Africa.

Sam Lapsley was born in 1866, only a year after Sheppard; his childhood could not have been more different. He grew up swimming in a creek on his family's four-hundred-acre farm in Alabama; his playmates were children who only a few years before had been his father's slaves. Between him and the blacks hung the veil that Du Bois described. Lapsley did his best to break through. Toward the end of his life, he wrote of the Congolese, "I like the black folks very much. They are not stuck up, though they are ready to stand up for themselves. . . . They are funny and lively, and make good company. . . . Those that live by the water-side . . . have skins like velvet."

As he grew up, Lapsley longed to help blacks; unfortunately, his parents trained the boy to preach to them rather than to talk to them as equals. In a church his family had built for field hands, the twelve-year-old had to deliver sermons to people three times his age. At first, he shook with stage fright. But soon enough, young Lapsley grew comfortable in the role of preacher.

If ever there was a captive audience, the ex-slaves who filed into the Lapsleys' church were it. Which is perhaps why Sam never learned the trick of listening—even with other whites, he seemed at a loss as to how to strike up a friendship without the aid of theology. This was most poignantly apparent in Africa, where Lapsley met a man he described as "a Russian, who was captain of an English steamer, . . . sick in a room at the other end of the court. . . . He is a gentlemanly fellow. An English Testament on his table furnishes a handle I hope to use on him." The Russian was probably Joseph Conrad on his six-month tour through the Congo, an experience he would transform into one of the greatest works of Western literature, *Heart of Darkness*. Lapsley, blind to all but the Bible, failed to learn the terrible secrets of the Congo that the Polish writer knew.

In contrast to Sheppard, the truths Lapsley believed in have gone as terribly out of fashion as the starched white collars he wore in photos. A talented student, a singer, an organist, he did struggle to overcome the softness of his upbringing. In his early twenties he burned with a fever to sacrifice himself to the poor, to travel to the most desolate place he could find and dedicate himself to the wretches he found there. A picture from that time shows him gazing shyly, just to the side of the camera: His delicate lips are a girl's, his skin appears translucent; his light hair creeps back from his forehead, already receding. He delighted in taking tea with ladies' clubs, playing shuffleboard, and reading the Bible—not exactly pastimes suitable for a future explorer. But he also was a man driven by his ideals, as a horse is driven by the whip.

In 1889, the Southern Presbyterians voted to fund their first missionary effort in Africa, and began the search for ministers to lead an expedition. Lapsley, the effete twenty-three-year-old preacher, might have seemed like an unlikely candidate to bushwack through the jungle and settle eight hundred miles from the nearest doctor. But he was the only white man willing to go.

CHAPTER 2

The Silk Top Hat

The *Adriatic* pulled out of the harbor and into open sea, and a few hours later the two men sat at a dinner together, bending their heads in prayer over steak tartare or roast mutton. For Sheppard and Lapsley, the meal would have been a dizzying induction into a new life together. They hadn't spent much time in each other's company; they'd both been too busy preparing for their trip, fund-raising, visiting with family.

Besides, up until now, the two men would not have dared to sit down in a restaurant or tavern together: In the South in 1890, laws prohibited mingling between black and white. But here in the watery realm, beyond Jim Crow laws, a sailors' code held sway, and the two men could share meals and sleep in cabins down the hall from each other. "If a man acts the gentleman we make him have a good time, white or black," the captain told Lapsley, assuring him that Sheppard would be treated with respect as long as he remained aboard the *Adriatic*. Lapsley greeted the news with relief; it seemed one of the many wonders of this aquatic domain. "It is strange to wake at night and listen, not quite recognizing the new world I am in," he wrote, delighting in the "shash-sh-w-wash" sound of the water against the sides of the boat. He and Sheppard prayed together at night, in an intimate circle of candlelight, as they asked God to help them reach Africa, the dark land where they would have only each other.

In London, the two men roomed together in a boarding house run by a Presbyterian family. "They spared no pains in helping us," Sheppard remembered. Each morning, an English boy brought the missionaries a pot of tea and hot water for shaving.

"As to Sheppard, the English don't notice at all what seems very odd to us," Lapsley wrote home. Sheppard ate at the host family's table and left his boots out for young Willie, the English boy, to darken with polish. The Alabama Lapsleys would have considered such a turnaround to be freakish and dreamlike, but their son quickly accepted it.

Sheppard must have been transported by those first few weeks outside his own country. Here he could venture into a tavern and order a pint; he could saunter into the Houses of Parliament or stroll through the British Museum, could buy a first-class ticket on a train. Each day, in his travels around the city with Lapsley, he socialized with English businessmen and ministers who treated him as a colleague. "Sheppard, Dr. Matthews and I are to meet a young man [who has been to Africa on] Friday, in Dr. Alexander's parlor," Lapsley noted down, indicating that his partner participated in most business discussions.

Lapsley remarked on his friend's exuberant exploration of the city: "He took a jaunt in the neighborhood tonight, and came in quite full of the sights—the railway coaches opening at the sides, and the market— 'such a market!'" Most wondrous of all for Sheppard—more so than the public squares and humming, chuffing, smokestacked, crowded railway stations—would have been his newfound liberation from the race hatred of the American South.

As the two missionaries hurried across the city together, Lapsley delighted in his companion's personality. He was discovering Sheppard to be exactly the sort of man you'd want to take along on an African expedition. "He is very modest and easy to get along with; also quite an aid in sight-seeing, and in anything else where I need help," Sam wrote home. The remark reveals just how ambiguous the relationship between the two had become. Though Lapsley struggled to lose his racial prejudice, he still regarded Sheppard as something between friend and servant—an "aid" and a "help." Meanwhile, Sheppard knew that his position on the team was precarious. If Lapsley found him difficult to work with, he would be fired, the first and last black missionary funded by the Presbyterian Church. Sheppard did not challenge his partner.

The young Alabaman needed all the help he could get. As he raced from appointment to appointment, Lapsley was wracked with worry. The church had hired him to travel deep into Africa, find an isolated spot yet to be staked out by other evangelists, build houses and a chapel and a school, then convince hundreds of native people to give up their culture and live like imitation Americans. It was a tall order, especially when you consider that neither he nor Sheppard would have owned a decent map of the Congo—even the most up-to-date maps were vague about what lay beyond the coast.

Furthermore, the young men knew little about the mechanics of traveling through the interior of the continent. Could you sail a boat up those dotted-line rivers on the sketchy maps? Or did you have to hike through the jungle? And if so, how did you go about hiring porters to carry your loads? How did you protect yourself against disease? Where was the best place to settle? And what of the African people themselves? Which tribes were friendly and which would greet you with a rain of arrows?

Lapsley had no idea how to answer these questions, and the Presbyterian businessmen he consulted in London weren't much help. He agonized about how to make contact with "old coasters," Europeans with significant experience in West Africa.

Just when Lapsley despaired of finding someone to advise him, a letter arrived. Decorated with a dollop of sealing wax like a smashed cherry, it came from General Sanford, an American expatriate, who had once owned a shipping company in the Congo. Sanford resided in Brussels, where he hobnobbed with other "Africa men." The general had been a friend of a friend of Sam's father; now this knowledgeable fellow promised to do whatever he could to assist the young missionary.

The offer, arriving in the nick of time, struck Lapsley as providential, a God-given coincidence. In a great hurry, the young man boarded a steamer and sailed to Belgium to meet with the mysterious benefactor, leaving Sheppard to amuse himself in London. After all, Sanford was an American-born businessman who'd formerly owned a plantation in Florida; he probably would frown upon the unusual partnership between the black and white men. It was best for Lapsley to go alone.

How did Sheppard spend his solo time in London? The adventurer leaves no record, but perhaps he passed a few hours composing a long letter to his fiancée, for he owed her an explanation. Just before he left the United States he had called on her in Birmingham, Alabama, where she was running a small school. But Sheppard neglected to tell her that he was on his way to Africa; it was only later that he broke the news.

Lucy Gantt's biographer, Julia Lake Kellersberger, a lady of a certain old-fashioned sensibility, explains the incident this way:

> [Sheppard] intentionally refrained from telling the woman he loved that he was on his way to New York to sail. It was better thus. She was young and romantic and would have been tempted to accompany him, which at this time would have been disastrous to them both. Years of hazardous living lay before him; years of waiting and working lay before her.

And so, sometime during his stay in London, William probably sat down at a writing table and stared at a blank piece of letter paper, trying to find a way to tell Lucy he no longer lived a few hundred miles away in Atlanta; that he planned to make his home on the other side of the world, where letters could take up to a year to reach him. He regretted that he'd held the truth from her, but she would be glad of it in the end. One day, the two of them would share a house in Africa grander than anything she could expect in America.

It's impossible to know exactly how William Sheppard kept Lucy engaged to him all those years. The letters he wrote her have not survived. We know only that she waited for him. That an intelligent and independent woman like Lucy would suffer through a decade-long engagement says a lot: William Sheppard was the kind of man who could fill up a woman's head with longing, could hook her with letters covered in that swooping, auditious handwriting that offered charming apologies.

In Brussels, Sam Lapsley perched on an ornately carved chair, nervously eyeing the splendor around him—marble statues, silk upholstry, gold-framed paintings. From the window drifted sounds of the city, the *clop-clop* of carriage horses and the bray of ladies' laughter. On the other side of the desk, General Henry Shelton Sanford hunched over some papers, monocle clamped to one eye. He wore a silk jacket and cravat of the best make, a silver-tipped walking stick by his side. With neatly coiffed gray hair and an imposing beard, he looked the part of the foremost American investor in the the Congo Free State.

Why would such a powerful man bother to help a twenty-three-year-old missionary? Lapsley could not say, but he preferred to think God had had a hand in the matter, for seemingly out of nowhere, the very secular businessman had volunteered to do whatever he could for the Presbyterians.

That day, Sanford proved just how useful he could be. First he provided tips for traveling in Africa, explaining that Lapsley would take a steamer inland to Matadi, and there, where the Congo River became impassible, he would hire porters; for thirty francs each, these professional carriers would lug baggage up to Stanley Pool, where Lapsley could catch another steamer. Sanford also recommended a London firm that would supply, pack, and ship everything needed for an African expedition, from tropical woolens to tinned mutton.

Most useful of all, the general escorted the young man to the palace of King Leopold II and inscribed Lapsley's name on the register.

Through Sanford, Lapsley had landed an interview with the ruler who controlled the Congo. It was an enormous coup.

Lapsley had shown up at General Sanford's office in a suit still dusty from the rigors of second-class travel. This outfit appalled the elegant businessman. "If you go to the king, you must have a top hat," he'd scolded.

It was mad advice to give a missionary, but Lapsley, awed by his brush with royalty and by Sanford's vast experience, never questioned it. He used his meager funds to buy a silk hat, and regretted that he could not complete the outfit with a swallowtail coat.

The truth was that General Sanford had no business dispensing fashion tips. Years before, his own lust for fashion had gotten him into deep trouble. As a diplomatic assistant in Paris, he had affected an outlandish outfit, a black suit with a sinister cape. The Parisian press went into an uproar over the young diplomat's clothes. Sanford lost his job.

Later, as a dignitary in Belgium, Sanford still longed to wear outfits that would distinguish him from the other diplomats. He decided that military dress would be just the thing. Sanford had never served in the army, but for the price of three cannons, he was able to buy the title of general from the state of Minnesota. That done, he designed his own martial uniform: "a close-buttoned swallowtail [coat] of dark blue, covered before and behind with a mass of gold embroidery, . . . a cocked hat adorned with startling white and orange plumes," and a sword.

Despite the stunning clothes, Sanford failed as a diplomat. He remade himself as a businessman, and failed again, tossing money at a series of get-rich-quick schemes, all of them duds. One of his most disastrous ventures was a shipping firm in the Congo. He had invested in the territory on the advice of King Leopold himself, who'd promised that Sanford would make a fortune. Instead, the American had lost every penny—and then some.

In short, when Lapsley walked into Sanford's office, he'd stumbled into the den of a ruined man. Had the missionary been more observant, he might have noticed squares of bright paint where portraits had once hung. Or it might have struck him that the valet wore the worried expression particular to all valets in doomed households. For Sanford had been selling antiques and sacking maids left and right.

Had Lapsley noted any of these signs of distress—or the terrible health of the General himself, who would be dead within a year—he might have thought twice before accepting help from him. But the young missionary saw none of it. He preferred to believe God had brought him to Brussels. And so he stepped blithely into what was more or less a trap. King Leopold—the man who controlled the Congo, quite a few crooked politicians, many bankrupted aristocrats, several journalists, and Sanford—also had plans for Lapsley.

On the morning of March 23, 1890, Lapsley agonized about what to wear. He reported to his mother that he had to be content with an outfit patched together from "Gus Hall's shoes, Birmingham pants, Chicago coat, 'Famous' collar, . . . Rogers, Peets & Co. Gloves (you bought them) and cravat of sister Gene's make." Then he took the top hat out of its box and popped it open. It would have made a sound like paper roaring into flame and emitted the perfume of the Brussels haberdashery from where it had just come. He balanced it on his head. Then he set out for his meeting with the king, walking carefully so as not to muss his fancy clothes.

At the gate to the palace, a livery man stopped him, checked his credentials, and then escorted him to a reception hall grand as a museum. There, another man, in a gold uniform and spurs, swept in and bowed to him twice. He was ushered into a vast hall lavish with gold leaf, and from somewhere among the crystals and carved cupids, a friendly voice called, "Good morning!" Amidst all the frippery, the king seemed remarkably down-to-earth—as if the splendor had been somebody else's idea.

Lapsley remembered,

> [He] is tall, erect and slender. . . . His hair, rather thin and
> gray, he parts a little to the right of the middle; his beard is
> long and fine, turning a little gray. . . . His expression is very
> kind, and his voice matches it. He wore a dark green military
> frock coat, epaulettes and sword, with no star or decoration
> whatever. His manner is both bright and gentle.

He was so taken with the king that "I quite forgot he was a Catholic."

King Leopold made it clear that he had distinct ideas about where
the Presbyterians should set up their operation: They belonged in the
Kasai, a remote region that lay deep in the interior of the Congo. And
then the meeting was over. Lapsley sauntered down the stairs half drunk
with royal flattery, pleased to have gotten exactly what he wanted out of
Leopold.

It never dawned on him that he now simply had become a pawn in
the king's own scheme: For Leopold needed settlers to move into the
Kasai, a forest bursting with ivory and rubber. Once the missionaries
had helped to westernize the territory—building roads and schools,
teaching the people English—Leopold would expel them. Then he'd
send in traders and make a fortune. Though they little suspected it, the
missionaries would work for the king.

Lapsley marveled at how easily his expedition to the Congo had come
together, the chain of lucky events that had led him to General Sanford
and finally to King Leopold, providing him with contacts and valuable
information. Had he lived in our time, with its CIA plots, Kennedy as-
sassination theories, deconstruction and decoding, perhaps he might
have suspected that his path had opened up too easily. For indeed, the
apparent coincidences that had brought the two missionaries together
and propelled them toward Africa were no happenstance at all. Sheppard and Lapsley had fallen into a web, its nearly invisible threads spun

by a network of politicians and fortune seekers. General Sanford was one of them. But at the center hovered the fat spider who controlled it all.

King Leopold II ascended to the throne just when it had become little more than an ornament; the Belgian parliament—not the crown—ruled the country. Had Leopold been a different kind of man, he might have been content to languish in his greenhouses and pleasure gardens, and to cavort with his parade of prostitutes, some of them as young as ten years old. But he considered such treats to be only appetizers. He wanted to become one of the most powerful men in the world.

In order to do that, he had to get his hands on a colony. For what could be better than hundreds of thousands of brown or black people under your command, lands bursting with natural resources, and best of all, no parliament to boss you around? To be an absolute ruler, that was the thing. It was the "African cake" that seemed the most luscious to Leopold. The continent, newly opened up by explorers, was dripping with copper, ivory, rubber—riches that made his mouth water.

But how could the figurehead of a tiny dot of a country hope to compete for a slice of this cake? Leopold was clever enough to realize he could turn his weaknesses into an advantage. His political insignificance made him invisible, and so he could do whatever he wanted without attracting notice. If he flattered enough politicians, if he started enough rumors, if he spoke stirringly about the evils of the Arab slave trade, if he kept a stable of spies, perhaps then he could win his colony.

Leopold understood that he lived at the dawn of the age of mass media, and that public opinion would be the new king. In the 1870s, the first illustrated newspapers appeared, along with the telephone and transatlantic cables. In the 1880s came celluloid films and the Montgomery Ward catalog. Rather than depending on their own eyes and ears to understand current events, people now expected the media to bring the world to them. Whoever controlled the newspapers controlled the world.

So Leopold mounted a thoroughly modern public relations campaign. In 1876, the king hosted a Geographical Conference in his palace, buttering up famous explorers and scientists by handing out medals and feting them in a throne room lit by seven thousand candles. After stuffing themselves in the banquet hall, the guests drew up plans for a scientific organization called the International African Association. Years later, when the distinguished founders had gone their separate ways and the IAA was defunct, Leopold replaced it with a new "philanthropic" society, the International Association of the Congo. He hoped that the public would confuse the two groups—and the plan worked. Hardly anyone noticed when Leopold used his front organization to wrest real estate away from African chiefs. All along the Congo River, stations popped up, flying the blue-and-gold flag of Leopold's philanthropy.

At the Berlin Conference of 1884–85, the representatives of European nations gathered under a chandelier in the music room of Prince Bismarck of Germany's palace to decide the fate of the Congo. Before them lay a map created by using Mercator's projection, a method that puffed Europe into a huge continent, while rendering Africa like a shrunken head, disproportionately tiny.

What it came down to was this: Britain and France were eager to grab control of the African interior. Meanwhile, Prince Bismarck, presiding over the conference in a blood-colored uniform, would swipe whatever crumbs he could get for Germany. The eleven other countries represented at the conference could only hope to lick the bowl. In a way, though, everyone wanted the same thing: to make sure that squabbling over African spoils didn't erupt into a world war.

What the conference needed was a referee, someone to preside over a compromise among nations. King Leopold, who billed himself as a philanthropist and who ruled a country so tiny it didn't even count, seemed perfect for the job. The delegates decided he could be a kind of caretaker, benevolently watching over free trade in the region, ensuring that business ran smoothly so all of Europe could profit.

The assembled representatives signed an act that made King Leopold the protector of the Congo. He now controlled more land than any other individual in the world.

General Sanford headed up the American branch of the king's public relations department. With his debts mounting and his diplomatic career a shambles, Sanford was eager to do any favors he could for the king. Perhaps it would lead to a job.

In 1883, Sanford sailed to Washington; the Congo, he told American politicians, would be the perfect place to dump their unwanted black citizens. One of his most interested listeners was Senator John Tyler Morgan of Alabama, defender of the white race. Morgan made sure that America became the first country to recognize the legitimacy of the Congo Free State; and it was largely because of Morgan's efforts that the Presbyterian Church chose to send missionaries to the Congo, rather than to other African countries.

In a roundabout fashion, Morgan was also the man responsible for bringing Lapsley and Sheppard together. When the senator heard that the Presbyterians needed a white volunteer to go to the Congo, he had urged the son of his former law partner to apply for the job. And so Sam Lapsley found his way into King Leopold's palace in March of 1890. A white supremacist and a shady entrepreneur had been just two of the many questionable parties who would help Lapsley carry out God's plan.

In May 1890, after several months in Europe, Sheppard and Lapsley stood at the rail of a ship, squinting as they tried to make out the first lights glimmering off the coast of the famously dark continent. At midnight, the ship anchored at Shark's Point; and in the morning the two took their first steps onto African soil.

It was as if they'd stepped out onto two different continents. Lapsley's Africa bore a suspicious resemblance to his native Alabama. The coast struck him as picturesque, white houses peeping through hedges.

He also noticed the "half-clad Africans, just like our own darkies; it made me feel quite at home to see them." He constructed amusing profiles of the whites they met and gossiped about the relations among the local missionaries.

Sheppard's Africa was an entirely different place. Human beings cowered before the throbbing Congo River, the ocean, and the ravenous beasts. For him, the natural world ruled.

As Sheppard tells it, Lapsley almost died soon after they arrived—an incident that his partner never mentions. "Mr. Lapsley called in a loud, distressing voice as he rushed out on the beach and lay speechless for a moment. . . . He exclaimed, 'I was nearly taken by a shark.'" In Sheppard's Africa, you might need more than a letter of introduction from King Leopold. You might need a heart, wits, and good aim. You might need what Sheppard had.

Lapsley never again mentions the silk top hat in his diaries or letters. Surely, though, he packed it with the rest of his possessions bound for Africa. The hat—its marvelous silk folded up tight as a bat's wing—would take up only a few inches, wedged in between the mosquito nets and bottles of medicine.

After they settled in the interior, Sheppard reported, most of the possessions they'd brought from home simply dissolved, eaten by white ants. Most likely, the ants devoured the top hat, too, burrowing into its box and discovering the silk flavored with the perfume of a Brussels boutique. White bodies wriggled, picking the hat clean, until it was just a skeleton, a bit of wire with some shreds of black still clinging.

"If you go to the king, you must have a top hat," General Sanford had said. Even then, as he entertained the young missionary in his office, the general had in his possession letters from an eyewitness in the Congo, who reported that he'd seen officers of Leopold's government buying slaves. Sanford was one of the few people outside of Africa who knew the truth: The king was in the process of erecting the largest forced-labor camp the world had ever seen, a system that would eventually kill as many as ten million Congolese.

For their part, the two young missionaries newly arrived on the coast did not even try to understand what lay behind the misery all around them, the skeletal African men who marched in chain gangs and cringed under the whip of overseers. One thing, however, was obvious. The top hat would not be needed here.

CHAPTER 3

Thirty-six Hippos

In the summer of 1890, a journalist sat in the sweltering heat of Central Africa and dashed off an open letter to King Leopold. Colonel George Washington Williams, a black American with a handlebar mustache and dandified good looks, did not bother to observe any of the usual formalities of royal correspondence. In the tone of a man upbraiding his equal, he spelled out the truth exactly as he saw it: The Free State government was a vast conspiracy bent on pillaging the Congo.

"Women are imported into your Majesty's Government for immoral purposes," he accused. "Black solders, many of whom are slaves, exercise the power of life and death. . . . There are instances in which [these soldiers] have brought the heads of their victims to their white officers . . . and afterwards eaten the bodies of slain children." And finally, "Your Majesty's Government is engaged in slave-trade, wholesale and retail."

The letter amounted to heresy. In Europe and America, Leopold was famous for humanitarian efforts; he had poured almost two million francs of his own funds into the Congo Free State. He himself had spearheaded an antislavery campaign, and was famous for having shut down the Arab traffic in human beings. Williams's accusations could only sound crazy, like the pathetic bleats of a one-man band.

Nonetheless, he sent the letter back to a publisher in Europe who promised to circulate it. The flimsy document, just a few pages long, was no match for the effusions of the king's media machine. "Who is Mr. Williams?" asked *Journal de Bruxelles,* one of Leopold's mouthpieces. "This man is not a United States Colonel. . . . He has never held even the lowest rank in the United States army. . . . In 1885, he succeeded in having himself appointed minister to Haiti by [President] Arthur's administration. In 1886 he resigned from the post. . . . In Brussels . . . he persistently offered his services to the king of the Free State, who declined them."

Leopold's accusations rang true. Williams had promoted himself to colonel simply by adding the title to his name, had burned through several careers, and had racked up a string of debts. Only death prevented him from becoming a bigamist—when he succumbed to tuberculosis at the age of forty-one, he was engaged to one woman and married to another.

But though he made a mess of his own life, Williams was endowed with a genius for understanding the sweep of events, a historical vision equaled by few of his contemporaries. He'd authored two voluminous history books, which even the white press had to acknowledge as "epoch-making" (the *New York Independent*) and "remarkable" (the *Boston Evening Transcript*). While working on *A History of Negro Troops in the War of the Rebellion 1861–1865* and *History of the Negro Race,* he had experimented with cutting-edge methods of historical research, such as traveling around the country to interview soldiers who'd fought in the Civil War. History, he believed, should capture the doings of ordinary people as well as of presidents and popes—an idea that was new and risky.

His letter to King Leopold shows that he used the same techniques in the Congo. He described the forced laborers, who "eat their rice twice a day by the use of their fingers; they often thirst for water when the season is dry"—the kind of information that probably came from the workers themselves. He listed the agonies of sailors and slaves, concubines and army conscripts. As such, his was the first human rights investigation in the Congo.

His letter led to a short-lived hubbub in the European press. A few newspapers demanded that the Free State answer the charges, and in time a government office did spew out a cursory report. And that was the end of it. Williams's conspiracy theory hardly caused a ripple.

Even those rare Europeans who had read the letter and believed some of its charges might not have shared Williams's outrage. If Leopold's government was a bit strict, what of it? Christianity, rail service, clothing to cover the private parts, and regular working hours—all these gifts were being showered on the heathen. The natives that resisted should be treated like spoiled children and spanked.

"The evolving of a great free people out of the present chaos I fear will be a bitter process," wrote missionary George Grenfell, whom Williams had stayed with during his travels in the Congo. Grenfell had witnessed enough atrocities to fill ten letters, but he saw no reason to speak up. To rule the Congo, he believed, one needed a strong whip and would often have to hit very hard. It was an opinion shared by most whites who lived in the Congo.

In May, while Williams was still trekking through the jungle gathering evidence, Sheppard and Lapsley dined in a hotel decorated with Portuguese tile and wedding-cake verandas. Around them, Belgian officials chatted in French and daintily picked at their plates. The missionaries, famished from their fifty-mile trip from the coast, ordered soup twice. "Thinking this was all, we ate like wild men," Sheppard wrote, going on to joke about how he and Lapsley squirmed with embarrassment as servants appeared with five more courses.

They'd just arrived in Boma, capital of the Free State. The government offices sat on top of a steep hill; the Belgians rode up to work on a toy-sized railroad with only two cars. Though tiny, the puffing locomotive promised wonders to come, for Leopold was funding the construction of a full-sized railroad that would skirt the cataracts on the Congo River. No longer would every bundle of ivory have to be carried out on the head of a porter. When the railroad was finished, the riches of the Congo interior could pour into European ships.

"When you are waked in the morning by the shrill whistle, and look out to see the engine . . . pulling the coaches up the hill, you almost forget that you are in Central Africa," Lapsley wrote approvingly of the dwarf train.

After Boma, he and Sheppard continued up river to Matadi, where work had just begun on Leopold's grand project. The ground shook with dynamite blasts. Laborers from Sierra Leone, Liberia, and Zanzibar dug away at the rocky hillsides. Some of them bore the long, puckered scars of the whip, like railroad tracks cut into their flesh.

No other writer has captured this place and time as well as Joseph Conrad in *Heart of Darkness* (Conrad had arrived in Matadi a few weeks after Sheppard and Lapsley):

> "I came upon a boiler wallowing in the grass, then found a path leading up the hill. It turned aside for the boulders and also for an undersized railway truck lying there on its back with its wheels in the air. . . . A horn tooted to the right and I saw the black people run. A heavy and dull detonation shook the ground, a puff of smoke came out of the cliff, and that was all. No change appeared on the face of the rock."

Trying to escape the blasts, Conrad's narrator hurries into the shade of the jungle. There he discovers a pit full of discarded slaves, men wasted by starvation and torture:

> "Black shapes crouched, lay, sat between the trees, leaning against the trunks, clinging to the earth, half coming out, half effaced within the dim light, in all attitudes of pain, abandonment and despair. Another mine on the cliff went off followed by a slight shudder of the soil under my feet.

The work was going on. The work! And this was the place where some of the helpers had withdrawn to die. . . .

"Near the same tree two more bundles of acute angles sat with their legs drawn up. One, with his chin propped on his knees, stared at nothing in an intolerable and appalling manner. His brother phantom rested its forehead as if overcome with a great weariness; and all about others were scattered in every pose of contorted collapse, as in some picture of a massacre or a pestilence."

Though these scenes may sound exaggerated, they are accurate reportage of the situation at Matadi. Disease was rife. Bodies piled up, several a day. Estimates for the death toll among African railway workers range as high as 1,800 in the year 1890 alone.

Neither Sheppard nor Lapsley seemed to grasp that they had stumbled into the middle of a massacre. Lapsley described the Lower Congo as a picturesque frontier filled with the babble of many languages, a parade of Kruboys, Loangas, Liberians. He knew that overseers whipped these laborers, but he thought that perhaps such discipline might be necessary.

"These imported workmen raise a question which is a 'live issue' among Christian men out here. If [the Africans] won't work, or are insolent, shall they be coerced with the lash?" he asked. Some of the local missionaries believed that beating the Africans was a necessary evil. You had to punish the workers in order to get houses built and crops harvested.

Lapsley reported, without comment, that "Sheppard preached to the Sierra Leone men . . . , after which they spoke to him freely of their condition. One of them said, 'No good here for Sierra Leone man; plenty sick, too much flog.'"

Sheppard himself made no mention of this incident. He noticed only that the white people in Matadi looked very sick. The humid course of the Lower Congo was a breeding ground for mosquitoes, and foreigners could be dead within a matter of hours. When the missionaries first landed in Africa, they heard a chilling story about a Swedish woman who had died in this very town. In the course of one day, her temperature had spiked to 110 degress Fahrenheit.

If this tale wasn't bad enough, the point was driven home when they visited a cemetery near Matadi. Out of the mucky soil sprouted gravestones bearing the names of missionaries. "Emaciated by deadly fevers, pelted by tropical storms, . . . fatigued and foot sore from many a tramp, they have laid themselves down in this pleasant dale," Sheppard wrote—neglecting to mention that the "pleasant dale" itself was so clouded with mosquitoes that no one dared live there.

How could the men have paid their respects to the white graveyard without noticing the mass graves into which the black bodies were dropped? And how was it that the Polish captain came so much closer to the truth?

Perhaps Conrad was more informed because when he stayed in Matadi, he shared a room with Roger Casement, the overseer of the railroad project. More than ten years later, Casement would pen one of the most famous indictments of the Free State, listing the same kind of atrocities Williams had described. Even as early as 1890, Casement had seen his share of outrages, and he must have given his bunkmate an earful.

There is this too: *Heart of Darkness* was published nine years after Conrad stood on the shivering ground of Matadi. As he wrote his novella, he surveyed that town through the backward binoculars of memory—it was distance that allowed him to compress all he'd seen into tiny, terrifying paragraphs. In 1890 he'd been too miserable, sick, and lonely to do much but scrawl a few notes in his diary. He had recorded compass readings, miles traveled, weather, the state of his health, and his own misery. "Today fell into a muddy puddle. Beastly. The fault of the [African porter] that carried me. . . . Getting jolly well sick of this fun," he wrote on July 5.

Sheppard and Lapsley, trudging through swamps and over piles of stones, were likewise preoccupied. They planned to travel deep into the interior, up rivers that had smashed steamships to bits and past warriors armed with poison arrows. Their goal: to build a mission station deep in the interior, among Africans who had never yet heard the name of Jesus; to reach natives who, without their help, would burn in the eternal torments of hell.

The missionaries didn't know exactly where they would settle or which Africans they would try to convert. The two men didn't worry about those details yet. For the present, they hoped only to pass through Matadi without dropping dead of fever.

The Congo River runs wide and smooth until Matadi, after which it turns to a boil, leaping and whirling off cataracts, and sometimes going backwards. Because no steamship could make it up these falls, the traveler of 1890 had to proceed on foot more than two hundred miles up to Stanley Pool, where the river once again became navigable. Everything had to be lugged past the cataracts on the back of an African—including sometimes the traveler himself.

Both the missionaries were recovering from high fevers on the day they'd decided to set off, so they began their journey riding in canvas hammocks that the Africans hauled on their shoulders. Other porters struggled on ahead, single file, carrying a bathtub full of cooking utensils, piles of cloth, the "chop box" loaded with tinned food, the tent, and the beds.

The first night, they camped by the river, and supped on jam, crackers, and water from the Congo. One of the porters swept clear a patch of ground, erected the tent, made the beds, and set up the mosquito nets. Into this canvas room the two missionaries retired for the night. They said their prayers together, and then each man disappeared under the shroud of his own net.

They were leaving behind the colonial towns huddled on the banks of the river, where Africans were only dusty wraiths who lived in shanties. They would be marching through a tunnel of trees toward the hallucinatory creatures and plants still uncategorized by Europeans.

The Africans they met now were proud people who hosted grand markets like lavish parties, who knew how to slice a boa constrictor up into steaks, who could kill an elephant with nothing but a few spears.

Sheppard found them most impressive. One day, as he and Lapsley clambered up the bank of a river where they'd been swimming, a local man gesticulated at them wildly. "He explained with much excitement and many gestures that the river was filled with crocodiles, and that he did not expect to see us alive on his side," Sheppard wrote. This became his theme: Far from being ignorant savages, the Congolese had a good deal more sense than did the arrogant foreigners.

Sheppard's attitude was unusual, even for a black American. George Washington Williams, for instance, despite his humanitarian efforts, had little appreciation for local ways; he regarded the Africans as lazy. Williams simply didn't notice that they had their own history, passed down in songs, masks, and traditions, or that they might think of work as something other than lugging boxes around for Europeans.

While Sheppard would have never suggested, as Williams did, that the Congolese should run their own country, he had far more sensitivity to them. He could *see* the Africans. He noticed how the women in the market had "faces, hair and loin cloths smeared over with a black preparation which trickled all down their legs. On inquiry we were told that it was . . . their mode of mourning for the deceased." When Sheppard says "we," he's being charitable, for Lapsley never did know or care why the women covered themselves with burnt oil. "Sometimes . . . [the women] make frights of themselves by smearing a black pigment over the face," was his comment on the practice.

Sheppard, such an apt observer of the Congolese, hardly mentions the white people they met, most of them fellow missionaries who acted as their hosts along the way. It appears that, although the whites nursed him through fevers and fed him hearty meals, they did not socialize with Sheppard. Lapsley studiously recorded snatches of conversations that took place at the mission stations they visited, and in these scenes Sheppard never speaks. Was he sitting at the end of the table, listening to the other men discuss the "labor question" and the whip? Or was he somewhere else in the compound, studying the insects and plants that fascinated him? He was, at any rate, silent.

All that changed when they reached the end of their road and settled for a few months in Leopoldville. The cosmopolitan Dr. Aaron Sims, of the American Baptist Union, gave them rooms in his house. There they could gaze out the windows at Stanley Pool, where the Congo River spreads into a lakelike expanse, a sheet of blue broken only by the tufts of islands.

For the first time in months, the two friends parted. Lapsley went off on a side trip, sailing on a steamship to Bolobo, where he would call on the famous explorer-missionary George Grenfell, a man who knew certain areas of the Congo better than any other European. Grenfell had explored the rivers of the Lower Kasai region and made maps; he knew how to navigate there, and what to expect from the various peoples who made their home along the riverbanks. Lapsley had been pointed toward the Kasai region by King Leopold, but where exactly should he settle in the vast territory? What village would be best suited to host a Christian mission? Grenfell would know.

It's not clear why Lapsley undertook the journey to Grenfell's compound in Bolobo alone. Perhaps he'd decided that showing up with a black partner would not endear him to men like Grenfell, men of a certain colonial frame of mind, who believed that you had to "hit very hard" to keep the Africans from running wild. Whatever his reasons, Lapsley decided to leave Sheppard behind in Stanley Pool, under the care of the eccentric Dr. Sims.

One of the few medical doctors in the Congo, Sims was also a freethinker who blamed most of the region's troubles on the "the evil lives of white men." Though theoretically a missionary, Sims wasted little time on the dull duties of catching souls. According to one traveler, "he was an accomplished physician, a skilled botanist and gardener, a versatile and thorough linguist, and a most extraordinary manager of practical business affairs. . . . He knew almost every white man in the Congo." He ran his mission as a kind of hotel for his patients, entertaining visitors like Joseph Conrad. Sims also spoke several African languages, and seems to have been a great favorite with the locals.

Sick people of every description had dragged themselves to Sims for treatment; he'd seen every variety of human misery, from smallpox to profound depression. Now he turned his attention to the tall and charismatic American who'd been left by his partner with no particular job to do, like some kind of undervalued valet. The doctor noticed Sheppard's extraordinary physical courage and his magic touch with people; he decided the black American was too talented not to be put to use.

Sims called a meeting with his guest. The doctor explained that the Bateke people who lived nearby were in danger of starving to death. If someone would dare to hunt down one of the hippos in the river, to shoot it and slice it up into steaks, the village would be able to eat. The mission would be dangerous, since the hippos charged on land or water, often faster than you could aim a rifle. The Africans, equipped with only spears and darts, frequently wound up crushed to death by the creatures. Would Sheppard do the job? Probably no white man had ever begged for Sheppard's help in just this way, appealing to him as a person equipped with superior skills. "I was delighted at the idea," Sheppard wrote. "Being anxious to use my 'Marteni Henry' rifle and to help the hungry people, I consented to go."

Within an hour, Sheppard was hurrying toward the cataracts with his gun. In America—and even around Lapsley—he had comported himself with a careful politeness; holding his body and face just so; hiding his talents behind careful modesty. Now he didn't have to. He burst into a blur of motion, a cracking of twigs under boots, a fusillade of bullets. You can see his sense of liberation in his language, which pours out in a rush, so different from the stilted sentences in which he describes some of his travels with Lapsley:

I raised my rifle and let fly at one of the exposed heads. My guide told me that the hippopotamus was shot and killed. In a few minutes another head appeared above the surface of the water and again, taking aim, I fired with the same result. The guide . . . cried to me to look at the big bubbles which were appearing on the water; then explained in detail that the hippopotami had drowned and would rise to the top of the water within an hour.

He bagged several tons of meat, leaving the two carcasses by the side of the river. The Bateke people leapt onto the bodies of the hippos and hacked them into pieces with axes, then paraded back to their village for a feast. Sheppard brought some meat back to Dr. Sims's place so that the missionaries staying there could also partake of steak that night.

After that first adventure, Sheppard spent his days hunting, not just to produce more hippo meat, but also to clear the dangerous animals from the river, so that the villagers could fish without fear. By all rights, he should have been preaching to the people—that is what the church expected of him. But he was far more interested in saving bodies than souls. Lapsley longed to keep the Africans from falling into the fiery pit of unbelief, but Sheppard preferred to see them clothed and fed and cheerful. So rather than hand out Bibles, he would hunt for them.

Far from feeling kinship with Sheppard because of his black skin, the Bateke regarded him as a benign alien. They called him Mundele Ndom, "the black white man," because like all other men who came from the other side of the sea, Sheppard kept his legs hidden in strange casings of fabric, and smelled of the disgusting foods he ate out of silver tins, and believed that same story about a god who had killed his own son.

For his part, Sheppard hardly regarded the Bateke as long-lost brothers either. They were full of half-baked ideas—insisting, for example, that he shoot only certain hippos, because others protected the souls of people they knew.

When the villagers refused to swim into the river to fetch a hippo he had just shot, Sheppard finally lost his temper. "You men are too timid, you are afraid of a dead hippo," he scolded. But even after this dressing-down, the men refused to jump in the river. "The wind will blow it to shore," one of them insisted, which must have struck Sheppard, who'd heard so much talk about lazy natives, as a particularly galling remark.

He'd show them. The missionary looped a rope around his arm and dove in to do the job himself. He swum out to the carcass and began tying his rope around its nose. The water around him churned. The carcass bobbed. A crocodile surfaced, reptile eyes glaring, and lunged at the neck of the hippo. Fat flew from croc teeth, so close to Sheppard's face he could smell the tang of blood. He dropped underwater, holding his breath while he fled through the murk, arms and legs flailing. The villagers lifted him to shore. "I begged their pardon and was ashamed of my bravery," he wrote.

The men had been right about the carcass—after a while, it floated to shore. "We enjoyed a hearty supper and retired for the night under a beautiful moonlit sky."

Sheppard says that this incident taught him to have deep respect for the locals. Far from filling the African heads with Bible verses, perhaps God had sent him here for another purpose—to listen. Perhaps the Africans were the missionaries and he the savage. The Bateke had humbled him.

Of course, Sheppard was not too humble to record the dizzying number of hippos he killed during his stay in Leopoldville: thirty-six. Or to treat another of the missionaries, a Mr. Rogers, to a fabulous hunting expedition, during which they camped out and ate wild duck for dinner.

On the second day of this trip, as Sheppard headed off in his own canoe to scout for prey, he heard a cry behind him. He turned and saw that Mr. Rogers was alone in his canoe—the rowers had all jumped out and swum to shore. A hippo was barreling toward him. The animal intended to crush Mr. Rogers to death, something that hippos could do quite easily. Sheppard squeezed off a shot and the animal immediately dropped.

Imagine how the hunting party looked as it returned to the mission station: Mr. Rogers skulking behind, the Bateke laughing and chatting, and Sheppard leading them all. With the encouragement of Dr. Sims and the Bateke people, he had bloomed into someone new. He'd grown big now, pith helmet pushed back on his head, gun slung over his shoulder, loud laugh, swaggering stride.

Meanwhile, Lapsley pored over maps and notes at George Grenfell's station in Bolobo. Ostensibly, the trip had been a success—Lapsley had gathered most of the information he needed to continue into the Kasai region. But lingering day after day at this remote outpost with the famous Grenfell had unsettled the young missionary. Yes, the station appeared to be comfortable enough, with its machine shop, photography studio, and observatory, its tall palm trees and its steamship, *Peace*, docked in front. But Mr. Grenfell himself was a mess—"very anxious," Lapsley commented. Grenfell hated the natives, and they hated him. They had even threatened him with murder, telling him, "We can kill you all when we like." Was this what it meant to be a missionary? Hiding in your fancy house, terrified that the people you'd pledged to help might shoot you in the head?

Lapsley sensed some injustice had been done to the native people, some misunderstanding had swelled into a blood feud. The young missionary sympathized with the local Africans, whom he described as "bold, free, good as anybody, willing to welcome a friend . . . but ready to fight, caring little for death." These were people better left alone. And yet the Belgian representatives of the Free State had been harassing them. The "State men"—traders and soldiers—had arrived in the villages all around Grenfell's station and demanded that the Africans supply them with food, free labor, fuel. For some reason—Lapsley couldn't figure out why—the Africans associated George Grenfell with the rough-and-tumble colonialists.

Lapsley did not know that only weeks before, the journalist George Washington Williams had stayed in the same visitor's house where he himself now slept. Grenfell had listened with interest to what Williams had to say, careful not to let on exactly how much he himself knew. "I wonder what [Williams] would say if he saw, as we did, nine slaves chained neck to neck in the State Station at Upoto and waiting for a steamer to carry them down to Bangala," Grenfell wrote to colleagues in London. But, unlike Williams, he was not willing to go public with what he knew, or even to protect the villages against encroaching State men. It's no wonder some of the Africans wanted him dead.

Lapsley had gathered the maps and notes he needed. But as he steamed back to Leopoldville, he was seized by depression, a sudden and uncharacteristic fear that his job here might be meaningless. "It seems as if the words and lives of the missionaries [at George Grenfell's station] were having no effect on these poor people," he wrote to his aunt.

By the time his ship pulled into Leopoldville, the miserable Lapsley must have gripped the railing of the deck, scanning the crowd for Sheppard, longing to see that familiar, mustachioed smile under the shadow of a helmet. But Sheppard had gone. He'd traveled 140 miles back into the cataract region to gather porters, a daring expedition he'd organized on his own, after he found there were no porters available in Leopoldville.

Dr. Sims's place buzzed with stories of Sheppard's exploits—the hippos killed, the famine averted, Mr. Rogers saved from certain death. The villagers, particularly, praised Sheppard's heroics. "The Bateke think there is nobody like 'Mundele Ndom,' the black white man," Lapsley reported. There was more to his partner than he had ever realized.

On the steamer to Stanley Pool, Lapsley had despaired: How could he hope to save a single African when the esteemed George Grenfell had failed so utterly? And then he'd returned to find that his partner had rescued an entire village from starvation. Sheppard, apparently, had found the secret. To earn the trust of the Africans, you must become protean, a shape changer, a man of a thousand faces. You had to be a black white man.

CHAPTER 4

Unraveling Rivers

If the continent of Africa is shaped like an elongated head facing east, with a cartoon nose upturned in disdain and a skull that bulges backward, then the Congo River meets the Atlantic Ocean at its nape. From there, the river arches upward, toward Africa's nose; about three hundred miles into this upward climb, it meets the Kasai River. At a narrow junction with walls of rock on either side, red water running furiously as boiling blood, the Kasai shoots sideways, straight into the interior, and then southward to form the border with Angola. Along the way, it unravels like a piece of yarn into smaller threads, waters flowing in a variety of colors. The Kwango River, for instance, is so sandy it looks yellow. Off of it splits the black Kwilu. At the junction of these two rivers, the black and yellow waters are reluctant to mix with each other "as cream and strawberry juice hold apart, with a wavy line of division."

George Grenfell had warned Lapsley that this region of unraveling rivers, the Kwango, was fever-infested and sparsely populated. He had suggested that the missionaries pass quickly through and head to the Lower Kasai. There, he promised, they would find a more hospitable spot to set up a town. But for some reason, Lapsley decided to scout around the Kwango anyway. Perhaps its desolation attracted him. After all, the Lower Kasai, newly opened to Westerners, was crowded with rival missionaries. Lapsley had dreamed of reaching out to the Africans who had never seen a white man or heard the Gospel. He hoped to discover such people in the Kwango.

To prepare for the trip, Sheppard hired Yansi tribespeople to steer the canoes—skilled rivermen who could detect jags and rocks underneath the cloudy surface of the water. Also joining the crew was Tippotib, Sheppard's pet monkey, named (probably by someone else) for the Arab slave-trade mogul who operated in the Congo. The monkey began the trip sitting up front in one of the canoes, but after he fell off the side a few times he was banished to a basket with the chickens.

While the group was traveling toward the river region, Lapsley caught a fever, and so Sheppard had to handle all the final details of the expedition. "Sheppard is a most handy fellow, and is now a thorough river-man. . . . His temper is bright and even—really a man of unusual graces and strong points of character," the recovering Lapsley wrote to his mother.

The white missionary would suffer fevers throughout the journey, sometimes riding bundled up in the bottom of a canoe. Sheppard, on the other hand, remained healthy—athletically so—except once when he made himself sick by drinking a double dose of quinine, the medicine used to ward off malaria. "[It's a] bad habit he has of taking two weeks supply at once, to save trouble," Lapsley reported, sounding like an exasperated spouse.

On Christmas morning 1890, they dropped their canoes into the blood-colored water of the Kasai. By the second day, Lapsley had fallen ill again. "Somehow whenever I am in the oven stage of a fever, I think of the dreadful fire to which these poor [Africans] are exposed, and then . . . it does not seem much to bear," he wrote as he huddled under blankets and coats.

They pressed on, coming to a series of towns along the river. Here they met Queen N'gankabe, who apparently glided out of the forest to greet all foreigners. The explorer Stanley had been most taken with her, saying that she resembled Martha Washington. Sheppard—never one to be awed by royalty—simply praised her broad shoulders. Lapsley could do little more than reach out of his canoe to shake her hand.

They left the queen's village, paddling on. The light waned. Storm clouds bruised the sky. They landed beside another village, hoping to set up camp, but as soon as the Babuma people spotted them, men ran toward them waving spears and guns. Sheppard stood his ground, holding out beads and cloth toward them. The men wanted none of it. They yelled, "Yaka! Yaka!"—"Go away!"

So the little party retreated to a sandbank on the other side of the river. Lapsley had to be lifted into and out of his canoe, carefully installed in a tent, and treated with a dose of calomel and jalap, purgatives then believed to help purge patients of their fever.

"A big storm came that night, but Sheppard was equal to it," the sick man remembered. "He ran here and there, always just in the nick of time, and saved the canoes from being swept down to Banana. . . . He swung on to the [tent's] guy rope, just as its peg gave way and the tent was getting ready to fly over land to Kintamo." Sheppard remembered how the angry villagers whooped all night and even took a potshot at them.

In the morning, Sheppard rounded up their hired men and traipsed down to the river, where he bagged a hippo. As they waited for the carcass to rise, other hippos gathered around them, so close that the some of the terrified rowers cried.

Then, like great sultans of the river, the missionaries paddled back toward the Babuma village, their canoes half submerged under hundreds of pounds of hippo steak. The people forgot their grudge and crowded around the carcass, arguing over who would get the best cut. Lapsley noticed one Babuma limping away from the scene, and then returning with an even stride. He was making off with extra meat by dragging it between his toes.

Hippo meat was currency here, Lapsley wrote; as they traveled up the river, they found that handing out steaks solved most diplomatic problems.

Meanwhile, Sheppard—the born trader—could procure anything

else they wanted, from bread to souvenirs. Lapsley watched with admiration as his partner haggled with people who had never before met a Westerner, transforming himself by turns into imperious customer, unctuous street vendor, and slapstick comedian. In one episode, when the Africans tried to sell a goat for a price Sheppard didn't like, the missionary pantomimed his disdain with a wonderfully grotesque gesture: "He puts his finger to one eye and gives that feature a pull more expressive than pretty"; then he waved to the other side of the river, as if to say, Take this goat to some unsophisticated customer over there. After Sheppard haggled down the price, he conducted the sellers to the edge of the river. "Gentlemen, let me show you to your canoe," he said with his gestures, so that the sellers paddled away in good humor.

One day the missionaries came upon a fast-running stream, golden with grit, that branched off the Kasai and into the grasses of the Kwango region. They turned down this river, and within an hour spied a village that hung over the water on a clay bank. When the missionaries stopped to buy some wood, the people scattered, afraid to come near. Undaunted, Sheppard bounded onto land, with Tippotib as his small ambassador. The monkey knew how to put on a show, "finding shelter on Sheppard's shoulder, where he devote[d] himself to pretending to hunt for game in his beard and even in his eyes, with busy fingers and smacking lips." The shy villagers soon gathered around, screaming with laughter.

The next morning, the missionaries peered out of their tent and saw a canoe, rowed by women, floating toward them. This was the barge belonging to Princess Antinobe, who had come to bring them "dash"— tribute. They offered her cloth and brass in exchange. By evening a crowd of several hundred people from the town—it was called Boleke— had gathered around their camp, curious and friendly, eager to trade. Lapsley, who'd retreated under his blankets with a fever, could hear them outside the tent—"such a hubbub!" It's not clear what Sheppard said to Princess Antinobe and her people, but he must have used his Southern charm. As the missionaries pulled out of town the next day,

Antinobe's father—whom they assumed was the king of the region—begged them to stay, promising them land if they would settle here.

Lapsley was inclined to go along with this plan. "These people are, first and foremost, fishermen, and seem a pure and simple race, as fisherfolk should be. Perhaps the Master will have his Peter and James and John from them before long," he wrote.

But he and Sheppard had not yet explored the entire Kwango region. And before they went to all the trouble of buying land and building houses, Lapsley thought it would be worthwhile to look around the region a bit more. So, with promises to return, the little party climbed into their canoes and pressed on again, deeper into the wilderness.

A few days later they turned off the Kwango River and paddled into the black water of the Kwilu, which narrowed to a thin channel as it passed through grassy swamps. They spotted fish-traps, similar to lobster cages, left by the locals. Here and there, they found a handful of people who would sell them some scraps of food, just enough to keep their crew of about twenty rowers on spare rations. Lapsley, down to his last candle, was saving a little stub for emergencies.

On January 15, 1891, two emaciated men crawled toward them out of the tall grass. They were refugees from the *Peace*, the steamship that belonged to George Grenfell's mission. Along with twelve or fourteen companions, they had run off to escape the brutal conditions aboard the ship.

The missionaries welcomed the survivors into their canoes. In a few days, they would come across another man from the *Peace*, so starved and disoriented that he couldn't speak. "We prevailed on him to get aboard, and gave him some [food], in which he took more interest, poor fellow," Lapsley wrote. "[It's] Friday today, so that shall be his name, by Sheppard's suggestion."

According to the refugees, they had run off after being starved and then whipped. Without enough rations, the *Peace* had become a floating torture chamber—hungry white men beating even hungrier black men—which is to say, it was a typical steamship making its way through the African interior.

The rowers refused to go any farther up the river; food was scarce in this lonely land, and besides, the Africans' work contracts were nearly up. Sheppard and Lapsley, especially sensitive to their hired men after hearing the refugees' terrible stories, complied. They turned the canoes around and let the river carry them the way they had come, back to Boleke, the fishing village that had been so hospitable. Having seen how desolate the rest of the Kwango was, they became certain that Boleke was the only place to set up a Presbyterian mission.

On January 24, they drifted into the town, singing African songs and waving bandannas, expecting hundreds to crowd toward them. They pulled their canoes onto land and set up a campground, but the villagers only watched them from across the river.

Finally, a man and a woman paddled up in a canoe and explained what had happened: A European steamship had passed through the area, stealing wood from a nearby town. War had broken out, and the white men set fire to the village. The local people wanted nothing more to do with foreigners.

"I can see the pillars of smoke now going up from the burning town," Lapsley wrote. Still, he was sure he could make a deal with the villagers.

To get plans started again, Sheppard and Lapsley paid a visit to Antinobe's father:

> We told [him] that we had come back according to his invitation, to see the land they had offered us, that we wanted to pay for it if we found it good, and would go back to [Leopoldville], get our stuff and come and live here.
>
> [Antinobe's father] replied, "We should be glad for you to settle . . . but can't sell you the land. We are not the kings. . . . If you want to stay here ask the king of this country."
>
> "Where is he?"
>
> "He is at his town."

"What is his town?"

"Kimbuta. . . . It is far away. Don't ask *us* for land."

Lapsley guessed that the town of "Kimbuta" did not exist. The chief must have invented it for the occasion. Rather than be openly rude, he preferred to send them off to an imaginary town to talk to an imaginary king.

Polite as it was, this brush-off was a terrible disappointment. Even more upsetting was the behavior of the ordinary villagers. Once so friendly, they now surrounded the missionaries' hired men, full of disturbing questions. "Who are these Mundele [white people]?" they wanted to know. They inquired whether Sheppard and Lapsley were water spirits who'd crawled out onto land. They were afraid the strangers would rape their women, and begged them to bring wives of their own.

Lapsley's hopes collapsed. The villagers were terrified of him and Sheppard. He began to wonder what had really happened when the steamship came through this area. Surely the Europeans had done more than steal wood. Lapsley suspected rape, murder, and torture—why else would the friendly Boleke villagers suddenly have become so terrified of foreigners? He and Sheppard would have to leave.

Heading down river, Lapsley saw more evidence of destruction. As they paddled past the place where the queen had come out to meet them, they saw refugees huddling along the sandbanks. A nearby town had been burned, and the Africans circulated further stories of destruction. The next day they learned whom the culprits had been: members of an expedition led by a commander named Guillaume Van Kerckhoven.

To Lapsley and Sheppard, the name meant little, but had they known the Congo better it would have sent a chill down their backs. A Belgian officer of the *Force Publique*—what would soon become the Congo's equivalent of the Nazi SS—Van Kerckhoven was a trim young man in pressed uniform with a waxed mustache that spread across his face like a snarl. He had an effective method of subduing those Africans who refused to supply him with free food and fuel: He declared war on the hapless villagers and then paid his men five brass rods for each severed head they collected.

A Congo governor-general called him "a hurricane which passed through the countryside leaving nothing but devastation behind it." Most likely, Van Kerckhoven did not do his worst to the people of Boleke—perhaps he gunned people down, raped women, torched a village, and stole wood and food. For him, this was just business as usual, the most efficient way to keep his men fed and his steamship trundling along the river.

Sheppard and Lapsley made their way back to Leopoldville in low spirits. They had exhausted all possibilities in the lower region of the Kasai river basin—and besides, after the Van Kerckhoven incident, the natives ran the other way when they spotted a foreigner. So now the missionaries would have to travel all the way to the Upper Kasai to scout around for a place to settle.

Only a few years before, it would have been impossible for any but the most hearty of explorers to reach this spot. In the center of the African continent, it was one of the most out-of-the-way places on the planet. But recently the Belgians had opened up the first trading station in the area, and the Upper Kasai was now connected to the rest of the world by a visit from a steamship once or twice a year.

As it happened, when the missionaries returned to Leopoldville, Sheppard learned that a steamship called the *Florida* was about to leave for the Upper Kasai, a rare and lucky event. Still, Lapsley was hesitant: If they took off now, they wouldn't have time to pack and prepare themselves for years of living in the outback. Worse, the steamer already strained under a full load. The captain would let them take only twenty bundles of supplies and eight servant boys.

We'll have only a small allowance for luggage, Lapsley complained to Sheppard.

Sheppard replied, If we don't go now, we'll have to wait five months. Sheppard's impulsiveness won out. The men would cast their fate with the *Florida*.

On the morning of March 17, 1891, the missionaries hurried to load their scant supplies into the hold. As the ship chugged out of its dock, Lapsley found himself humming a snatch of a hymn:

> *Wherever He may guide me, no want shall turn me back;*
> *My Shepherd is beside me, and nothing can I lack.*
> *His wisdom ever waketh, His eyes are never dim;*
> *He knows the way He taketh, and I will walk with Him.*

The Alabama missionary didn't notice that he was singing a double meaning—an ode not just to God but to the partner who had made sure he survived the Kwango, and would surely protect him through the dangers to come.

Like most of the ships limping up and down Stanley Pool, the *Florida*—a remnant of General Sanford's failed business—was a sorry specimen. A paddle wheel powered its climb up the river, turned by a fire at the heart of the ship that had to be continuously fed with wood. Often the engine broke down, but even when it worked and could be coaxed into going full steam, the vessel sometimes made no headway against the current.

That's exactly what happened when the *Florida* tried to leave the Congo River to enter the mouth of the Kasai. Sheppard wrote:

> The captain called me to the wheel house and asked that I take the wheel as he directed the course. I did so with plea-sure. We steamed off, turned the nose of the steamer around the sharp point and into the strong current of the Kasai. The captain rang his bell for full speed. The *Florida* did her best, but the current was too strong. She quivered under the strain

and was forced backward. . . . Not a man spoke a word; all as still as death. . . . We steamed for five hours, only making a half mile. While the steamer was under such an awful strain the rudder chain snapped and there we were in that awful current. . . . I called out to the captain to keep her going, and then ran back to the stern of the boat, got hold of the iron bar which governs the rudder, and as the captain signaled to me with his hand, guided her safely to a sand spot.

They had barely left the Congo River, and already the ship's fire bars, ruined by hours of straining against the rapids, needed repair. By the time the steamer began moving again, the crew had not eaten a decent meal for days. Buying food was impossible; the few people they glimpsed along the shore melted into the woods, still wary after the recent Van Kerckhoven incident. Sheppard and Lapsley ventured out to hunt, but came up with little.

On March 25, Sheppard wrote that the African workers were starving, and the captain had threatened that if he didn't get food for them soon, he himself would go insane.

The next day, Lapsley woke up to the sound of the lash. The captain was whipping one of the crew members for refusing to collect wood. "Chicot is a strip of hippo hide slit, and the ends twisted for thongs, leaving a handle. . . . It makes a terrible mark where it strikes, at first a white streak, then a long welt. The culprit, if he happens to deserve the name, seldom shrieks, but writhes and gasps piteously after the tenth or fifteenth blow," Lapsley vented into his diary. The preacher who had once so loftily debated the labor question with his colleagues—who had even defended the whip—was now disgusted by the captain's cruelty. He retaliated in the only way he knew how—by opening up precious boxes of supplies he and Sheppard had packed for their expedition and handing out tins of meat to the African workers.

Sheppard, meanwhile, lay on one of the benches in the dining room of the ship, sweating with fever and nausea. His partner tended him with an air of desperation, administering just about every medicine he had—ipecac, Dover's powder, quinine, calomel, and jalap. On the deck outside, the captain was unraveling. He paced up and down, exclaiming, "I shall go mad, I shall get sick." Sometimes he followed such outbursts by laying into the backs of the Africans with his whip.

Conditions improved a bit as they steamed into the Upper Kasai. Sheppard had recovered his health; the local people they met were eager to trade; the climate improved; and the missionaries began to spot Kuba towns, where the gorgeous inhabitants wore velvet clothing decorated with pom-poms and carried elegant handbags.

Though the captain no longer muttered about going mad, the whippings continued. One day, Lapsley could stand it no more. He stepped between the captain and one of the bleeding Africans lying on the deck of the ship. "If you please, this is Mr. Simar's man," he admonished. Simar was a Belgian officer, another passenger on the ship, and the captain had no right to punish African soldiers under his command.

"Why do you stop me?" the captain grunted. As he saw it, all Africans came under his control. These brutes had lost the axes he'd given them to chop wood. They had to be taught a lesson.

Lapsley argued that the Africans should be given a chance to explain themselves. Wouldn't the captain at least give them a fair trial?

"The captain, having lost all control of his temper, asked me to consider myself as only a passenger," Lapsley wrote. Nonetheless, the missionary's outburst had an effect. For the rest of the journey, the captain put away the whip.

After two months of floating through the Kwango with Sheppard, Lapsley had changed; he'd watched how Sheppard coaxed the Africans, charmed them, fed them, flirted with them. He understood now that there was another, more humane way of handling the Congolese. It was as if for most of his life, Lapsley had never bothered to look closely at any whip—it was only a faraway curlicue riding on some overseer's belt. But now he had changed into the kind of man who did look. The whip zoomed into close-up. Lapsley described the long tentacles of it, the way it was fashioned out of cured hide. He described the wounds on the victims' backs with such sympathy as to make us, a hundred years later, wince.

Lapsley seemed not to know which tribe he belonged to anymore. Would he side with the men who wielded the whips or the ones who cowered from them?

The nightmare of their journey melted away as they neared their destination, a town called Luebo, center of the fledgling Free State government in the Upper Kasai. The missionaries had heard about the dry weather of this region, which made for far healthier surroundings than the Lower Congo. But they hadn't been prepared for its beauty.

"The whole country was filled with palm trees; the hills and valleys and everywhere, beautiful palms," Sheppard remembered. Local people zipped around in canoes. Huts peeped out of the wooded hillsides, blue mountains in the distance.

On the riverbank, a crowd cheered and gestured at the ship with the eerie enthusiasm of castaways, for they hadn't heard news of the outside world in almost a year. The men who swarmed around the *Florida*—greeting friends, shaking hands—were mostly African soldiers and workers. Only a few Belgian traders lived in this area. The Belgians welcomed the newcomers, and then hungrily tore into their mail, exclaiming over world events already long familiar to the missionaries.

As the crew unloaded the steamer, the captain said his good-byes, promising to be back in nine months. Until the *Florida* returned, the residents of Luebo would have no contact with the outside world. Sheppard reflected that they were now eight hundred miles from the nearest doctor.

That night he and Lapsley stayed at the trading post, where they consulted with the local Free State commissioner about how to proceed with their work. The commissioner suggested that they begin evangelizing at the nearest village, Bena Kasenga, a forty-minute walk away, at least until something better came along.

The missionaries hiked with the servant boys and their supplies out to a field that sloped down to the bank of the Lulua River. There they pitched their tent and set up a camp. The sound of their hammers on the tent stakes must have floated into Bena Kasenga because soon a band of Africans strode toward them, carrying bows and spears. These dusty, scrawny people had never before seen an outsider, and they chattered in a tongue the missionaries could not understand. The missionaries smiled for all they were worth, jabbering to the villagers in English. The warriors whirled and ran.

Night came. No light at all from the village. In the profound darkness, stars wheeled like slow-motion fireworks; the moon was the battered face of a Belgian trader eyeing his spoils. The river made slurping sounds against the shore. Jackals howled.

The tent glimmered, shroud-colored under the cold light. The missionaries lit one of their few, precious candles and ducked inside. Each man climbed under his netting and curled up in his cot. The candle guttered, casting woozy shadows on the walls of the tent. Sheppard thought about how they were so far from home, surrounded by people and yet alone.

In his memoirs, he admitted, though Lapsley doesn't, that they sobbed all through the night.

CHAPTER 5

Choosing the Kuba

The next morning, the partners hiked into the village and found themselves received with more fanfare than the day before. Children danced beside them on the dusty road, as if two missionaries amounted to a parade. Sheppard handed around a mirror, and even the shyest villagers drew near to watch the magic of faces and fingertips and sky sliding over its surface.

Lapsley charmed them with other trinkets. "Mr. Lapsley's gold watch always drew a crowd," Sheppard wrote. "When the lid flew open, how [the villagers] would jump back and laugh! . . . Then the back [of the watch] was opened and they saw a little wheel, a forward and backward movement. They then asked us to show them the little men down inside who do the pushing. Mr. Lapsley tried to explain, but it was useless."

The pocketwatch might be marvelous, but what the villagers really wanted to see—this they indicated by pointing to Lapsley's boots—was whether the white skin went all over his body, or whether it had been painted on. So the missionary unlaced his boots and modeled his feet for them, and the people laughed at the novelty of toes as pale as maggots and an insole the color of the moon.

As for exactly what the villagers made of the men, it's hard to say. If they were like most West Africans, they regarded the visitors as spirits who'd returned from Mpoto, the land of the dead. In the same way that Victorians believed that soulless heathens dwelled in the Dark Continent, the Congolese believed that America and Europe were where spirits walked in limbo. Sometimes the dead managed to return to their home villages from the across the sea, with all the color sucked out of their skin—white ghosts.

"There must be something in the appearance of the white man frightfully repulsive to the unsophisticated natives of Africa," Livingstone observed. "On entering villages previously unvisited by Europeans, if we met a child coming quietly and unsuspectingly towards us, the moment he raised his eyes, and saw the men in 'bags' [European clothes], he would take to his heels in an agony of terror, such as we might feel if we met a live Egyptian mummy at the door of the British Museum."

And just as the Victorians had decided that Africans were cannibals, the Africans were certain that the silvery cans the white men carried contained human flesh, ground and tinned for their convenience.

So when Lapsley and Sheppard first sauntered into the village near Luebo, they had to overcome many of the prejudices and terrors of the local people. But the missionaries found that fear quickly melted into curiosity, and soon enough, they made friends.

Though Sheppard and Lapsley could not yet distinguish among the various peoples of the Kasai, they learned that they had settled among the Kete. In the hierarchy of African politics, the Kete hovered somewhere in the middle. Unlike the true unfortunates (the Luba), they were not usually harvested as slaves. Instead, the Kete eked out a simple existence as farmers and hunters, paying tribute to the wealthy Kuba people who controlled the region.

The missionaries had chosen to settle in a Kete village that was little more than a collection of huts surrounding a dusty market square. Here, little boys herded goats; men farmed manioc root and chickens; women toted around bundles of wood and barrels of water; everyone, from the toddlers on up, knew how to trade. The town's buzzing conversations centered on how many knives should be exchanged for a hut, how many eggs for a monkey. Bartering was a branch of philosophy. A simple exchange might take all day, with buyer and seller sitting together on a blanket, sipping palm wine as they tit-for-tatted; when they came to an agreement, they sealed it with a ritual that could be as complex as a marriage ceremony.

In the doorways and in crossroads, the Kete had propped up some hastily carved depictions of guardian spirits. Sometimes the statues were so halfheartedly made that they had only slashes for eyes. When Lapsley tried to convince the people to throw out these "idols," he was surprised at their stubbornness. They absolutely refused to part with their statues. Nor would the villagers give up their own ideas about the universe: When the sun sank into the water, a team of men caught it in a canoe and ferried it across the ocean, so it could rise again in the morning.

In short, the villagers would probably never pledge themselves to Jesus—and though this irritated Lapsley to no end, it didn't particularly worry Sheppard. He delighted in the Kete's earthy culture. Buying a plot of land for the mission, he sealed the bargain in the African way; he broke off a piece of straw, spat on the end of it, and threw it over his shoulder.

Sheppard mixed easily with the Kete, enjoying their sophisticated sense of humor and their wisdom. Even if they were poor scientists in a Western sense, they excelled at the observation and mastery of their environment; they had studied all the animals, from the boa constrictor to the tulu. He also praised the Kete for their social organization: "The people had their judges, jurors, lawyers and officers of the town." Their cleverly designed houses could be taken apart, rolled up, and moved. Every ten years, according to Sheppard, the people took down the entire town and paraded like a traveling circus to some new spot. This was done for sanitary reasons, presumably to throw off insects and parasites.

In the new location, they would set up the buildings exactly as they had been before.

Sheppard seemed to have fallen in love with the African land and the vigorous athleticism required to survive in it. Special clothes were helpful, for one thing. Sheppard wore his own version of high-tech gear: a white linen suit that repelled mosquitos and a pith helmet that protected him from the blazing sun.

He organized hunting parties, cleared fields, went exploring, oversaw construction projects. Photos show him performing dentistry on the locals, posing with a python skin like a long red carpet, leading a group of men on a hunting expedition. In these pictures, he dwarfs the Kete around him, those tiny men with arms hardly thicker than their spears, their faces neat and gleaming. Sheppard is huge and rumpled, his cheeks cracking with smile lines, his chin sometimes hidden under a goatee. He has shoved his pith back off his forehead, and his suit is wrinkled with wear. He's tucked his pants into puttees; his feet end in white lace-up shoes so oddly insubstantial that they give him the look of a ballet dancer. He's often laughing, his body a blur of motion.

His countryman Henry Morton Stanley had publicized Africa as a sweaty hell teeming with monsters, its jungles shrouded in continual twilight. Even Lapsley found the landscape eerie and morbid: "In the early morning, the dew drops from the leaves in the woods around us like rain—a dismal sound to hear in the gloom."

But where the others saw shadows, Sheppard observed stunning light. He insisted that the continent was not dark at all, but more luminous than any other place—"the moon and star light is glorious. . . . [The heavens] seem to shine nowhere so brightly and beautifully as in 'Darkest Africa,'" he wrote in his autobiography. And in a letter to Dr. Henkel, his boyhood employer, Sheppard gushed, "I always wanted to live in Africa, I felt that I would be happy, and so I am."

He must have also written to Lucy, but unfortunately those letters probably have been lost forever. Whatever he chose to tell her about Africa, surely it was as positive as any salesman's pitch, for he hoped to convince her to spend the rest of her life with him there. Instead of wooing with the usual suitor's repertoire of flowers and bon bons, he offered her the Congo moon and the rings of a deadly boa curled in a tree.

It is impossible to know what Lucy made of her first letter from the Kasai. It would have taken almost a year to reach her; would have become battered, ink-smeared, and frayed after its long journey; would have betrayed more passion for Africa than for Lucy herself. But still she remained loyal. Perhaps she detected a streak of practicality beneath his poetry: Here was a place they could settle far from Jim Crow laws. Here they could be free.

While Sheppard delighted in the Kete's exuberant culture, Lapsley was repulsed.

> [Their] dances are all, more or less, lascivious in intention and effect. . . . A pitiable sight was the little baby girls in the crowd, all innocent-looking, many bright-eyed and pretty, imitating the immodest gestures of their big sisters and even their mothers—immodest? Often frantically obscene.

Another, later Presbyterian missionary expressed how exasperating it could be to work among the Kete:

> We had hoped to find a people glad to receive our message; and that we would have only to learn the language and tell them the wonderful story, and then see them coming into the church. We were not prepared for the utter *indifference*. They are not exactly idol worshippers, but they have *bakishi* or charms and fetishes, and *these* they allow to go into decay through *indifference*.

In the first weeks after they arrived at Luebo, Lapsley comforted himself with thoughts of home. He began constructing a Lilliputian replica of the Alabama plantations he had known in his childhood, a tiny Dixie in the Congo. He landscaped the nine-acre spread with palm and plantain trees, dotted it with one-room buildings, and planted it with fields of "goobers," a crop familiar to the two Southerners. Each missionary had his own hut, and Lapsley delighted in adding extensions that reminded him of the grand homes of Selma. "I haven't been able to keep my hands off these buildings, and indeed I made the frame of the little veranda to my house myself, because my boys don't [know how to build] a hip roof, like those in the front and rear of our old Vine Hill home," he wrote to his brother.

Two dirt roads ran through the plantation, and it was probably Lapsley who gave them their tongue-in-cheek names: Pennsylvania Avenue and the Boulevard de Paris. He was determined to transplant Europe and America to this patch of the Kasai, to impose his own pastiche of civilization on the village. He opened a school for the village children and offered daily church meetings.

The Kete showed little interest in his cultural offerings. They much preferred it when he opened up his medical case to reveal rows of glass vials that made chirping sounds when they rattled against one another, and handed out potions with magic names: calomel, jalap, Livingstone rousers, cathartics. "As for castor oil, they would lick the spoon and call for more. . . . Honestly, those people would swallow pills just as long as you would deal them out," Sheppard wrote. But they would not swallow the story of Jesus Christ.

So Lapsley turned to the one group he could control: the servant boys he and Sheppard had brought up from the Lower Congo. The budding sex drives of these Congo boys began to preoccupy—even to obsess—Lapsley, especially when two of them took a fancy to two sisters who lived nearby. Lapsley, who saw himself as surrogate father, responsible for safeguarding their morals, agonized about what to do. If he prevented the boys from marrying, the youths might engage in fornication. And if he allowed them to wed in the Congo fashion, the marriage might not "stick." Only a Christian marriage would do—but could he force it on the Africans?

The sisters belonged to the Zappo-Zap people, a notorious group whose name probably came from the sound of gunfire. The Zappo-Zaps (a subgroup of the Songye people) were the chameleons of the Kasai region, who survived by imitating their European and Arab oppressors. Most notoriously, they worked as middlemen in the slave trade, abducting their neighbors and selling them to foreigners. The Belgian traders rewarded their best workers with wives, bought from the Zappo-Zaps for a few lengths of cloth.

So, had he wanted to, Lapsley could have simply bought the Zappo-Zap sisters. They would then have become his property for seven years—under King Leopold's laws, missionaries and State men were allowed to practice this sort of temporary slave-buying. The seven-year slaves were called "libres," even though they were hardly free.

Everyone, from the Congolese servants to Mr. Engeringh, the Belgian trader at Luebo, urged Lapsley to buy the girls. The missionary politely refused. Instead, he decided to force American ideas about marriage on the girls' mother. He sat opposite the woman on an animal skin in the shade of Sheppard's house and attempted to explain his terms to her.

"'God's white men' [prefer] people who marry to live together forever afterwards. We don't want to rent your daughters [for] twelve moons like some folks here," he told the woman. When the boys went back to their homes in the Lower Congo, the wives would have to go too, Lapsley insisted. Would the mother let her girls migrate to faraway Congo land?

The mother refused.

And so Lapsley pronounced the engagements off.

That night, he checked in on the boys. Swinging a candle around their quarters, he glimpsed a tangle of arms and legs, and heard the fluttery hush of teenagers trying to hide. His eyes adjusted to the gloom, and he took it all in: the sisters huddled next to their would-be husbands, drums and bowls of food stockpiled in the back of the hut. The young people admitted that they'd planned to hold their own wedding, Congo style. They might have already fornicated. On ground that belonged to the Presbyterian Church, they might have fornicated.

Lapsley plunged into the woods, breathing hard. He broke off two branches, made switches out of them, and then whipped each of the teenage boys until his own arm hurt. No food tomorrow, he yelled at the rest of the boys cowering in their hut.

The next day, he hurried over to Luebo and bought the girls for a pile of scarves—it seemed the only thing to do.

Lapsley held the ceremony in Sheppard's tiny house. The young Africans bowed and marched like puppets in a penny show. Lapsley told them where to stand, how to hold their candles, what to say, even what to wear. He dressed up one of the boys in Sheppard's coat and hat; the other in his own red-and-white jacket.

"The two ex-cannibals [sisters], who still sometimes speak of [eating] *me (!)* are thus introduced within the pale of civilization and Christianity," Lapsley wrote after he had performed the ceremony.

The girls settled in to live on the plantation with their husbands, and Lapsley developed an avuncular concern for them, especially the sister named Vwila. "So fond of her sweetheart in a pretty way, and good to everybody, while as mischievous as a kitten. I like her immensely." Although he hadn't wanted to buy slaves at first, it pleased him to have the young people under his control.

A new idea began to grow inside his head. Why not give up on evangelizing the Kete? Why not instead try to make Christians of some other group, perhaps the Zappo-Zap?

They "have been cannibals very lately, without doubt. The [Kete] say they eat dogs and people," he wrote. "But the Zappo-Zaps are the finest people about—magnificent men and handsome women, and carry themselves quite as an aristocracy." Though they might be slave traders, the Zappo-Zaps prided themselves on their cultivation. In Arab-dominated parts of Africa, they spoke Swahili and wore robes. Among Europeans, they learned French or English, ate on China plates, and wore pants. They were, in other words, much like the Lapsleys of Alabama—people who moved in the best of circles.

Sheppard despised the Zappo-Zap. He had been shaken by what he'd witnessed when their traders marched through town. Sometimes they were bold enough to strut through the missionaries' plantation with a procession of emaciated men, women, and even tiny children, all joined at the neck by swinging chains.

One day, Lapsley bought a little girl, about six years old. He records the incident in his diary but never mentions—perhaps out of propriety—the horrific reason why he chose this particular girl. Sheppard tells the grisly tale in full. Not only had the girl been enslaved, she had been compelled to consume the flesh of her own mother. According to his account, the Zappo-Zaps had killed the sick woman, cooked her, and forced the other slaves to eat her.

Sheppard and Lapsley did not think much about the ramifications of buying slaves—namely, that they were encouraging the slave traders to round up yet more victims, and were helping to create a market with the beads and scarves they offered in exchange for human beings. They simply bought slaves whenever it would have broken their hearts not to.

Sheppard took up guardianship of at least one slave, a strong woman named Kafinga. It's unclear whether missionaries granted their slaves freedom outright, since most of the captives had no homes to go back to. Instead, the ex-slaves settled on the plantation, working for freemen's wages.

But little N'tumba—or "the Girl Who Ate Her Mother," as Sheppard called her—could not stay with the missionaries. Lapsley would have liked to adopt a child, but he didn't dare to "in this awful hot-bed of corruption. . . . [For] when seven or eight years old, she would be considered my wife by all these people." By this point he had become fed up with the Kete, and thought about abandoning them. He recognized that the hardscrabble farmers cared more about getting the best price for their chickens than engaging in theological debate.

Lapsley would have liked to live among the Zappo-Zaps, but Sheppard wouldn't hear of it. And so the white missionary kept his eyes peeled, searching for a people worthy of the Christian message. There were plenty to choose from in the Upper Kasai, a crossroads of African cultures. On market day, a Bamoyo woman swayed into town with a bundle on her head, smiling to reveal teeth filed into triangles. A few

Bangala men, who'd hiked all the way up from the Kwango, squatted in a yard with their spears tipped at casual angles, their scarred foreheads giving them a perpetual look of worry. And in the center of town, a group of Kuba people set out their tapestries for sale—chocolate-colored velvets studded with pom-poms. The Kuba towered over the other Africans and arrayed themselves in kilts as carefully pleated as tuxedo shirts, hats that ran the gamut from beanies to showgirl confections fluffed with feathers. "Very proud, don't take insults," Lapsley noted. "The most artistic race I know. Even [their] commonest utensils have an attractive shape."

In the end, he picked the Kuba—despite the warnings of Mr. Engeringh and Mr. Stache, the local Belgians. It was impossible, they said, to meet the Kuba king. He dwelt in a city that lay at the end of a labyrinth of secret paths; anyone who told the way into the city would be beheaded. The explorer himself would also be executed if he made it into the city, in order to protect the secrets of Kuba geography. For nine years, the Belgians had been trying to gain entrance to this African Shangri-la, this hidden utopia rumored to be rich in ivory, gold, and rubber. Several Belgian traders had sent gifts to the king, only to have them returned, sometimes accompanied by death threats. The Belgian trader Ernest Stache had tried to reach the kingdom and had failed, confounded by the network of hundreds of narrow paths in the jungle.

Why did Lapsley choose the xenophobic Kuba, arguably the worst candidates for conversion to Christianity? Perhaps out of a need to compromise with Sheppard. Unlike the Zappo-Zaps, the Kuba had enchanted both of the missionaries. Lapsley identified with them as patricians—their language included a word (*bakon*) that meant "hick" or "yokel," which they used to dismiss ordinary villagers such as the Kete. As for Sheppard, he relished the prospect of spending months or years tracking down a hidden kingdom. He also must have been entranced by Africans who comported themselves like Parisians, whose very existence confirmed what he had always suspected: that the people on this continent were as brilliant as the night sky above them, their costumes spangled with a silver lamé of tiny shells like stars.

In June 1891, Sheppard set off on an expedition toward the south, a first stab into some outlying Kuba towns, where he could study the geography and the "dialect of the strange and strong people" without threatening the king. Accompanying him was Ernest Stache. In his book, Sheppard says little about this trip, though he does note modestly that "a lake was discovered" on the way—hiding one of the most celebrated accomplishments of his lifetime behind the passive tense. The body of water would later be named Lake Sheppard.

Left alone on the plantation for two months, Lapsley began to unravel. Where he had once strolled down the Boulevard de Paris with Sheppard in the evenings, now he rattled around by himself. He hated to sleep in the hut with its flapping walls made of palm. Sounds floated up from the village—deep drumbeats that sent tremors through his cot. Down there, the Kete jumped and whirled around their fire, women shimmying so that their bare breasts rolled like mad eyes, baby girls twitching their bottoms seductively.

Drifting off to sleep, he must have feared the driver ants that attacked people in their beds. He might start awake to find his nose and mouth clogged, ants crawling desperately up into his nostrils.

His own thoughts had become like driver ants—they suffocated him, stopped up every pore. Why had he ever allowed women to settle on the plantation? Why did he fail to stop the villagers from their dances? Why not silence the yelps of sexual pleasure that issued from the huts?

He might become a savage himself, a fear he expressed in a letter to his brother. "The isolation from Christian influences, even of all books except my Bible and English hymn book, and the constant contact of godless influences, has certainly lowered my level of Christian life, chilled me, and kept me always in a series of inward apologetics."

When he learned that his partner had reached a town only about a day's journey distant, Lapsley was elated and decided that he and Engeringh, the other Belgian trader and a friend of Stache, should take a holiday in order to have a reunion with their friends. Decision made, the pair hurried to the Kuba town, where they found Stache and Sheppard "growing quite wild . . . living much like the natives, though hardly so well."

Lapsley's depression melted as he enjoyed a feast with the three other Westerners, and it surely helped that Sheppard convinced him to sample some of the Kuba's palm wine. Lapsley might have been tipsy when he jotted in his diary that night—he admits to feeling a rush of fatherly fondness for one of the servant boys in his care. Interestingly, in that same entry, he refers to Sheppard and Stache as "the two white men." Months later, he would again make the same slip in a letter to his aunt.

Sheppard, too, had grown disoriented when it came to skin color, his language hinting that he, like Lapsley, had begun to regard race as mutable, a temporary state. African babies, he claimed in his book, started out pale as fly grubs and only darkened as they took human form. Maybe one day Lapsley would darken, too.

In November, it was Sheppard's turn to live alone on the plantation. Lapsley had left on a journey to Luluaburg, a town that teemed with migrant workers, where he planned to hire farm hands for the plantation. In his partner's absence, Sheppard occupied himself with vigorous landscaping feats, such as planting a line of banana trees up Pennsylvania Avenue. "While he was away, I went into the forest and cut down timber and built two houses and fences, whitewashed [the] inside and outside, made walks and planted trees. Flowers began to bloom. . . . [I] bought chickens, dogs, monkeys, ducks; made it look like home. [The Africans] were always asking, 'Mr. Lapsley not coming? We want to see him.'" Sheppard kept himself too busy to suffer much loneliness. Still, he must have looked forward to the moment when his friend marched home with the new workers.

Lapsley had expected that the trip to Luluaburg would be easy, a holiday tramp in the company of a laughing group of African women he'd promised to escort there. Instead, the trek turned into a tribulation. Hit by repeated fevers, he could no longer shake the exhaustion that gripped his ravaged body. After a few days' march, he found he could hardly put one foot in front of the other. In a fog of pain, he stumbled along, depending on his African companions to take care of him. His friends led him through a region where sages puffed on hemp, into a village where he dined on roasted bees, and past gardens grown wild around destroyed villages. All the way, Lapsley felt "as if I had been beaten with rods from my waist down."

It was an interesting turn of phrase: When he first landed in Africa, he'd sympathized with the overseers who carried whips on their belts. And then, as he watched the Africans writhing under the lash of the chicot whip, he'd felt moved to help them. Now it was he who took the beatings—the blows meted out by an invisible hand. In his distress, he seemed to hallucinate himself into a body welted with the marks of the chicot.

Lapsley's diary entries from this period are sketchy. He jotted down notes in the flickering light of the campfire, exhausted, one painful leg thrust out before him. But in the spaces and silences of his words, one can guess at the enormous transformation that had gripped him. Suffering opened his heart in great gashes. Pain taught him compassion. As he dragged himself though the jungle on lame legs, the differences between himself and the Africans melted away. What did it matter if they worshipped other gods, or married according to other customs, compared to this one great sameness? They hurt. They suffered as Jesus had, and they longed for comfort. He saw them now as human and holy.

In Luluaburg, a Zappo-Zap prince presented the missionary with three young slaves. Lapsley reassured them. "You are my children now," he told them, and his first act as father was to hand them clothing and food.

He had gone on his trip to hire workmen, but in the war-torn country he found it easier to acquire ex-slaves and refugees. There were many miserable people who'd been burned out of their homes or abducted by Zappo-Zaps. As Lapsley hobbled back home to Luebo, people begged for work from him—and refuge for their families as well.

"All along the route, natives who had fallen in love with [Lapsley] joined the caravan. In many cases men with their wives, children, goats, sheep and all their belongings followed him," according to Sheppard. People who had nowhere else to go fell in line behind the limping missionary, and let themselves be led to the promised land.

Sheppard scanned the grassy hill, waiting for his young friend to come running down with his arms waving in triumph—that familiar, sand-colored face under the bobbing shadow of a pith helmet. Instead, a band of refugees wended its way toward him, their backs bowed under household possessions: pots, rags, bags of meal and peanuts. Their leader, an old man who humped along on stiff legs, wore a queer-looking European coat, much tattered, that flapped around him.

"Sheppard, how are you? I am glad to see you," the old man called, as if nothing were the matter. His face had been broiled by the sun, the features twisted into some new expression Sheppard didn't recognize; but those eyes peering out from the blistered skin, those were familiar. You forgot about such eyes when you lived among the Africans. Blue as the Wedgwood plates in shop windows back home, Lapsley's eyes seemed too delicate for this bright place.

Sheppard ushered the sick man back to his hut and helped him pry off the ruined shoes, bringing him a pan of water to soak his feet. Seeing his partner so broken-down, Sheppard wrote, "I could not refrain from withdrawing to the bushes nearby . . . [where] I broke down in spirit and wept." He gave his last pair of shoes to Lapsley, though they were two sizes too large. Since every other piece of his clothing had rotted away, Lapsley regarded his pajamas as his best suit. When he'd washed and shaved and put on his cleanest outfit, he looked like a hospital patient. Wan and feverish, he still managed to tell his story and to explain how he'd accumulated the ragtag band of "seventeen men, four women, one baby, three pigs and two dozen chickens" that had followed him back to the plantation.

The twenty-two people Lapsley brought home were just the beginning. As rumors spread about the Presbyterian mission, ex-slaves and refugees began to show up, asking for work. The missionaries' place, once a fanciful replica of an Alabama plantation, had become a refugee camp, dotted with hastily built huts, outhouses, laundry hanging every which way, a baby squalling, and chickens foraging along the formal row of banana trees.

Despite the growing settlement at Luebo, Lapsley stuck to his plans. He still wanted to resettle among the Kuba. Their future lay in the forbidden kingdom.

In January 1892, the steamship *Florida* arrived with a whistle blast, painting the sky with its white puffs. The missionaries hurried to meet it, eager to tear into long-awaited mail from home—though for Sheppard this ritual must have been bittersweet, since both his parents were illiterate.

The missionaries' pile of mail included an ornately penned and sealed envelope from the governor-general of the Free State in Boma. It contained devastating news. The Presbyterian Church had been denied permission to its land near Luebo; the missionaries would have to vacate the premises—refugees, ex-slaves, chickens, goats and all.

On an impulse, Lapsley decided to board the *Florida* and sail down river to meet with the governor-general; along the way, he would stop off and visit Dr. Sims, for he still felt weak and hoped the doctor could cure him. He shuffled on board, wearing his best set of clothes—pajamas and goatskin shoes. Once on deck, he called out, "Goodbye, Sheppard; God bless you. I will return by the next steamer."

It would be half a year before the next ship came up the river, the longest time the two men would be separated since they stood together on the New York pier. Sheppard must have gazed after the steamer until it rounded a bend and the tree branches blotted out the silhouette of his friend, the tiny figure on the deck of the ship, still waving even as he disappeared.

Lapsley found that steamship travel had greatly improved since his last trip. Now passengers enjoyed opulent dinners, three courses that came in succession, European-style. But despite these comforts, he was in a good deal of pain. He had become so prone to fevers that he dared not spend much time on the windy deck, and though he rarely complained, his every bone ached.

Years before, the chitchat of the Europeans would have fascinated Lapsley—he would have filled his diary with gossip about their way of dressing and speaking; he would have noted who was Catholic and who Protestant and who a nonbeliever. But now, perhaps because he himself suffered, he spent time among the African crew. He noticed the lines of worry that wrinkled their faces; the scabs on their legs; the glances they traded among each other; the ways that they, Nigerians, were different from the Kete he'd come to know.

They were, he understood, fellow-sufferers: disease-ridden, lonely for their families, haunted by what they'd seen in war camps and burned-out villages. Lapsley dedicated himself to easing their pain. He wrote, "[Every morning] I come down to my seat on a box among the Lagos boat hands. . . . They hang their sore legs overboard for the rushing water to wash them for treatment, and come and present them in turn for medicine. There were nearly twenty sores this morning, some twice the size of a silver dollar. I find a solid satisfaction in easing somewhat their pains."

The Africans also carried wounds that Lapsley's medicines could not heal. In such cases, he simply witnessed their pain, touched it, breathed in time with it. "Today a poor soldier from near Lagos . . . died aboard. His countrymen, though strangers to him, helped me to make his last experiences of this world a little more tolerable—he didn't die friendless. . . . I spoke and prayed with the living, and they made a neat mound over the dead."

Lapsley had sailed to Africa believing that a missionary's job was to convert as many people as possible. He would preach to the half-clad heathen, and they—weeping with joy to hear Truth—would dress in three-piece suits or billowing skirts and file into the makeshift churches he built for them. Every year, he would send a figure back to the Presbyterians at home, and it would be published in the Foreign Missions annual report under the heading "Converts to Christianity." Lapsley, the dreamy young man, must have imagined that his number of converts would someday be very high indeed.

But things had not gone as he hoped. After a year and a half in Africa, he hadn't managed to make a single convert. Instead, he kneeled before the Nigerian boatmen, swabbing pus from the cankers on their legs. And as he did so, something quite unexpected happened. Without the permission of the Presbyterian elders or their Foreign Missions board, Lapsley humbled himself before the men he once called savages. He emulated Christ.

Back in the Kasai, Sheppard had sunk into melancholy. Left alone with the Kete, he found them more alien than he'd imagined. His admiration began to sour. In his diary, he complained about their strange beliefs— one of the few times he ever did so. "The twitching of the eye, the itching of the hand, the flying of a crow across one's house, the hooting of the owl in the jungle, a snake crossing one's trail were all bad signs. . . . Truly the souls of these people were enveloped in the blackness of an awful midnight."

It was the witch trials that bothered him most. One midnight, he woke to find the village roaring with grief. A man had just died, and every one of the villagers mourned with frantic sobs, squeezing their eyes to make tears come. Anyone showing insufficient grief could be accused of killing the man through witchcraft. Should that happen, Sheppard learned, a trial would be held. The accused would be forced to drink a cup of poison, while his neighbors gathered wood for the fire that would finish him off.

Sheppard itched to leave the town. How good it would be to set off on an expedition to find the Kuba city, how good to have Lapsley swinging beside him on the trail, and at night, to pray together in English, a language Sheppard hadn't heard for months now.

He busied himself with preparations for the journey. In order to learn the Kuba tongue, he hosted a series of feasts and invited traders and tax collectors. "They were not hard to entertain. I don't believe anyone is when you spread a table before [him]—nice elephant steak!" By passing around plates and filling wine cups, Sheppard became the first Westerner to gain fluency in the Kuba tongue.

Finally, one afternoon in May, the villagers ran up to him and announced, "Chuck a chuck! Chuck a chuck!" It was their onomatopoeic word for steamship, evoking the chug of the engine. Sheppard joined the crowd at the riverbank and narrowed his eyes against the blaze of water. The ship labored up river, and the figures on board waved and yelled. He couldn't tell which one was Lapsley. The boat swung toward them, the crew leaning vertiginously off its side to push toward shore with long poles.

When it had anchored, Sheppard climbed on board.

"Where is Mr. Lapsley?" he asked the captain.

"Mr. Lapsley has not come," the fellow said. "But here are some letters for you."

Sheppard grabbed them greedily, searching for that delicate, meticulous handwriting of Lapsley's. Nothing. So he ripped open a note that came from a fellow missionary in the Lower Congo. His eyes passed over the few sentences, but the words refused to march into meaning.

And then, as he wrote later, "My head became giddy. My knees smote together. I staggered from the deck."

On shore, the villagers crowded around him. "Where is N'tomenjila?" they asked, calling Lapsley by his pet name, "Pathfinder." "Hasn't N'tomenjila come?"

Sheppard declared, "N'tomenjila will come no more." He staggered up the path to the plantation and disappeared into the woods. Lapsley had died in Matadi.

Two months before, Lapsley had reached his destination, the town of Boma, where he would meet with the governor-general. He had managed to stumble into the government offices, and though he was so frail he could hardly walk, he had negotiated a deed to the Presbyterian mission. Task accomplished, he made his way to Matadi. There, he collapsed onto a cot, to be cared for by a Swedish missionary named Petersen. When the patient's urine turned dark red, Petersen made his diagnosis: Lapsley had blackwater fever.

This disease, still a deadly one in Africa, is a potent form of malaria. As the victim's red blood cells disintegrate, his urine becomes purplish or black. His fever can spike past 107 degrees. He vomits blood and bile and suffers from severe pain in his loins. Sometimes, because his overworked kidneys cannot clear away all of the destroyed red cells, the victim's skin will darken. So as Lapsley died, he may have become like one of those babies Sheppard imagined, born white and growing into its color.

"I had good hopes of his recovery until the early morning of the last day, when I found that the temperature did not fall as low as usual. Instead, it gradually rose," his caretaker, Petersen, wrote. "When I told him we wished to try a cold bath, he said, 'Yes, and if that doesn't succeed, you will find my will in my bag.'"

Hours later, after Lapsley died, Petersen looked through his satchel, and as promised, found the will meticulously prepared. Lapsley had left his pocketwatch and his English Bible to his father. All the rest of his scanty personal effects he left to the Presbyterian mission. Sheppard and another missionary were named executors of the will.

When Sheppard learned of the death two months later, he stumbled away from the river and into the woods "to pour out my soul's great grief." After the first shock, his thoughts kept returning to one memory—that New York pier, Sam's worried mother yelling last instructions to him, her words almost lost in the wind.

By the next day, he had composed a letter to her, in which he told how much he had loved her son, and also made his excuses.

"Dear Mrs. Lapsley, I know that you have wondered why I have not written you, or why I was not the first to break the sad news, but as you may know . . . at this point of the interior we get a steamer once, perchance twice, a year." He reminded her of that morning in 1890 in New York, when he'd promised to guard her son against the perils of Africa.

He assured her that he'd done everything he could to keep that promise: "We had never been separated for any length of time since we left America. I can place my hand on my heart and look straight up to God and say conscientiously, 'I have kept the charge you gave me; I have loved and cared for him as if he were my own brother.' . . . I have nursed and cared for him in all his sickness, and he has done the same for me."

Sheppard's missive speaks not just of grief but also of guilt. It asks for absolution. Alone in his hut, dipping a quill into improvised ink, he composed the letter that would travel thousands of miles to arrive in an Alabama parlor, in the soft hands of a woman he hardly knew. And surely, she would pass on the precious note to prominent Presbyterian newsletters. Sheppard would have known that it would be widely circulated.

He asked for forgiveness, then, not just from Mrs. Lapsley but also from the church. Why did he feel guilty? Perhaps because the death of his friend gave him an opportunity he had never dared hoped for: He was now head of the Southern Presbyterian Mission.

CHAPTER 6

Becoming Bope Mekabe

The most famous missionary of Sheppard's boyhood had been David Livingstone. Wandering through the outback accompanied only by a few Africans, the British hero had collected specimens, made maps, and searched for the source of the Nile. Livingstone rarely bothered to preach or hand out Bibles to the Africans; in fact, the so-called missionary failed to make a single convert—except among the English. In a series of best-selling books, he celebrated the grandeur of the continent and the essential decency of the Africans themselves. "If one behaves as a gentleman he will be invariably treated as such," he believed. Denouncing the Arab slave trade, he lectured his fellow Europeans that they had a duty to bring the "three Cs" to Africa—Christianity, commerce, and civilization. As naive and culturally insensitive as this plan sounds now, Livingstone had a point: He wanted to see Europeans invest in Africa rather than feast on it.

Sheppard followed the Livingstone model. He treated the missionary job title as an umbrella under which he could pursue his multifarious ambitions. Explorer, big-game hunter, celebrity speaker, fund-raiser, art collector, anthropologist. He would excel at roles that were closed to nearly every other black person of his day.

But in the 1890s, the era of Livingstone was drawing to a close. The empty swathes on the map had been filled in, and now Westerners were settling the interior of the Congo as traders, bureaucrats, preachers, and teachers. Soon there would be no need for explorer-missionaries at all.

More to the point, the last the thing the Presbyterian Church wanted to do was fund lavish expeditions into the wilderness. Every year, the Foreign Missions department issued a newsletter that listed success in exact figures, divided up into categories and columns. If the format looked suspiciously like a corporation's annual report, that's because in a way it was. Charity donors would want to know how many churches had been built, how many schools founded, how many persons aided by medicines. But by far the most important figure was how many converts had been made.

Saving souls, the most crucial part of Sheppard's job description, was a task for which he was ill-suited—literally. In a group photograph from 1909, his colleague William Morrison wears a dark woolen jacket, cravat, and battered black hat; he's dressed for the mundane duties of teaching and preaching and desk work. Sheppard, on the other hand, has costumed himself as a cowboy-explorer in a blinding white suit, Panama hat, and lace-up boots buffed to a high shine. He poses with his chest puffed out, one hand on a hip. He looks ready to hunt, not preach.

In 1892, when his partner's death left him suddenly in command of the Presbyterian station, Sheppard needed converts desperately. The church might close the Congo mission entirely unless they saw some results.

But when it came to dressing Africans in cheap calico cloth and forcing them down on their knees to pray, Sheppard was profoundly ambivalent. He had too much respect for Africans to strip them of their culture and teach them to imitate Americans.

Had he wanted converts, he could have found them within easy preaching distance. The ex-slaves and refugees who had settled on the Presbyterian plantation belonged to the Luba/Lulua tribe. This bedraggled and deracinated people, who'd been scattered all around the Kasai region by the slave trade, bore an uncanny resemblance to early Christians. Fleeing from slave traders, exiled from burned villages, forced to labor by the Free State, orphaned, widowed—the Luba had nowhere to go besides missionary stations. In years to come, they'd flood to the Presbyterians in such numbers that the missionaries would have to turn many of them away.

Sheppard could have hunkered down in Luebo and tended to these unfortunates, setting up a school, a church, and a health clinic. Had he done so, he would have become like many of the missionaries who followed him, social workers who taught orphans to farm and preachers who translated English hymns into the Luba dialect.

Instead, he modeled himself on Livingstone. He wanted to open the door to Africa's secret places so that the next wave of missionaries could follow.

Of course, by 1892, most every door in Africa was already open, at least a crack. That's what made the Kuba people so special. They had refused contact with the West. For nine years, Europeans had been battering at the gates of the Kuba kingdom, without success. Whoever did find a way into the forbidden city would be hailed as a great Christian *and* a brilliant explorer. He would pave the way for future missionaries *and* he would prove his own genius. It was a challenge worthy of Livingstone himself. Sheppard would take it.

Hours after he learned of his partner's death, Sheppard burst into action. He gathered Africans from the plantation and made his pitch: He needed a party of men to join his search for the elusive Kuba kingdom. "We may all be marching to our graves," he warned the men who stood before him. Nine were sufficiently devoted to him to volunteer. A day later, he and his men packed up and headed down a sandy path into the jungle. They possessed no map or guide, only an idea: In remote parts of Africa, roads tended to run between markets, zigzagging around to accommodate traders. Rather than trying to plot the entire route to the forbidden city, Sheppard would hop from market to market, posing as a wanderer who hoped to buy food for his men. He would approach the city in the manner of a sailing ship, tacking back and forth against a headwind.

That first night, the group camped in a Kete village, joining the locals for evening festivities around their fire. What a strange vision they must have been. Sheppard led his men in singing "We Are Marching to Zion," a hymn about a city of God that could be reached on foot. Their hosts reciprocated by carrying drums and ivory horns from their houses. Soon, dancers swirled around the flames of the fire under a red moon that sat in the sky like a poppy. The villagers cavorted all through the night. What with revelers tripping over their tent ropes, drumbeats shaking the ground, and goats rooting around in their possessions, Sheppard's footsore men hardly got any sleep.

After a few days, Sheppard sidled up to the village chief and asked how to get to the next marketplace. The chief refused to tell, explaining that the king had decreed such information should be kept from foreigners. "I dare not disobey him."

So, Sheppard wrote, "I slipped out of the village quietly and stood in the road at a place where three paths met. By and by I saw a man starting out to the marketplace. I stepped out and followed him without asking any questions, making a mark so my men could come after me."

In this next town, he ingratiated himself by buying quantities of eggs. Perhaps aware of his hidden agenda, the people presented him with yet more food, goats, and chickens that kept his men stuffed and stuck in the campground. "I knew we couldn't dispose of all that food in one day, so I concluded to have a sit-down for four or five days; but the food rolled in without abatement."

Generous as they were, the villagers refused to reveal the path to the next market. So Sheppard tried a new approach: He pleaded that he and his men needed eggs. They'd managed to eat every last one in the vicinity—wouldn't his hosts consent to take one of Sheppard's men to the market, on an innocent errand of egg-buying?

His ploy worked. The villagers consented. Sheppard's man learned the way to the next town, and soon enough, the little band sneaked off and continued meandering toward the heart of Kubaland.

Sheppard used the egg trick over and over. "Day after day we moved along this way. . . . We did nothing but buy and eat eggs," he wrote, joking that in villages well stocked with chickens, the plan backfired. You want eggs? the people would say. And then they would drag out baskets full of them. Once, Sheppard had to gobble thirty before he could beg his hosts for more.

Eventually, when the expedition reached the town of Ngallicoco, the villagers would not offer help. At night, a town crier strode through the streets, announcing that no one should give directions to the strangers.

Still, Sheppard's luck held. He struck up a friendship with a fellow traveler, a Kuba man who offered to take him along on the path to the next village. "I was delighted, knowing that this man had full knowledge of [the king's] edict and yet cordially invited me to his town."

The next leg of the journey would be different from the other hops between villages. The travelers would be entering Kuba territory, the first of the towns in the sprawl around the capital. Like a pawn jumping into a strategic square on the chessboard, Sheppard would be one step closer to checking the king.

The village was called M'boma, and here he got stuck again. The egg trick would not work, of course. Nothing, not even hard cash, would persuade the locals to show him the way. Sheppard despaired. Every day he lingered in M'boma, he risked drawing attention to himself and bringing down the king's wrath. For almost a month he paced before his tent, watching for an opportunity.

Finally, it came. Some travelers emerged from the forest and announced themselves to be the king's ivory traders. Sheppard slunk off and found his most trustworthy volunteer, N'goma, one of the servant boys from the Lower Congo, now grown into a man. N'goma was as much a foreigner in Kuba country as Sheppard. Still, he—carrying a spear and wearing a loincloth—would attract less attention than his pith-helmeted boss.

"Follow those men's tracks in the soft sand," Sheppard instructed N'goma. "Make a cross mark in all of the off trails. . . . I will follow your trail at once with the caravan."

The plan would only work if the next few days continued to be dry—even a brief downpour would wash N'goma's marks away. As Sheppard led his men through the maze of paths, watching for the crosses drawn by a toe in the sand, his luck held. So did the weather.

After they'd walked for two days, the woods opened out, spilling Sheppard's men into a marketplace in the middle of a town called Pish aBieeng. Amid the tall Kuba people, parading about in their elegant drapery, Sheppard spotted wiry N'goma. He was buying—what else?—eggs. Perhaps the young man hoped to use Sheppard's favorite ruse to get to the next village.

For N'goma had lost his quarry. The traders had noticed him following, and in the middle of the night they'd pulled out of Pish aBieeng, leaving not so much as a footprint to tell where they'd gone.

As Sheppard's men massed in the village, and the local people began to understand the missionary's intent, they grew terrified. "If the king hears you are here all our heads will come off," they said, pleading with him to leave their town.

Should Sheppard stay and risk the lives of these strangers? Or should he retreat, which would be tantamount to giving up? He settled on the awkward compromise of camping in the jungle—close to the village but not technically in it.

Once again he'd been beached. He had no idea how to get any closer to the capital. To pass the time, he pulled out a two-year-old edition of a newspaper he called the *Daily News*, probably the *London Daily News*, most likely purchased before he left Europe. Its presence here in the jungle was somewhat miraculous—for two years it had survived the ravages of the white ants that had eaten up nearly every other piece of paper.

The words on the yellowed pages must have spoken to him like messages from another world: news stories about political debates, reviews of theater shows that had long since closed, advertisements for a new box camera from Kodak and a strange contraption called the phonograph. It would have reminded him of the wonders of London: thundering trains, ladies' eyes flashing under ostrich plumes, the smell of coal smoke, the leaden shine of the Thames and the Houses of Parliament lit up golden in the wash of a winter sunset. And Lapsley beside him, Lapsley fussing with the foreign coins and eager to visit Livingstone's grave.

How far away all that must have seemed on a sweltering morning in the Kasai outback. The clothes that hung on Sheppard's back had grown gritty with sweat. He had not shaved, and could only bathe in an improvised fashion. It had been months since he'd spoken to anyone in English.

So he paged through the moldy newspaper, trying to lose himself in the imaginary city, London two years ago, bursting with luxuries he could have never explained to the Africans around him. Perhaps he was reading an article about the new spring hats or a recipe for coq au vin when the screams began.

The village had erupted into noise and motion. Voices sobbed, moaned, begged for mercy. People were crashing past him into the woods. From between the trees, Sheppard could just glimpse the soldiers who had marched into town, a band of men in feathered hats and kilts, brandishing knives.

"Now hear the words of [the king]," one of them proclaimed to the fleeing people. "Because you have entertained a foreigner in your village, we have come to take you to the capital for trial."

Sheppard lifted himself out of the chair and strode in the direction of the soldiers. The leader, over six feet tall, bronze-colored, half blind, regarded Sheppard haughtily with his good eye. This was N'toinzide, one of the king's sons.

In his ragged white suit, Sheppard must have been an odd vision. These Africans had never before seen a man clothed head to toe, his legs encased in "bags," his feet hidden inside contraptions that dangled string, his face half hidden under a kind of roof. The stranger stood tall enough to stare into the prince's single eye.

"The chief of this village is not guilty," the stranger insisted. "He . . .

told me to go away, . . . and I did not." Furthermore, he said, no one had helped him find the outskirts of the capital. He'd figured it out for himself. If the soldiers wanted someone to blame for his presence here, well then, they'd have to convict him and him alone. He was the guilty one, not these hapless villagers.

"You are a foreigner and you speak our language?" the dumbfounded prince replied. He spoke with a foppish lisp, for his two front teeth had been removed, according to Kuba fashion. Then he swaggered away, conferred with his retinue, and led them off in the direction of the capital.

After the soldiers had disappeared, the village fell silent. People huddled in groups, hardly bothering to move. Someone explained to Sheppard the exact manner in which they would be killed. Their necks would be stretched over bent saplings, and when the executioner swung his sword, their heads would fly into the air and land at the feet of a delighted crowd of aristocrats.

Sheppard couldn't eat. A piece of chicken on a banana leaf, a fried plantain cut up into yellow coins—these things made as little sense to him now as jokes without punch lines. Why bother to choke down food he'd never have a chance to digest? Why bother to do anything?

They were all corpses-to-be, everyone in this village, right down to the youngest Congo boy, Susu, who had been with Sheppard for almost two years now. Soon their bloody heads would fall with the hollow sound of hail.

The prince marched back to the palace and briefed the king: The intruder spoke the Kuba language, knew the secrets of their geography, and wore the strangest clothing he'd ever seen.

Intriguing news indeed. King Kot aMweeky called a meeting with his advisers. He reclined on two slaves—as a demigod, he was forbidden to touch the ground, could not come in contact with anything as mundane as dirt, and so must be cushioned by warm human flesh. The advisers wore the dress costume of the Kuba aristocracy, later described by the ethnographer Emil Torday:

All men wore the kilt, very like that of the Highlanders; . . .
a leaf-shaped knife about a foot long with a beautifully en-
crusted handle stuck in the belt on their right hip; in front a
long pocket of skin, from which the hair had not been removed, dangled like a sporran; their heads were surmounted
by a conical cap of lace-like fibre, fixed to their hair by needles ornamented with a miniature bell.

The men conferred. King Kot aMweeky needed to strengthen his
hold on the throne, in order to keep power away from the many rival
clans that vied to control Kubaland, and to awaken even more terror and
awe in his people. What could be a better addition to his entourage than
a ghost—or even better than that, the ghost of a long-dead king? The
advisers decided then and there that the stranger would be called "Bope
Mekabe," and that he'd be introduced as a reincarnation of one of the
ancient kings.

As one ethnographer has noted, Kuba oral history contains no record
of a "Bope Mekabe"—which is all the more reason to assume that the
king and his advisers came up with the story during a brainstorming
session. They may not have believed that Sheppard was a ghost, but
they knew a political opportunity when they saw one. A royal ancestor
come back to life in order to endorse King Kot aMweeky—it was a brilliant political move.

One day Sheppard had been a condemned man, and a few days later the
prince's delegation marched into town and declared him royalty. "You
need not try to hide it from us any longer. You are Bope Mekabe who
reigned before my father and who died," the prince told him. "His spirit
went to a foreign land; your mother gave birth to it, and you are that spirit."

Now, rather than sneaking through the mazelike paths of the jungle,
Sheppard promenaded beside the prince, marching to the capital behind an honor guard.

Giddy with his good luck, he was also overcome by the beauty of the land around him. He described the jungle they marched through as a place of fairy bowers and grottos. "Festoons of moss and running vines made the forest look like a beautifully painted theatre or an enormous swinging garden." Above, someone had strung what appeared to be hornet's nests through the trees. Even these charms to ward off invaders, filled with poisoned arrowheads, had a festive look to them, like a string of Chinese lanterns.

And then he caught his first glimpse of the city itself, spread out before him on a vast table of land above forests of cultivated palm trees. As he marched through the gate, he knew he'd entered a place unlike anywhere else in Central Africa. Emil Torday gives us some idea of the scene that must have opened up before Sheppard:

> Stepping out of a lovely grove of palm trees we faced a long street, at least thirty feet wide, as straight as an arrow. It was bordered by oblong huts, each standing alone at an equal distance from its neighbors; they were all the same shape and differed only in their walls, which were made of matwork [*sic*] ornamented with beautiful designs in black. . . . The houses were as spick and span as if they had just been finished; the road was swept clean. Though the day was still hot the village was busy as a hive. . . . The very children were bent on some task, some working the smith's bellows.

As they passed a guard post, hundreds of Kuba urbanites swarmed around Sheppard, pressing against each other to get a glimpse of the spirit king. Prince N'toinzide led Sheppard through the crowd to a house—a high-ceilinged place with walls made of cleverly woven screens—and presented it to him as a gift. Sheppard's men were shown to their own quarters. Their goats and chickens were led away, to be cared for until Sheppard required them. Strict sanitation laws prevented anyone from keeping sheep, dogs, ducks, pigs, or chickens within the walls of the city.

The next morning, Sheppard woke to the ringing of horns and a commotion of people scurrying around the town square. Today would be his debut—his first ceremonial meeting with the king—and he was dismayed that he had nothing better to wear than a suit "that had once been white linen," with the broad-brimmed pith helmet and the white canvas shoes. His men, too, rooted around for something fancy to put on. One of them donned a necklace made out of string and a brass button, only to be told that he had to remove it, because brass and copper ornaments were reserved for the king.

In the city square, to the beat of drums, a crowd of thousands gathered before a horseshoe-shaped stage. Seven hundred women—the king's wives—preened and jostled each other around rugs of leopard-skin and an ivory throne. The crowd parted, and a carriage made its way through the river of people, an elaborate hammock inlaid with cowrie shells carried by sixteen men. They installed the king on his throne, careful to keep his feet from touching the ground.

Torday, who visited the capital in 1908, a decade and a half after Sheppard, described it this way:

> A comparison with Japan, in the middle of the last century, is forced on one's mind, [except that the Kuba king] was the Shogun and the Mikado in one person..... [He represented] the living link that alone can join [the Kuba people] through the chain of his one hundred and twenty predecessors to Bumba, the founder. The spirit of Bumba lives in every one of them; it is the life of the living, the memory of the dead, the hope of future. . . . Any weakening of [the king's] power, every affront to his dignity sends a tremor through all.

If the king died, the majestic ceremony of the city would turn into cacophony: Aristocrats would plot against each other; royal heirs would be assassinated in droves. Eventually, a new king would be installed, and the city would return to its calm. The king represented order.

Kot aMweeky's hair had gone white—Sheppard estimated him to be about seventy-five years old—but he'd lost none of the vigor of youth. "I judged him to have been a little more than six feet high and with his crown, which was made of eagle feathers, he towered over all." He wore blue cloth studded with cowrie shells, which gleamed so white that they hurt Sheppard's eyes, and a dusting of camwood powder from toe to ankle.

The king reached out a hand to Sheppard and proclaimed, "Wyni"— "You have come." Sheppard, who had already mastered the niceties of Kuba court manners, bowed and clapped, then gave the appropriate response: "Ndini, Nyimi"—"I have come, King."

Reaching toward his belt, the king pulled out a knife, its blade snicking against a hilt. The weapon gleamed, a foot long. The king turned it so that the hilt protruded toward Sheppard. "In the red halls of the Kuba royalty, this has been handed down for seven generations," he announced. "It is now yours."

And then he invited Sheppard to join the entourage on stage, the royal family and the army of wives. Dancers strutted into the square, whirling and ducking. Singers called out choruses. Drums and orchestras played. One by one, the seven sons of the king performed military ballets, leaping about as they cut the air with their knives.

Sheppard kept stealing glances at the king. The old man was absorbed in the entertainment, laughing sometimes at a particularly clever bit of footwork. After perhaps an hour, Sheppard screwed up his courage and leaned toward the throne. "I understand, King, that your people believe me to be a [Kuba] who once lived here," he whispered.

The old man turned to him, beaming. "True."

There was no way to put it delicately, so Sheppard blurted it out: "I want to acknowledge to you that I am not a [Kuba] and I have never been here before."

At that, "the king leaned over the arm of his great chair and said with satisfaction, 'You don't know it, but you are *muana mi,* one of the family.'"

"They knew me better than I knew myself," Sheppard joked. The more he insisted that he was a foreigner and a missionary, the more smug the

Kuba grew. Having been reincarnated in a land across the ocean, they allowed, he might be discombobulated. He might have forgotten his true identity and his real name. But at least he hadn't lost his ability to navigate the secret paths of his own country. At least he hadn't forgotten the customs and manners of the palace.

They had a point, for no matter who Sheppard said he was, he conducted himself exactly like a reincarnated member of the Kuba elite. He made friends with his new "brothers," most especially Prince Maxamalinge, who feted Sheppard with a lavish dinner party; the two men became close enough that, a decade later, Maxamalinge would become a fixture in the Sheppard household.

Most important, Sheppard handled the king like an old pro. "I was rather careful not to ask him too many questions," he said later. He learned to cough when the king coughed; he clapped after every sentence; he talked in the strange, low voice he'd observed other courtiers using around Kot aMweeky. In fact, Sheppard proved to be so deft a politician that he might have been able to take the throne, had he wanted to. A few years later, when Kot aMweeky finally did die, Sheppard was looked upon as a serious contender, despite his frequent protests that he had no connection to the royal family. Had he been a different kind of man—say, a fellow like the bounder in Kipling's "The Man Who Would Be King"—he might have ruled hundreds of thousands of people and commanded untold wealth.

So why not agree to become Bope Makabe, prince, magical spirit, and Kuba sophisticate? Sheppard had found a far more alluring role for himself. He would be the Kuba's documentarian, bringing back to America evidence of their grandeur. To this end, he hurried around with notebook in hand, observing the city's inhabitants and recording details of their myths, customs, clothing manufacture, child-rearing practices, laws, and civic behavior. He collected piles of art, from stunning velvet cloth to witty pieces of pottery. Fifteen years later, Picasso would shock Europe with *Les Demoiselles d'Avignon,* a painting that incorporated West African masks. The revolutionary work helped give birth to cubism—and eventually, to a European love of African art. But in Sheppard's day, the pieces he gathered would have been regarded as curios, far less valuable than the ivory tusks that the Kuba used as doorstops.

Despite his lack of training in anthropology, Sheppard somehow guessed the significance of what he saw in the Kuba capital—"their knowledge of weaving, embroidering, wood carving, and smelting was the highest in equatorial Africa," he asserted. Later scholars would prove him right. According to Jan Vansina, the region's most eminent ethnographer, Sheppard had stumbled into the last of the stately courts in Central Africa, kingdoms that hundreds of years before had rivaled the courts of Europe in technology and culture.

But in the nineteenth century, few people knew about Africa's grand past. In anthropology books, engravings of African and European skulls sat side by side, offering "proof" that the owners of the former had tiny brains. Scientists described the peoples of the Congo as hardly human. "Lord Mountmorres states that he saw in the vicinity of Avakubi a more primitive and simian type of Pygmy than the Babbute," reads one anthropology book. "These [people] he first took to be a group of chimpanzis [sic], springing from branch to branch, and stopping from curiosity to look at the intruder in exactly the same way as do the larger apes."

Sheppard had stumbled onto proof not only that the Africans were fully human, but that they could be as elitist and tradition-mad as Westerners.

Like feudal Japan or the Europe of the Middle Ages, Kuba society was one of high formalism. About half of the men who lived in the capital had a title—and with each aristocratic office came unique insignias, names, hats, rituals, privileges, and philosophies. You might be, for instance, a provincial governor; with that office came a white oxpecker feather, a copper hat pin, a special wooden staff, and tiny bows to wear under your shoulders. These accoutrements spoke volumes about your position in society, your family, and your history.

Ethnographer Torday described one such provincial minister: "Isambula N'Genga did not look down on the common people any more than we look down on a fly crawling across a wall. The rabble did not exist to him; I am quite certain that their voice never reached his ears. . . . He did shine like a diamond in the sky; groomed, oiled, combed to perfection, he would walk down the street, slowly, his staff over his shoulders and his hands negligently slung over its ends. . . . When I asked him a question he would just wave his hand towards one of his courtiers—that was that fellow's department!"

The Kuba's household possessions—stools, boxes, pipes, and cups—were as ornate as the city's aristocrats. Lapsley had observed that even the least of their utensils was plastered with designs. Vansina noted that the Kuba learned to carve the way children in Europe learn to read. The best artisans had developed methods unknown outside of the kingdom—drilling tiny holes in shells, creating detail work with copper inlay, making velvet out of palm fiber, weaving fabric into pom-poms and wavelike folds. The artists delighted in trompe l'oeil, visual puns, sight gags: They made pots that balanced atop human feet and carved clay cups so that they appeared to be woven out of basket material. For those in the know, the pipe bowls lampooned the faces of famous people, much the way political cartoons caricature politicians.

Kuba dynastic history—ancient kings and the stories surrounding them—was also a favorite theme. On a hilltop in the city, four statues represented the Kuba's founding fathers. The most important of the ancestral kings, Sheppard noticed, held a game on his lap that resembled a checkerboard.

Indeed, the checkerboard was a fitting symbol for the city itself. Sheppard described the streets as a grid, but beyond that, the city's extreme cleanliness, the origami folds of its social classes, the complicated decorations on every wall, and its draconian laws, gave it the atmosphere of a life-size game. The citizens moved in ballet-like harmony. After lights-out at about nine o'clock, the entire town went dark. Only the king could flaunt the law—behind the walls of his palace, seven hundred wives sang him to sleep. In the morning, prisoners scurried out to clean the streets and pull up weeds. Every family had to sweep the public way in front of their house every day.

Aside from the king, the Kuba were monogamous. "A young man sees a girl whom he likes; he has met her in his own town or at some other, or perhaps at a market place or a dance. He sends her tokens of love, bananas, plantains, peanuts, dried fish, or grasshoppers. She in turn sends him similar presents," Sheppard noted. He praised the Kuba as moral people, with a high sense of duty to their own families and their city.

The Kuba were so well behaved it was downright eerie. Sheppard's description of one man's death captures the essence of what is so beautiful and also so disturbing about Kuba culture:

> [A man named] Nnyminym took to his bed. . . . I visited the patient; also treated him, but Nnyminym grew weak and was moved from his bed to a mat on the dry ground. . . . [One day], earlier than my usual time for calling, his wife sent for me, saying that Nnyminym was dead. . . .
>
> I found the family bathing him and putting on his burial clothes [even though the man was alive].
>
> I remarked, "You are hasty, I fear, in dressing him for burial."
>
> But the wife remarked with grief, "No, he will be dead soon."
>
> When they had fixed his hair, shaved his face and shoulders, anointed his body with palm oil and adjusted his legs back under him, they all sat in a semi-circle. . . . This was all done in a businesslike way. . . .
>
> The wife asked in a calm, gentle tone, "What of your debts are unknown to us?"
>
> Nnyminym answered calmly, "I have settled all my debts; but listen, I will tell you the names of those owing me." And without effort, he called name after name as his wife broke

small pieces of bamboo for each name. These pieces of bamboo were kept and the debts collected after death.

Now and then Nnyminym in his sitting attitude looked at his hands growing pale, watched the heaving of his breast, looked at his family and friends before him, drew a long breath as though very tired, and actually watched death steal his life away. As soon as his eyes were closed a scream went up from his wife, and the rest of his family joined in.

The Kuba had an enviable bravery. They faced death squarely, performing a ritual around it as profound as a tea ceremony.

And yet this dignified grief could turn murderous. Anyone not displaying sufficient sorrow might be accused of witchcraft and forced to drink poison. The "witches" were almost always women of low caste.

Sheppard recounts the following story to illustrate how one family's grief could spin out of control and turn into a witch trial:

> A child died suddenly in the town. The wise men said, "It is bewitched."
>
> So they rushed through the street, crying out, "Where is the witch? Where is the witch?"
>
> They saw an old woman sitting alone in a house. Some cried out "There is a witch." They seized her. She said, "No. I am no witch."
>
> . . . They dragged her to the poison house; gave her poison; she drank it, and in a little while was seized with pain, but could not throw off the poison, fell down and died in agony.

Witchcraft ordeals and divination existed side by side with the kind of legal proceedings more familiar to us: courts, juries, trials, sentences. For the Kuba, the poison cup was a kind of DNA test—scientific evidence of guilt or innocence. If you drank the poison and lived, you were proved innocent. But Sheppard regarded the poison cup as nothing less than the African version of lynching. He became distraught when the victims staggered through the streets, vomiting up bile or dying in contortions.

Nor would he look the other way when it came to human sacrifice. Though they did not trade in slaves, the Kuba used captive men and women to ornament their funerals. "The burying of the living with the dead [is] far beyond [what the Kete do], who only bury goats with their dead," the king once bragged to Sheppard. "Our kind of people," he seemed to be saying, "aren't so cheap as to send our loved ones off with a smelly pack of animals." The king's own mother had glided off to the afterlife with a thousand servants in tow.

Weeks after he arrived, Sheppard confronted the king about the poison ordeals and funeral sacrifices, arguing for human rights "in the strongest language." It was the first time he had violated court protocol, had dared to challenge the divine authority of the king. But instead of beheading Sheppard for his insolence, King Kot aMweeky only laughed; he took the foreigner's suggestion as a joke. Had Sheppard traveled to King Leopold's palace and argued that the Congolese deserved to run their own country, he might have received a similar response. The idea was simply beyond the pale, too absurd to be a threat.

It was a different matter entirely when Sheppard began to weave his magic spells.

One day, Sheppard's servant was observed sprinkling foamy powder into a stream. A few hours later, a tornado whipped through the city, flattening several houses. Kot aMweeky was furious. Only kings—and the spirits of kings—could create storms like that. Sheppard must have caused the cyclone with that bubbling powder; he'd been showing off with his high winds; he'd been spitting rain down onto the palace. And for what purpose? To steal the throne? To stir up a storm of political unrest?

At noon, two court messengers showed up at Sheppard's house and told him his presence had been demanded at the palace. Sheppard stood before a looking glass and brushed his hair, then shrugged on his coat.

He followed his escorts along the streets, through a succession of gates, and into the cool darkness of the palace.

The king's face twisted when he saw Sheppard. "What caused that storm?" Kot aMweeky demanded.

Sheppard offered some sort of meteorological explanation—the rainy season, weather patterns in the Kasai, high pressure systems.

He might as well have poked the king with a stick. Eagle feathers flailing, neck cords bulging, Kot aMweeky screamed out his accusations: Sheppard had brought that storm down on the city. Sheppard would have his head lopped off.

The missionary froze—terrified, tongue-tied.

And then he found himself speaking in a tone you might use to croon to a baby, a voice he'd heard all around the palace, a Kuba way of talking, the only known antidote to the king's tantrums. He borrowed it for the occasion. He put it on like a velvet hat.

"It is true, King, my people were at the creek, but they were washing my clothes and it could not cause a storm," he said. "They used in washing what we call in the foreign country 'soap,' and it caused the whiteness and foam on the water, but it is something innocent and cannot cause a storm." The moment had passed. Even the king had grown bored with his own tantrum. "Well, don't have your clothes washed anymore," he snapped.

Sheppard left the palace and emerged into the pounding heat of the day, shouts of leapfrogging children, smells of peanuts drying in the market, the drone of the snake charmer's horn, ladies chatting in a doorway, the whole parade of ordinary life around him. Later, he joked about how anxious he'd been in that palace, wondering whether the king would take off his head. He needed his head, as "it is the only one I have."

But as Sheppard stumbled back to his quarters that afternoon, he probably could not see much humor in the incident. Soap flakes, gunshots, a bit of brass worn on his clothing—any of his Western habits could be misinterpreted as a political statement and lead to a death sentence.

Kubaland must have reminded him of the American South. In both places, his survival depended on his ability to play-act, to go under a false identity, to hide his true impulses and feelings—and most important, to stay on the good side of men who could easily kill him. Of the many explorers who could have wandered into Kubaland, Sheppard was uniquely equipped to live through the experience. His years in America—where he'd had to step into a variety of roles, from the "son" of a white dentist to the leader of a black church—had taught him to be a shape changer. Sheppard was a whirlwind of smoke and air and glitter, a dazzling sideshow of a man who could cough like a Kuba courtier or preach a sermon to a Virginia congregation. But the cost of such stupendous adaptability must have been high. Who was he under all the different masks and costumes?

It was soon after the storm, and his near-execution, that Sheppard decided he'd had enough. After several months in Kubaland, he wanted to return home with the tremendous artifacts and notes he'd collected— for surely he would be celebrated for the coup.

But leaving would be no easy matter. First he asked the king point-blank whether he might be dismissed. "Oh no," Kot aMweeky said, "you must stay with us."

Sheppard visited the palace several more times: "I told [the king] that I loved him and his people, and that it was a real pleasure to live in his town, but that his [Kete] subjects at Luebo were looking for my return. . . . The king replied . . . that he wanted me to remain with him and not to return again to Luebo."

Finally, Kot aMweeky relented and granted Sheppard a leave of absence: "You may go and remain a year."

In his negotiations, Sheppard did not forget his duties to the church. He convinced the king to grant him nine acres of land in the center of town on which he could found a mission station. Perhaps Sheppard eyed that lovely green field and imagined children running across it, and his future wife Lucy leaning against a doorway of a cottage—for she still waited for him back in the States, and he planned to bring her here as soon as he could.

He carried so many artifacts out of the city that his men had to walk single file, like porters struggling along one of Stanley's old trails. For years, the Belgians had been attempting to get into this kingdom and plunder it, to carry out ivory, rubber, and gold. Sheppard took art instead—what would later become one of the most valuable Kuba collections in the world.

"The parting with King Lukenga was touching. He was king, but he had a kindly heart," Sheppard wrote, suddenly forgiving Kot aMweeky for his moods. "The king furnished us with two guides and his royal mace for safe conduct. Hundreds of men, women and children followed us out on the plain, waving, singing and shouting a farewell."

As Sheppard traveled back to Luebo, he reveled in his freedom, away from the intrigues of court and the whims of the king. In small villages, he shared meals with farmers and hunters, humble people who called him simply "Sheppate."

One night, he gathered with some villagers around a leaping fire. They told him of the jackals and leopards that stalked the woods; how the people stayed up late at night in the safe circle of firelight, entertaining each other with stories to pass the time. They asked Sheppard about his own country, questions that must have struck him as refreshingly honest after all the subterfuge of the capital. "How do you get to the foreign country?" they wanted to know. "What do you eat?" They laughed at some of his answers, for the place he described seemed a fairyland.

"When I tried to tell them that we had a season of the year that . . . got so cold you could walk over streams without breaking through, and that some of our houses were taller than a palm tree, they incredulously shook their heads," he wrote.

Did he also tell them that across the sea, in a palace far taller than any palm tree, a king paced around his throne room, plotting their fate? Did he break the news that they were doubly cursed by kings, not just their own but also Leopold?

Most likely not. That night, as the cups of palm wine went from hand to hand, and people leaned against each other, enjoying the scratchy sound of tired voices, Sheppard's far away home must have seemed far away indeed. He was, that night, a man born in the land of the dead, come across the sea to this place of light, before this snug hearth, to tell his tale. He was Bope Mekabe.

PART II

The Poison Cup

CHAPTER 7

The Wedding Dress in the Coffin

In photos of Lucy Gantt Sheppard, you notice her clothing more than anything else about her—the collar that chokes with its scratchy lace, the voluminous dress that hides any hint of a body beneath, the pleated collar that flares out from her shoulders like stunted wings. She appears every inch the Victorian—refined, polite to a fault, secretive.

Two biographers who tried to document Lucy's life came away with little. When a male interviewer visited her in the 1940s, the aged widow answered his questions in sentences that wouldn't have looked out of place if they had been engraved in a greeting card.

A female biographer had a bit more luck. To Julia Lake Kellersberger, Lucy provided an account of her whereabouts during her busy life—but said almost nothing about what it all meant to her. The author was forced to color in the story, adding dramatic touches the old lady never mentioned.

"The long fingers of the pale February sun gripped the icy arms of the great oaks that line the broad streets of Tuscaloosa with the same gestures of friendliness as in Februaries past; crowds of freed slaves jostled together in the market square," Kellersberger begins, describing a scene surrounding Lucy's pregnant mother. "Indeed there was nothing to mark the day as different from others save to one orphaned ex-slave girl, deserted by her husband at her crucial hour." The book goes on that way, the author engaging in a kind of speculative biography in which she imagines the views outside the windows and the lessons taught to Lucy in school. In the absence of Lucy's opinions and impressions, the author makes them up.

I find myself resorting to similar tactics. Little remains of Lucy besides a few fading letters, those fragmented biographies, and some polite articles she wrote for *The Missionary*. And yet, after sifting through these scraps I have become quite certain of one thing: It was no picnic being William Sheppard's wife.

He dragged Lucy through malarial swamps while she was pregnant, installed her in a mud house, stuck her with the dirty work, cheated on her. When he sat down to compose his autobiography, Sheppard never thought to mention his wife; nor did he refer to Lucy in any of his widely published articles. In other words, he was typical of the adventurers who traversed Africa, women and children following behind them, until the hapless wives went back home or perished.

Livingstone, for instance, subjected his wife to many of the same hardships Sheppard did: Mary Livingstone hobbled pregnant across Africa, lost one child, suffered from paralysis, and then traveled home to live in poverty while her husband tried to raise funds for further expeditions.

Mary's mother was so disgusted with her son-in-law that she wrote him a scathing letter: "Was it not enough that you lost one lovely babe, and scarcely saved the other, while the mother came home threatened with paralysis? And will you again expose her and them in those sickly regions on an exploring expedition? . . . A pregnant woman with three children trailing about . . . through the wilds of Africa, among savage men and beasts!"

When Livingstone ignored the warning and brought Mary on yet another mission, she perished from malaria. Only then did Livingstone acknowledge his guilt: "There are regrets which will follow me till my dying day," he wrote.

Like Mary Livingstone, the wives who traveled to the Presbyterian Congo mission during its early years suffered terribly. Most died. Lucy was one of the few missionary wives to survive her ordeal. For this accomplishment alone, she was exceptional.

The heart is conservative; it loves what it knows best. What Lucy knew best was heroic women and absent men. Her father abandoned her mother when the child was born. Lucy probably never met him; she rarely dared speak of him. Even when she had reached the age of seventy-three, when an interviewer asked her why her father left and what happened to him, she said nothing. "[I] very much desired to question Mrs. Sheppard upon this point for fuller facts; but regarded her reticence," the interviewer wrote, explaining that he was too polite to push Lucy further. Perhaps he suspected that Lucy's father had been white. Why else would she have hidden his identity under such a thick blanket of silence?

Whoever the father had been, her mother more than made up for his absence. When Eliza Gantt's only daughter was born, the former slave owned little besides a *Webster's Blue Back Speller*. Still, she was determined that her girl would acquire all the accomplishments of a Victorian lady. Lucy would never hump around with a slosh bucket and a scrub brush, as her mother did; she would work with her mind.

In 1877, when Lucy was eleven, Eliza sent her to one of the best black schools in Alabama. Eight of the ten dollars the mother earned a month as a maid went to the girl's tuition. Lucy distinguished herself as the school's star soprano. She performed at graduation every year, always wearing the same dress, which had been cleaned for the occasion—a cost covered by an extra fifty cents sent by Eliza.

After graduating, Lucy scraped by as a teacher in a one-room schoolhouse; her students were the children of field hands who snatched their learning in brief reprieves from picking cotton.

It was on one of her trips back to Tuscaloosa to visit her mother that Lucy met William Sheppard. He was then a theological student living in a rented room, a fellow in a frayed suit with only a penny or two to jingle in his pocket. But the way he carried himself, towering over her with shoulders like great wings, she knew he was headed somewhere grand. He talked to her about Africa—how a colored man could make his name there—and she believed him.

More than the white laundered dresses, more than her trained soprano voice, more than the patched-together education, more than the ladies' magazines that taught her how to maintain proper hygiene, more than anything else Lucy had been able to sew or read or learn to do, William Sheppard promised to lift her out of poverty and shame. She would hold on to his shabby coattails and they would magically change into fine wool and silk. Stick with him long enough, and one day she was sure to find herself in a fine brick house on the most respectable of streets. It would be the kind of place her mother had always dreamed of—like the mansions Eliza scrubbed and scraped for other people. And Lucy would make sure that the house had a sweet little bedroom in the back, where her mother could move in, and finally, after all that drudgery, be able to rest. That, most likely, was the point of marrying William Sheppard: to repay her mother.

For the first three years of their engagement, the lovers lived in different cities. Lucy waited five more years while he disappeared in Africa. During much of that time, she lived with her mother, the two of them settling into what must have become a comfortable spinsterhood.

Then one day a telegram arrived from London. William had returned, and would be home soon to marry her. And her faith in him had paid off—her fiancé had just visited Queen Victoria. Her penniless minister had become one of the most eminent black men in the United States.

And what about William Sheppard—how did he view his impending marriage to a woman he had not seen for years? It seems he did not think about her much. He was, after all, rather busy in London. In the summer of 1893, he stopped there to be honored: He had been asked to join the Royal Geographical Society, the group that had funded Livingstone's trips.

Thirty years before, when Henry Morton Stanley swashbuckled into London after his first trip to Africa, the Royal Geographical Society snubbed him, and would not so much as hold a meeting in his honor. Stanley, after all, was the sort of man who wouldn't do in polite society. Born a bastard in Wales, he masqueraded as an American. One didn't know which was worse—the coal-dusty village of his true origin, or the self-promoting circus of a country that he pretended was his own. The pug-faced parvenu was the very opposite of the gentlemen explorers who gazed out of portraits in grand homes. He'd gone to Africa not to Christianize the heathen but to make himself famous. He even had the gall to serialize his search for Livingstone in a tabloid newspaper. And so the Royal Geographical Society refused to fete him—that is, until Queen Victoria sent Stanley a snuff box and invited him to visit her at her castle in Scotland. Then the old boys had to give the adventurer his due. Stanley had broken down the barriers of snobbery and become the first tabloid explorer.

Upon arriving in London, Sheppard found himself celebrated in somewhat the same manner as Stanley. He received a medal and met Queen Victoria. Dapper in his swallowtail coat, his face settled into a beaky, hooded-eyed handsomeness, Sheppard was all of twenty-eight, three years younger than Stanley had been.

And now, with a medal hanging from his chest, he would sail back to America and his true work would begin. Presenting himself as a man who had penetrated into the forbidden city of the Kuba kings, he would pack huge crowds into churches, would tell them all he had seen, and the wonder of it would challenge Southerners to reexamine their notions about Africa. The story he told was a reverse *Heart of Darkness*, a tale of a man who travels deep into the jungle and stumbles into a city of checkerboard order.

And he would ask them: If Africans possessed shriveled, inadequate brains, then how did the city of Mushenge come to be, with its courts and juries, its history spanning hundreds of years, its magnificent art?

"Perhaps they got their civilization from the Egyptians," Sheppard said once, echoing the attitude of his day, which held that the best Africans could do was to steal culture from their neighbors. But then he'd added mischievously, "Or [perhaps] the Egyptians [got their civilization] from the Bakuba!"

Sheppard gave the first of his great speeches in London's Exeter Hall, where he showed off Kuba artwork. Upon returning to the U.S., he called on President Grover Cleveland and presented him with a cleverly woven rug, proof that African creations rivaled the maddest of New York fashions. He sent the rest of his artifacts down to the Hampton Institute, his alma mater, establishing the beginning of a collection that he would contribute to over the years, eventually amassing over four hundred pieces of art.

Sheppard also regaled Hampton students with the story of his journey into the Kuba kingdom. When he came to the part where the prince threatened to execute him, he conjured up a knife from his bag. This, he explained, was a duplicate of the ritual blade that would have been used on his own neck; then he detailed exactly how the Kuba planned to kill him:

> The victim's hands and feet are bound, his arms strapped to his side; a strong sapling is bent down and his head is so tied to it that the neck is stretched and held taut. The executioner whirls the knife—a broad murderous blade with undulating edge like an exaggerated "Christy knife," and with one stroke severs the head from the shoulders and cuts the cord that holds it, so that it is flung, ghastly and horrible, at the feet of the awe-stricken spectators.

One can imagine the effect these theatrics had on the students at the Virginia school. In many parts of the South, a black person could be lynched for brandishing a weapon like the one Sheppard held. And yet the explorer was proud of the murderous beauty of the blade, for it was

An early photo of
William Sheppard.
*Courtesy of the Hampton
University Archives*

Sheppard's partner, Samuel Lapsley,
before he left for Africa.
Courtesy of the Presbyterian Historical Society

Kuba dignitaries act as extras in this very staged photo. Resplendent in the linen suit and pith helmet favored by colonialists, Sheppard also leans on a Kuba spear and stands on an animal skin—drawing on both Western and African symbols of power to create a dual identity. (The Kuba man to his right wears brass anklets, marking him as a chief or royal.)

Courtesy of the Presbyterian Historical Society

Sheppard extracts a tooth. He picked up this skill from his first boss, Dr. Henkel.

Courtesy of the Presbyterian Historical Society

(*Right*) Sheppard poses with a freshly killed boa constrictor in one of his many trophy photos.

Courtesy of the Presbyterian Historical Society

(*Below*) Maria Fearing. A former slave, she paid her own way to the Congo. In Luebo, she bought children out of slavery for a pair of scissors or a few beads, then raised them herself.

Courtesy of the Presbyterian Historical Society

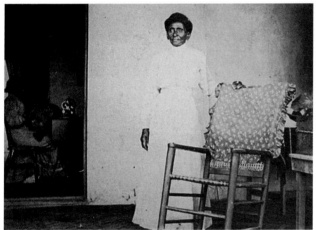

The croquet players in this undated photo appear to be Lucy and William Sheppard, Maria Fearing, and Lillian Thomas. Perhaps it was taken during the brief period when Sheppard presided over an all-black Presbyterian mission.

Courtesy of the Presbyterian Historical Society

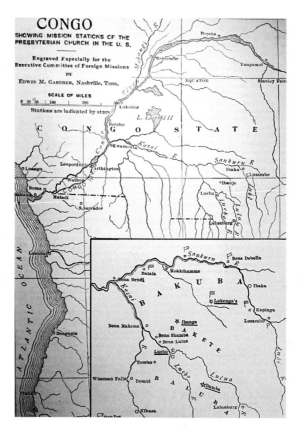

CONGO

SHOWING MISSION STATIONS OF THE
PRESBYTERIAN CHURCH IN THE U. S.

Engraved Especially for the
Executive Committee of Foreign Missions
BY
EDWIN M. GARTNER, Nashville, Tenn.

SCALE OF MILES

Stations are indicated by stars

(*Above*) A 1909 map of the Congo shows the Presbyterian triumphs.
Note that the church claims to have a station in the forbidden city
("Lukenga's")—which was not exactly true. Ibaanc ("Ibange") lies just
on the edge of Kuba country.

Courtesy of the Presbyterian Historical Society

(*Right*) A gathering of
missionaries in 1900, or
thereabouts. Standing:
William Morrison and
Lachlan Vass. Sitting:
Joseph Phipps, William
Sheppard, and Henry
Hawkins.

*Courtesy of the Presbyterian
Historical Society*

Morrison and Sheppard show off a buffalo carcass.
Courtesy of the Presbyterian Historical Society

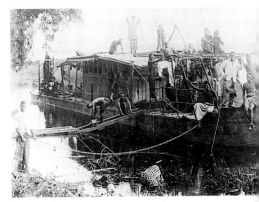

The wreck of the SS *Lapsley*. Sunday school children had saved their pennies to help pay for the Presbyterians' steamship. It capsized in the Congo River, killing twenty-four people.
Courtesy of the Presbyterian Historical Society

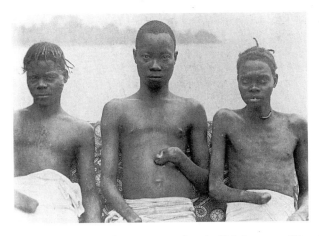

Lachlan Vass took this photo to prove that the Belgians cut off hands of villagers who refused to harvest rubber. Photos like this one helped to bolster Sheppard's controversial report.
Courtesy of the Presbyterian Historical Society

Max Sheppard had to wear a pith helmet as protection from the sun whenever he ventured outside. On the back of the photo his father wrote, "Our baby with his big cannibal friend."

Courtesy of the Hampton University Archives

The Presbyterians printed this 1905 Sheppard family photo as a souvenir card; on the back, the card lists handy facts about the missionary effort in the Congo. "A Woman's Missionary and 'Sunshine Band' [have] been organized and [are] doing much helpful work. . . . A simple text book and parts of the Scripture have been put into the hands of 2,000 children."

Courtesy of the Hampton University Archives

A picnic party (for the Fourth of July?) gathers in Ibaanc. Sheppard positions himself front and center.
Courtesy of the Presbyterian Historical Society

A convention of Presbyterian missionaries in 1909. Lucy and William Sheppard sit second and third from left; Morrison is second from right. In the middle, Althea Brown Edmiston poses with her child and husband. She sailed to Africa as a single woman, but later married one of her colleagues.
Courtesy of the Presbyterian Historical Society

In Leopoldville for the libel trial, Sheppard and Morrison stand with the Kuba witnesses.
Courtesy of the Presbyterian Historical Society

The Sheppards in Louisville, Kentucky. William had been demoted from "Black Livingstone" to "Children's Friend."
Courtesy of the Hampton University Archives

Dr. Wm. H. SHEPPARD, F.R.G.S. and family, Our African Missionary.
Better known as "The Children's Friend."

a symbol of the African kings who crafted their own swords, the black rulers who doubled as artisans.

He spoke all over the South—to black college students in starched and mended suits; to beneficent volunteer ladies; to would-be missionaries with crosses glimmering at their necks; to white students from the best schools.

It was, after all, a time when audiences were hungry for Africa, the more exotic the better. They associated the continent with bare-breasted "Hottentots," Tom Thumb–sized Pygmies, and wild men wearing leopardskins. No World's Fair or exposition was complete without an ersatz African village, a collection of huts in which imported Pygmies or Dahomeyanas or Ubangis shivered in their "authentic costumes" and hawked curios to the public. In one Chicago sideshow attraction called "Darkest Africa," a barker yelled to onlookers that if they only went inside the tent, they would hear from the very lips of Captain Callahan how he had had his penis cut off by cannibals. "He will remove his robe," the barker promised. "And after you see with your own eyes that the captain is absolutely devoid of sexual glands . . . then, and only then, will you be expected to pay fifty cents."

Sheppard, of course, was no sideshow attraction. The explorer inspired his audience with G-rated tales, suitable for Sunday school classes, and he frequently made mention of the Christian duty to save heathens. Still, like the carnival performers, he knew how to entertain, as his wedding would prove.

The ceremony was planned for February 1894 in Jacksonville, Florida, where Lucy and her mother lived together in yet another shack. She must have pictured the wedding as a modest affair—she had almost no family and could afford nothing but orange blossoms in the church.

On the day before the ceremony, William arrived in town and burst into their house. That laugh, that flash of teeth, that smell of gunpowder, that gangly stretch of arms knocking the doilies off chairs. The teacups shook in their saucers. The Bible on the table splayed open under his thumb. He threw his top hat on their chair and made himself at home.

A small wedding? Not if Sheppard could help it. He had only one day to gather a crowd, and he went to work immediately. Barging into a nearby schoolhouse, he regaled the children with tales of Africa, narrating the adventures in the third person and never letting on that he himself was the hero. He concluded with a pitch for his own wedding: "The man who did these things is to be married tomorrow right here in your own city." And so when Lucy marched down the aisle, she did so not only before her dear mother but also in front of pews full of children, who squirmed to get a better view of the man at her side, the explorer who'd shot thirty-six raging hippos and taken tea with sawtoothed cannibals. It was a fitting start to their marriage, the hero decked out in a London-tailored suit that made the bride all the more invisible behind her veil.

The couple's honeymoon—if it could be called that—was a whistle-stop tour through the South during which William drummed up support for the Congo mission. More than money, it was volunteers that the church needed—a circumstance of which Sheppard must have been painfully aware. He'd left the Luebo plantation under the care of George Adamson and his wife, a Scottish couple of questionable ability. Mrs. Adamson entertained the Africans by opening and closing her parasol for them, but seemed at a loss as to how else to communicate. Mr. Adamson bought supplies with a bad check. Unless Sheppard found recruits, the mission might die, never to be funded again by the Presbyterians.

He found three. Henry Hawkins, like Sheppard, was a preacher who'd been trained at the Stillman Institute. Hawkins wanted to take his wife, Victoria, with him, but for obscure reasons, the Presbyterians turned her down. This forced him to make a wrenching choice between wife and avocation. He picked Africa.

The other two recruits, Lillian Thomas and Maria Fearing, came from Lucy's alma mater. Fearing was a particularly remarkable woman. Born a slave in the 1830s, she had to wait thirty years until she was free to begin her education. As a middle-aged woman, she put herself through school at Talladega College. The oldest student at the school, she bunked with and baby-sat two of the youngest girls: Lillian Thomas and Lucy Gantt. Now the triumvirate of roommates had been reunited.

In May 1894, the five missionaries met at the dock in New York to sail to London.

Lucy might be headed for a wilderness prowled by jackals and infested with the tsetse fly, but that didn't discourage her from trying to scrape together some nice things, the kind of accoutrements that would look proper in a middle-class Southern home. Upon arriving in London, she hurried around with her husband, amassing supplies for the expedition. "Her feminine instincts craved a cooking stove and pretty china," according to Lucy's biographer Kellersberger. "Later, at a trading post in the Congo she was able to purchase a few blue and white porcelain plates and platters, but never a stove." It was as if she planned to paste over the horrors of Africa with doily and chintz, hoping that somehow a bourgeois existence would be possible in the outback.

When the Americans reached Boma, the capital of the Free State, Lucy must have realized just how rough and frightening her new life would be. The five missionaries pushed their way through a square teeming with Belgian bureaucrats, Congolese whores, railroad workers paid in jugs of rum, overseers with whips coiled on their belts. To top it off, William came down with a fever; he huddled under blankets, sweating and talking nonsense. With no idea how to tend him, Lucy hurried through the dusty streets of Boma, searching for a doctor, or indeed, any respectable person. The only medical man turned out to be dead drunk, but an English missionary gave her instructions and she managed to nurse her husband back to health.

Then began the 260-mile march past the cataracts on the Congo.

Sheppard and Lapsley had taken this same trek together a few years before, the feverish men riding in hammocks that swayed from the shoulders of African porters. Now it was the three ladies who would ride in the canvas hammocks, wrapped up like delicate larvae. Lucy, lounging Cleopatra-like above the naked backs of the porters, grew flustered. She confused the Congolese words for "stop" and "go," and ended up tumbling out of her perch to fume by the side of the road, until William straightened everything out.

Several weeks later, she found herself swaying on the deck of a steamship that puffed along the Kasai River. For William, the trip was a tiresome repeat of three years before, when he'd shivered with fever on a dining-room bench, the captain pacing on the deck declaring, "I shall go mad," Sheppard and Lapsley watching the ship's rations dwindle to nothing.

If Lucy had any illusions about Africa, they would have been dashed now. Even for a woman who grew up in the maid's quarters, the ship was horrifically squalid. When she dared to stand on deck at all, she would have had to peer out through a wire net that had been draped over the ship to protect passengers from arrows that flew from the thickets along the river. The steamer jumped and bucked over rapids. The captain had pocketed the tins of meat they handed over to him at the beginning of the trip—"Chop fini," he told them, in a patois of Congo dialect and French. Instead of their own delicacies, he fed the missionaries on rancid hog meat and hardtack. Lucy improvised some vegetables by boiling potato vines in an old tin can, but still, the travelers were often hungry.

She might have felt entitled to at least a scrap of comfort—if not for herself, then for the baby that banged against the drum of her belly. In the late stages of pregnancy, Lucy was sleeping on bare wood decks in sweltering heat, was suffering morning sickness on a ship that whirled woozily underneath her.

Judging from the couple's itinerary, William had not scheduled a pregnancy. Instead, he raced toward Luebo. Preoccupied with his beloved Kuba and the fate of the Presbyterian mission, he hardly seemed to notice the distress of his young wife.

In Luebo, the pair moved into a mud hut. It's not clear what had happened to the comfortable palm house William had built years before. Perhaps he chivalrously gave it to one of the lady missionaries. Or perhaps it had never been as comfortable as he imagined. At any rate, Lucy found their new home alarming: The roof leaked; the dirt floor was swampy; the windows let in only the murkiest light; their possessions rotted in the gloom.

The Presbyterian station itself had become a shambles. A series of white couples had tried to run the place, but all had admitted defeat or simply expired. Mrs. Adamson had died from fever. Mr. Adamson had been demoted by the church and sent down river. A Mr. and Mrs. Rowbotham had zipped in, brimming with good intentions, but soon decided that the climate would kill them. By the time the Sheppards arrived, the only Westerners left on the plantation were Dr. Dewitt Snyder and his wife, a couple from New York. Dr. Snyder had volunteered to act as the mission's medic, though it's not clear why he was able to append the title "Doctor" before his name, since he'd been trained only as a pharmacist.

He and his wife had inherited a terrible situation. Years before, Lapsley had invited former slaves and orphans to move in. Now the place had turned into a refugee camp, with about eighty adults and dozens of children. The adult Africans had to be given work, the children educated. "It forces me to be overseer over this lot of people," Dr. Snyder complained. He had expected to be their preacher and doctor, but found himself instead a reluctant governor.

And so it was in a mud hut, among ex-slaves, that Lucy gave birth just before Christmas. The labor pangs came much earlier than expected, and the baby emerged sickly and shriveled. Lucy had no doctor to consult, only Snyder with his valise full of malaria medicines. She did her best to nurse her little Miriam, but within a few weeks the baby was dead.

Lucy used her own wedding dress to line the coffin, yards of foamy lace wrapped around the tiny corpse. In the end, she had been able to give her daughter nothing but this—a tidbit of luxury, a final cushion.

In a letter to a friend back home, Lucy told the brief but terrible story of her daughter's life: "Mrs. Snyder often said [to me], 'Mrs. Sheppard, how dainty [the] baby is.' . . . She did seem too dainty for earth, yet we prayed so earnestly that God should spare her to us, but he saw best to take the little treasure to Him. None but a mother who has had her little one [taken] away knows my suffering. Oh, my Father, *help me.*"

The next baby would not be born in a mud hut—Lucy would make sure of that. She convinced the men to build a five-room house for her; she did the rest. The floors she made in the native way, dirt from anthills packed down and burned until it formed a kind of cement. She sewed a ceiling out of cotton sheets. Because she had no glass, she used muslin to cover the windows. In the empty room she called the nursery, she strung up Kodak film over the window, strips of celluloid that had gone bad and never been developed or negatives that had spoiled. The result must have looked like a black-and-white version of stained glass. Instead of the lives of the saints, this window told the story of Lucy and William, their reversed images glowing in the late morning sun. Here Lucy posed beside Westminster Abbey; there William waved from the deck of a ship. In the negatives, they would have had dove-colored faces and licorice teeth, their white linen clothes gone black as funeral garments.

Because she had a husband and hoped for children, Lucy struggled to build a Victorian home in the middle of the outback.

"I called it the *Ladies Home Journal* house, because so many of the ideas for making furniture and for simple colorful decorations came from that magazine," Lucy wrote later. She went on to describe a domestic situation that would have confounded the editors of most ladies' magazines:

All of the furniture that I had was made from packing boxes of various shapes and sizes. These I draped with bright cretonne and the results were both practical and attractive. I never possessed a cooking stove. For years my cooking was done out of doors, the kettle or saucepan resting on three stones, or upon several hard anthills. I managed to bake by putting live coals above and beneath a clay pot. Constant vigilance was required to keep the bread from burning. A small brick oven, later, made baking a less precarious adventure. Lights were another problem. Candles were a luxury. These were supplemented by a tin can filled with palm oil, with a rag serving as a wick. When I was finally able to obtain a glass lamp in which I could burn palm oil, I was so overjoyed that I felt certain no light in the homeland was any brighter.

Congo girls took their turns, by twos, working in my home learning new methods of more abundant living. . . . Boys were trained in my kitchen to cook, for I had ever in mind the future homemaking of young Christian men and women.

How different was the experience of the women who went to Africa without husbands, and did not have to conform to domestic expectations. Althea Brown, who would become Lucy's colleague several years later, chose to sail off to the mysterious continent because she craved adventure and independence. Proud of her African and Native American heritage, tomboyish, brilliant, Brown had graduated at the top of her class from prestigious Fisk University, putting herself through school by starting her own beauty shop. She could have stayed in the United States and become an entrepreneur. Instead she headed for the frontier, where she would one day write the first Kuba-English dictionary.

Hers was not a *Ladies' Home Journal* house. In Africa, she invited dogs, cats, and parrots to roam through her rooms. She trained monkeys to greet visitors and remove their hats. "We did have two pretty little leopards," she lamented, "but they died." She delighted also in the African cuisine. "Come into our nice dining room and have a cool drink of spring water and a good dinner of either native or European food," she wrote, inviting her audience in America for an imaginary visit. "If you like, I can serve you an elephant steak, or a monkey stew. Both are very good!"

The difference was, Althea Brown had chosen Africa—and as a single career woman, she found herself liberated from the stultifying conditions in the States. She survived the deadly climate for several decades.

So too did Maria Fearing. Another single woman recruited by William Sheppard, Fearing was a tiny woman with jug-handle ears. She weighed about a hundred pounds and was in her fifties when she volunteered to go. The job had killed men half her age, and the Presbyterians, not wanting to be held responsible, refused to pay Fearing's way. Undeterred, she funded the journey herself by selling her house to Sam Lapsley's father.

This sliver of a woman would outlast many of her younger colleagues in the field, enduring the Congo eight years longer than the Sheppards themselves. She would found an orphanage and run it on a frugal budget, buying children out of slavery for a pair of scissors or a few beads. Fearing quit at the age of eighty-one, but only because the church insisted she retire.

Unlike unattached women such as Fearing and Brown, the missionary wives traveled to the Congo out of duty rather than passion for the frontier. This may be why they tended to die as speedily as European flowers transplanted into African soil. Mrs. Snyder, Mrs. Morrison, Mrs. Adamson, Mrs. Rochester—these women dragged after distracted husbands to a swampy hell they'd never wanted to see. They drudged from the first flattening heat of the morning until the last stabbing light of the evening, looking after not only their own children, but dozens of orphans as well, and attending to their adventurer husbands. They expired so quickly that they had to be buried in the remote villages where they had fallen ill. Even in death, they troubled their husbands as little as possible, their headstones tilting in out-of-the-way spots, demure and proper, ready to be forgotten.

Mrs. Sheppard and Mrs. Snyder must have grown fond of each other. Lucy remembers the way the white woman tried to comfort her when her "dainty" baby grew sick. So when Mrs. Snyder also became ill in the spring of 1896, it must have been a terrible blow to Lucy. The missionaries had run out of the medicines that could cure her, and the nearest doctor was over eight hundred miles away.

When a steamship docked in Luebo, Dr. Snyder decided that he and his wife must get on board. If she could survive the trip down to Leopoldville, she might live. Frail and feverish, Mrs. Snyder struggled onto the steamship and waved wanly from the deck. She would never return.

The Snyders had been the only white people at Luebo. Now they were gone, which made for an interesting situation. The Congo mission, funded by a segregated Presbyterian Church that believed in bringing white people and white values to Africa, was run by a black man and staffed entirely by black people. It was a situation that the Presbyterians back home regarded with horror.

Posthaste, the church hired Samuel Phillips Verner. He would become the business manager in Luebo—but more important, he'd act as the token white until others could be recruited.

That the church hired an unhinged fellow like Verner attests to just how hard it was to find a white man, any white man at all, willing to risk his life in the African outback. Only twenty-five-years old, Verner had already suffered a nervous breakdown; under its influence, he'd believed himself to be a Hapsburg emperor. Now he was recovered—more or less. After reading David Livingstone's books until "Africa became as familiar to me as my own blue hills of Piedmont," Verner had come up with Nietzschean ideas about the Dark Continent. He fantasized about an *American* Livingstone who would bring democracy and capitalism to the savages—and make a tidy profit along the way. "The land which all the nations of history could not conquer at last has thrown open its doors, given up the keys of its treasure house, and over the crumbling dust of the heroes who died that it might live, the invincible Caucasian is marching on," he wrote.

He must have been disappointed when he arrived in the Congo and he found out just how far from invincibility his fellow Caucasians were. The Snyders, he learned, had left Luebo early, and Mrs. Snyder had died in Leopoldville, still far from the coast. They had left the Congo mission in the hands of American blacks, a situation that Verner would have found deeply worrisome, since he believed that dark-skinned people had mental aptitude enough only to be "second-class missionaries."

He rode the last few miles toward Luebo in the customary hammock, suspended from the shoulders of the porters. Peering over the canvas walls, he watched the scenery go by, peanut fields and palm groves. And then a bend in the road revealed the first sign of the missionaries. An African boy waved an American flag—apparently, he'd been sent as an honor guard to welcome Verner, a pint-sized escort to transform hammock into motorcade. Soon, Verner's porters began shouting, "Sheppati!" And then Sheppard materialized in the road: "A large, well-built man came across the grass, and in the old familiar accent [of the South] gave me greeting and welcome." He did not appear to have been stunted by the absence of whites. Cheerful and honey-tongued as ever, Sheppard gushed about the church he was building, the banana trees, the hunting. He showed off a gleaming plantation house surrounded by flowers.

Verner hadn't thought the American Livingstone would turn out to be black. But with the flexibility of the half mad, he took this new revelation in stride. After meeting Sheppard, his views on race began to change. Eventually, he gave up his theories about second-class missionaries and effusively praised his black colleagues. But the true measure of Verner's admiration was the way he modeled himself on Sheppard. He too would soon tramp off in search of his own Kuba city—it was as if he hoped to steal Sheppard's mythic adventures and make them his own.

His first night in Luebo, in September 1896, Verner dined in the house that had been so lavishly decorated and primped by Lucy Sheppard, the palm palace with its muslin ceilings and *Ladies' Home Journal* touches. Wearied by months of travel, he reveled in the comforts Lucy had conjured from the jungle: "a long house with low verandah and large white pillars, and Mrs. Sheppard in the doorway. My first impression was how faithfully the place and surroundings reflected the old Southern home life to which [the Sheppards] had been accustomed; one could almost imagine himself, save for a few details, in old Virginia again. My welcome was all that heart could desire."

As she plied the newcomer with biscuits and chicken, waddling because of her ponderous pregnancy, her new hope for a child after the untimely death of Miriam, Lucy must have felt exhausted but pleased. Her baby would arrive any minute now, born into an airy mansion, with its own room and plenty to eat. One day, the little girl or boy would trace a finger along the faded Kodak negatives and ask to hear stories about them. "That," Lucy would say, "was a terrible time. But no more. No more bad times for us."

As she cleaned up Mr. Verner's dishes, the contractions started. By the end of the night—with no doctor to watch her, no anesthetic, not so much as a trained midwife—she gave birth. In the morning, she drowsed with a healthy girl on her chest: Lucille.

Within days, the new mother was back at work. Her stamina astonished Verner: "It was wonderful to see how well she attended to her domestic duties, even continuing to teach school, notwithstanding her maternal cares, and that with cheerfulness and a happy spirit." Lucy ran the school, teaching the barefooted orphans without benefit of desks, schoolroom, or books. Her husband had also put her in charge of the makeshift hospital; after the Snyders left, Lucy became the reigning medical expert.

But not even her endless roster of duties could cut through her joy: Little Lucille was no "dainty" baby. Lucy knew this baby would live.

And on top of that, Mr. Verner's arrival meant all kinds of improvements. He and William would roll up their sleeves and work together to overhaul the transport system. With a white man acting as their representative, the missionaries at Luebo could be assured of better service from the Belgian captains and traders, men who might refuse service to blacks. Cloth, tinned meat, vials of medicine, needles, tea, coffee—all of it might soon come steaming up the Kasai River, to be packed tidily in Lucy's pantry.

In the spring of 1897, Verner neglected his duties in Luebo—bookkeeping bored him—in order to go off in search of diamond mines and cities made of gold. After a few weeks, he stumbled into a remote Kuba city, called Ndombe. Years before, he had rhapsodized about the kind of man who "walks down the street and his very air names him an uncrowned king." Now he had the chance to test his theory. If he waltzed into a Kuba town and met with its leader, would he be recognized as a god, a reborn king, as Sheppard had been? Would the people hand over their riches?

Instead of a god, the people of Ndombe took him for a fish. When they saw Verner's translucent skin, they decided he must have come by it sleeping deep in the ocean, lost in caves of coral, shielded from the sun in the blue-green murk. Nor did they turn out to possess any diamonds—just a lot of goats and peanuts and tapestries.

So, after poking around, Verner decided to return to Luebo. He and his African crew climbed into two canoes, to float down the Kasai River toward home. "It was the historic Fourth of July," he wrote. "The two boats were now packed for our departure. . . . In the boat with me I took all the smaller boys and the weaker women, leaving the second boat to be rowed by my strong hammock carriers."

Soon Verner's canoe shot out front, its occupants losing sight of the other boat in the twists and turns of the river. Toward evening, when the sky dimmed, they pulled over to wait for the other canoe. The tea-colored water of the Kasai lapped at the shore. The dark air pulsed with insects. The woods turned black. The African women and children gathered driftwood and cooked their dinner. And still the other canoe did not come.

Verner did not sleep a wink that night. The next day, he paddled down river to deliver the women and children to safety; then, with some African volunteers, he headed back to search for the missing canoe. The rescue party paddled against the bash of the current, their pace agonizingly slow as they scanned the shores for any evidence of their lost friends. Finally, Verner spotted something:

> We approached a small low sandy island, and I saw an object lying on the beach, resembling at a distance a piece of manioc root. . . . As the boat was halted, I bade Kassongo [to] descend and see what the thing was.. . . . Kassongo got out, turned the object over, and exclaimed, "It's a man's arm!" . . . I leaped ashore, followed by the others. Surely enough it was part of a yellow arm from the elbow down. . . . Kassongo looked closely and exclaimed, "Kelala's arm!" The others confirmed him. I turned away and ran up across the isle, and sat down on the shore, bursting into tears. There could be no mistake. I knew that arm too well. Over many a swollen streamlet had the strong arm borne my tired body. . . . There it lay, mute in its silent and terrible appeal.

The canoe had been attacked by the Baschilele, a fierce tribe known to kill all intruders into their land. Had Verner asked any of the local people for advice, they would have told him to avoid Baschilele country; but the American, in his ignorance, had led his faithful servants straight into a trap.

With ten deaths on his conscience, Verner stumbled toward Luebo, feverish, blistered, and suffering from what he called "brain troubles." When he arrived home, he learned that tragedy had struck here, too.

While the Baschilele had been dismembering his men, the Sheppards' baby, Lucille, had taken a fever. She had just died.

"My faith was surely needing its rock-bottom foundation in those days," Verner wrote about the pileup of terrible events. One can only imagine Lucy's state of mind as she dragged herself back into the house after the funeral. Nothing to do now but clean the litter from the days before—the compresses hardened into tortured shapes, the pills ground up for an infant's consumption. The African sun blazed through the Kodak negatives in the nursery window, bleaching away all the images.

When her second baby died, Lucy was two months pregnant with a third child, which left her with no choice: She would have to give birth in the Congo again, without a doctor, without anesthetic, without any hope the new baby would survive. William, too, must have been wracked with grief after the death of two children, though he left no written record of his grappling with the loss.

But he had his work to distract him, for the situation at Luebo was more precarious than ever. Samuel Verner—the token white man, who lent an air of legitimacy to the mission—was teetering on the brink of a nervous breakdown. He would soon drift away entirely. By the turn of the century, Verner would wrench off his minister's collar and find employment in the sleazy, dreamy realm of the carnival sideshow, where he'd always belonged. As a "special agent"—a polite term for a slave buyer—for the World's Fair, he returned to the Congo in 1904 to collect Pygmies and "red Africans" for exhibition in St. Louis. The specimens he procured in the African markets were shipped overseas, where they were forced to dance for gawking Midwesterners, their bare feet slapping the frigid soil.

In 1897, with Verner clearly on the way out, Sheppard must have agonized about his own future in Africa. If no other white man volunteered to become the token leader of the Presbyterian station in Luebo, the church would surely shut the place down—and Sheppard might have to sail home, never to venture inside the Kuba kingdom again.

CHAPTER 8

A Basket of Hands

Like so many martyrs, Samuel Lapsley proved to be a more forceful leader in death than he had been in life. Who could contradict the long-ago policy decisions of a saint? Years before, Lapsley had wanted to plant a mission in the middle of the Kuba kingdom. Now the Presbyterians hoped to honor the wishes of their lost brother—wishes they would have remembered every time another of his articles appeared. Even in death, Sam Lapsley continued to publish; he'd left behind hundreds of diary entries and letters. These appeared in church newsletters, extolling the virtues of the Kuba.

In 1897, everybody, including Sheppard, was waiting for Lapsley to rise again and return to the Congo, to lead the way into the forbidden city of the Kuba. Never mind that Sheppard was the one welcomed by the Kuba as a king; never mind that he was perhaps the only Westerner who spoke their language with any fluency. He knew that the Presbyterians would never give him the go-ahead to found a mission in the Kuba capital. He needed a white man through whom he could operate. Preferably the new fellow would be as sweet-tempered, sickly, and easy to influence as Sam had been.

William Morrison arrived in Luebo in the spring of 1897. He was so sick that he had to be lugged up the hill in a canvas hammock. When the porters lowered the stretcher and Sheppard peered at the fellow inside, he must have thought the contents very promising—here was Lapsley all over again. The stranger, emaciated from his long journey, burned with fever. He mumbled in the salt-cured drawl of an upper-class Virginian. Thirty years old, he was just about the age that Sam would have been, had he lived.

"He is so much like dear Mr. Lapsley," Sheppard told his wife. "We must save him."

But soon enough, the likeness faded. Morrison easily shrugged off his fever—he had never been one to wallow in illness. Nor did he physically resemble Lapsley in the least. He had a thatch of oily black curls on his head, beneath which he wore a beard that emphasized the sharpness of his chin; his eyebrows were so thick, they appeared to have been pasted on, like the masking-tape brows of Groucho Marx. Nature, it seemed, had not outfitted him for the part of the South's brief-blooming lily, its pale and perfect martyr.

That, however, was exactly what his parents had decided he would be when he was born. They'd begun training him early to become a missionary. Morrison resisted. In college, he became a caustic writer and a skilled debater, and he looked forward to becoming a lawyer.

But his resolve to follow his own path crumbled after his father, dying, used his last breaths to command his son to follow the missionary's calling. Years later, when Morrison read an article in a church newsletter about Lapsley, he felt he could not escape his fate: Here was the boy his father had always wanted him to be, a golden angel of the South who wandered to Africa and ended up beneath a gray stone tilting from a malarial swamp. Morrison gave up his dreams of the law and volunteered to take over Lapsley's job.

The new recruit could translate Greek and Latin, could debate and sing, and though his grades had been mediocre, he was known for his punctuality. Most important, he was white. To the Presbyterian Foreign Mission, these seemed like ample qualifications to take charge of a town full of refugees in one of the most remote areas in the world. He would become the new leader of the Congo mission.

On the journey over to Africa in December of 1896, how many times did Morrison curse himself for succumbing to his dead father's orders? How many times did he wish that he'd simply defied the old man and become a lawyer? Now he would never have the billowing black robe, the magic spell of Latin words, the hushed courtroom and the flight of his own impeccable logic.

Instead, he was sailing away from everyone he loved, possibly to his death, to take up a job that he'd always had doubts about. He comforted himself by indulging in unmissionarylike tirades against the foreigners he encountered in each port. He saved his worst invectives for the Belgians, "a nasty piggish lot of fellows who would make a decent man sick without a storm."

Morrison had no reason to resent the Belgians—not yet—but he seemed to guess at what they were up to in the Congo. "We sailed from Antwerp Sunday morning Dec. 6th amid the hurrahs of ten thousand voices & the screeching of a brass band; such a howling mob of jabbering idiots I have never seen," he wrote. "The Belgians think they have one-half the earth because by courtesy of the powers they were allowed control of the Congo Free State." Before he so much as set foot on African soil, Morrison understood that King Leopold's famous philanthropy was a lie.

This was yet another way in which Morrison differed from his predecessor. Lapsley—sentimental, prudish, self-searching—had been a thoroughly nineteenth-century man. When he caught a steamship captain whipping the African crew, Lapsley, as described earlier, jumped to their defense, yelling at the captain and halting the abuse. To us, this behavior seems heroic. But Lapsley immediately regretted the outburst and prayed to God for forgiveness. He had lost his temper and strayed from the lamblike behavior that was his ideal.

Morrison was no lamb. He wouldn't have hesitated to chew out that steamship captain. Born only a year later than Lapsley, he belonged to a different era, surveying the world with the wide-angle lens of twentieth-century mass media. He was angry about injustices all over the world, and hated the greedy individuals and governments that preyed on the meek.

The trouble was, he didn't always know how to contain his anger. Years later, when he wrote letters of protest, Morrison was as likely to ridicule the Belgian bureaucrats' misspelling of French words as he was to object to their slave trading. He did not hesitate to insult the men he despised. Even some of his friends worried about the activist's indiscreet letters and tactlessness.

Morrison did not care to be polite; he only cared about being right. He was gifted—or perhaps cursed—with blue eyes that pierced through the gilded uniforms of Free State officials to the shriveled hearts within. After only months in the Congo, he had grasped what others, Lapsley most especially, had never been able to understand: that each bit of brutality he witnessed in Luebo was not an anomaly; that the Free State government was carrying out systematic massacre of the Africans; that the "philanthropic" King Leopold was nothing but a swindler. And he, Morrison, had an obligation to stop the murders and tell the world the truth about the Congo.

In early 1898, Lucy nursed her third newborn, a little girl named Wilhelmina, in the cool of the five-room house. She must have enjoyed the drowsy naptimes of a Kasai afternoon. The muslin ceilings rippling in the breezes. Sounds from the village echoing, faraway, dreamy, as she rocked her child, marveling over the miniature fingernails and feet and bow-shaped mouth.

But mixed in with the contentment would have been the terror, nights when Lucy woke with her heart pounding and hurried to the crib to check. Did the baby's eyes still flutter open? How hot was her skin? Had she gained weight? Lucy's first baby had died after a few weeks, the second after several months. She knew all too well how quickly fever could descend on her child, deadly and mysterious as the African driver ants that sometimes ate the flesh off of infants. The Congo interior was a hard enough place for adult Americans to survive; babies were even more likely to succumb. For this reason, many missionaries sent their children back home to live with relatives.

When the baby was five months old, Lucy bundled her up and boarded a steamer on the African coast. She would visit her mother in Florida, then take her girl to Virginia to be raised by William's sister, an arrangement that bordered on adoption. Leaving her child behind, Lucy would return to her husband and her duties as a missionary. Though she would see Wilhelmina in the meantime, it would be more than a decade before she would live with her daughter again. Strange as this arrangement may seem to us, Lucy regarded it as a heartbreaking necessity. Her husband's career came first.

William must have suffered from bouts of loneliness during the year and a half of Lucy's absence. He appears to have had few close friends. Morrison treated Sheppard with grudging respect, but made it clear that the black man would take his orders. Certainly Sheppard knew better than to expect the soulful intimacy he had shared with Lapsley.

Morrison, however, did encourage his colleague's long-standing dream to reach out to the Kuba—and because of Morrison's support, Sheppard had the church's aid as well. The Presbyterians would fund an expedition into Kubaland, and perhaps even provide enough money to build a Christian town there. Now Sheppard was ready to take possession of the plot of land that King Kot aMweeky had given him.

But since Sheppard's last visit in 1892, a new clan had taken control of the palace, installing a ruler named Mishaape on the throne. Mishaape regarded Sheppard as a son of the last king, a pretender to the throne, and a threat to his own political power. Not only had he banned Sheppard from Kubaland, he had vowed to kill the missionary.

Still, though Sheppard had heard he was on Mishaape's most-wanted list, the explorer did not give up. In 1898 he walked thirty-five miles into the jungle to set up a new station in a remote town called Ibaanc. There, on the edge of Kuba country, he would keep trying to woo the tribe and forge a treaty with the hostile King Mishaape.

Sheppard may have left Luebo for other reasons too. Not much was left for him in the town that had once been his home. Lucy had taken their baby and gone back to the States, and now he wandered alone in the house with the *Ladies' Home Journal*s stacked up in trunks, the fading Kodak windowpanes, and the bassinet that yawned open like a grave.

Furthermore, he must have found Morrison—who was dwelling in a hut nearby—to be a galling presence. For years, Sheppard had been running the mission on his own. He knew more about the Kuba people than any other Westerner alive; he spoke several African languages; and thousands of local Congolese regarded him as a leader—indeed, a prince. And then Morrison showed up in Luebo and treated him as an inferior.

So Sheppard packed up and moved—and he did it with Morrison's blessing. The two men must have recognized that Luebo was not big enough for both of them. Better that each man rule his own town. Morrison would stay behind in Luebo and oversee the Presbyterian school, the plantation, the orphanage, the church, the two lady missionaries (Maria Fearing and Lillian Thomas), and the huts full of refugees. His colleague would do what he preferred: disappear into the wilderness to live among the Kuba. Though he traveled only thirty-five miles, Sheppard found a spot so deep in the jungle that most of the people who lived there had never seen a man in Western clothes before. As far as the villagers in the town of Ibaanc knew, their own King Mishaape was the most powerful ruler on the planet. They had yet to learn that a king in a land far away had claimed them as his own personal property. Along with the rest of the people of the Congo, they would soon be annexed by King Leopold.

By the mid-1890s, the Belgian king was consumed with two obsessive fears: bankruptcy and germs. In damp weather, he wrapped his beard in cellophane to prevent it from becoming infested with microbes. For similar reasons, he had a servant iron each page of the London *Times* when it arrived; if the newspaper seemed to pulse with infection, perhaps that was because it contained discouraging updates on stock prices and financial events.

Leopold had gone deep into debt in order to build his African railroad. It had been a gamble, a huge investment that could ruin him and force him to sell off the Congo. But despite the considerable risks, he continued to pour money into the construction project, even as it fell further and further behind schedule and went far above budget. Other men would have given up. But Leopold had guessed that within a few years the Congo would be worth more than anybody had dreamed. The reason could be summed up in one word: rubber.

By the 1890s, phone lines stretched between houses; telegraph cables snaked under the sea; electric lines, studded with glowing bulbs, crawled like creepers over Coney Island; telephone switchboards grew hairy with wire connections. Within only a few decades, the Western world had been stitched together. And what held together this new high-tech infrastructure, providing insulation from water and electricity, was a low-tech material that had been around for years. As the twentieth century dawned, rubber began to look like gold.

The Congo was full of it. When Sheppard traveled toward the forbidden Kuba city for the first time, he had described a forest hung with green streamers, like bunting in an enchanted theater: rubber vines. If Sheppard had known then what would happen later, he might have compared those vines to telephone lines and electric wires, for they just as surely connected the remote region of the Kasai to the stock markets of Europe. Without realizing it, he had hiked underneath what would turn out to be the Kasai region's spectacular wealth—and its ruin.

At the turn of the century, the Belgians had just begun to despoil the Kasai, chopping down forests and burning villages in order to get at the precious rubber. For Sheppard, the reign of terror began in September 1899, when a runner huffed into Ibaanc with an urgent message: The Zappo-Zaps had set about destroying an entire Kuba district. The massacre was unfolding only a short march away, in a region called Pianga. And rumor had it that Belgians had ordered the attack. They had hired the Zappo-Zaps to subdue the region and confiscate every last ball of rubber.

"The Zappo-Zaps, the cannibals, have come down and are catching our people and murdering them . . . , and we have come to ask you to help us drive them out," the messenger explained.

Sheppard asked who was leading the raid.

"Malumba N'kusa," came the answer.

Sheppard knew Malumba well. He was a man with whom one could not expect to negotiate, especially when he was backed up by hundreds of warriors.

"If Malumba N'kusa is leading them there is no use of my going," Sheppard told the messenger. "He will never hear me."

Still, the embattled people of the Pianga expected Sheppard—perhaps their only ally who possessed a rifle—to defend them. They brought him gifts of goats and chickens. Sheppard refused.

He had rarely, if ever, ignored a cry for help. It must have been a wrenching decision for him to back away from the hero role, especially since he had several friends in Pianga. But battling the Zappo-Zap would be suicide. He said he might as well "take a rope and go out behind the house and hang myself."

A few days later, Sheppard was sitting on the porch of his house when another runner hurtled up to him. This man had come from

Luebo; he carried a bamboo baton, inside of which was a rolled-up letter from Morrison.

As Sheppard remembered it, the letter was brief, its wording so formal as to be almost rude. Morrison ordered him to immediately stop the raid. He did not offer to help Sheppard in this impossible task, nor was he forthcoming with men or arms.

It's not clear why Morrison was so adamant about his orders. Perhaps he recognized in Pianga an opportunity to gather the one thing he needed most right then: a weapon against the Belgians.

Half a decade before, when Sheppard and Lapsley had settled in the Congo, they ran into few Europeans, and so they found it easy to stay out of politics.

Not so Morrison. By the time he took control of the Luebo station at the turn of the century, the area teemed with soldiers, would-be rubber moguls, fortune hunters, and petty bureaucrats. These men, with deeds to land tucked under their arms or military orders folded up in the pockets of their uniforms, regarded the missionaries as interlopers. After all, didn't the Kasai region belong to the Free State and its rubber companies? What right did the missionaries have to challenge the Belgian laws of the Congo Free State?

Morrison had only disdain for Belgian law. If slaves ran away from their masters and sought asylum at the Presbyterian mission, Morrison figured that was their right—after all, several international treaties had declared slavery to be illegal. So Morrison paid no attention to the edicts of the State men who propped their heels up on desks in backwater towns in the Kasai; just because these petty bureaucrats decided to endorse slavery, that did not make it legal.

Still, these State men controlled the local armies and the police forces. They could make life exceedingly unpleasant—and short—for anyone who stood up to them.

Morrison did. In 1898, a Belgian officer named Fromont led his soldiers into Luebo to steal food and gather slaves. All the other missionaries in the Kasai region had looked the other way when the Belgians plundered villages. Not Morrison. First, he filed a protest with Fromont, reminding him that the looting was illegal. That action only inspired Fromont to become more violent, and to order his soldiers to round up thousands of people—the entire Luba population of Luebo—and take them into custody. Fromont planned to march this huge crowd back to the State barracks, and there force them to become his soldiers or laborers.

Without the backing of the American government, without troops of his own, without guns, Morrison retaliated using the only weapon he had at hand: the media. "I told [Fromont] that to tear the people away from the homes which they had built . . . was not only cruel and most inhumane, but was a distinct violation of rights which were guaranteed to the natives under treaties." Morrison threatened to tell his humanitarian friends in London what he'd seen so they could wake up the world.

At the turn of the century, this tactic must have seemed wildly original, bordering on insane. No one had ever launched an international human rights campaign before. It could take months for a letter to go between Europe and the Kasai—so who would imagine that the threat of a negative article in the London *Times* could change the behavior of an officer who lived in a hut in the Congo?

And yet it did. "When [the officer] saw that I was in earnest, he was most surprised," Morrison wrote. Fromont left town without taking any slave laborers with him. The missionary had won.

But what had he gained, really? All over the Congo, State officers raided villages, confiscating whatever they wished and terrorizing the people. Even though Luebo was safe for the moment, the Belgians were sure to return. And one day, they might ignore Morrison's protests and lead his African friends away in chains.

Morrison decided he *would* go to the media. And he would do it in a way that was sure to produce results. What he needed was a scandal, a situation so horrific that it would jolt Europeans and Americans out of their apathy. He needed a story so grisly that not even Leopold could explain it away. Photos of mutilated bodies. Eyewitness reports fleshed out with gut-wrenching details. Names of victims. A list of the weapons used. Not only would Morrison have to catch an atrocity as it was happening, he would have to document the whole event as well.

Morrison heard about the tragedy in the Pianga region soon after Sheppard, but while Sheppard preferred to keep his distance from the violence, Morrison saw it as the opportunity he was looking for. He sent a message to Sheppard in Ibaanc, demanding that his colleague face down five hundred Zappo-Zap warriors, that he wander through the killing fields with a notebook and a Kodak camera. Morrison wanted evidence of atrocities, even if it cost Sheppard his life.

"These were orders," Sheppard wrote. "I had to go; there was nothing else to do." The words sound mild, but considering Sheppard's usual accommodating tone, they ring with resentment. He had been ordered to take on a terrifying mission by a man who had nothing near his expertise or understanding of the Africans.

If he still clung to any illusions that Morrison would someday turn out to be another Lapsley, they were dashed now. Lapsley would never have commanded Sheppard to risk his life alone—instead, he would have accompanied his partner into the Zappo-Zap den, or, more likely, would have listened to Sheppard's opinion, waiting for a safer opportunity to help the Pianga villagers. And whatever decision the partners came to, they would have carried their plan out in style, Lapsley insisting that his friend eat the last tin of mutton, Sheppard peeling off his own shoes and lacing them onto the sore feet of his companion. About them had hung the camellia perfume of the nineteenth-century South in its best moments—they were unfailingly gallant.

Morrison, on the other hand, was not. He would use any weapon at hand to stop the Belgians, even if that weapon was to be Sheppard.

A boy jumped up and down, pulling a rope to make the church bell bob, clapper swinging like a tongue. Hundreds of villagers hurried out of their houses and fields to gather in the town common, before the pale-garbed figure who waited, his face hidden under a helmet that shadowed his eyes and nose. You could see only his mouth, with its orderly array of teeth like cowrie shells—the neat teeth of a foreigner. When the people had found their places and settled into a hush, he called out to them, "We have just received a letter from Luebo that we must . . . stop the raid [in the Pianga region]. You who are willing to go, stand in line. You who are not willing, go to your homes." And then he waited confidently for the men to rush toward him.

But instead, the villagers fled from the square, until nothing remained but an expanse of sandy dirt, scuffed with footprints.

"Everybody had gone!" Sheppard wrote. "To tell the truth, I . . . wanted to join them, for I did not want to go to Pianga at all." The villagers' reaction confirmed what he suspected—to go to the Pianga would be to march to one's death.

Still, he had to obey orders. He walked around the village appealing to his friends individually, so they could not disappear into the crowd. In this way, he mustered eleven men to follow him.

After only a few hours of marching, Sheppard's party came upon a deserted village. And then another. And another. They called out greetings to the air, to the barkless dogs that wore bells around their necks, to the palm huts that creaked in the breeze. No one answered.

Finally, after hours had gone by without a glimpse of any villagers, a man stumbled out of the forest. He had been shot in the hand, and the bullet had shattered the bones. The swollen hand reeked of infection.

The man told Sheppard a horrific story: The Zappo-Zaps had demanded that the people of the Pianga region travel to their stockade and pay them taxes. What choice did the villagers have? The Zappo-Zaps were hundreds strong, hardened from years of slave trading and armed with expensive European rifles. The Pianga people couldn't hope to resist them.

On the appointed day, crowds of villagers obediently filed into the Zappo-Zap headquarters, a corral of high fences that had been hastily banged together for this very occasion. Malumba, the leader of the Zappo-Zaps, towered before the villagers. He demanded a sum so high it amounted to extortion: sixty slaves, herds of goats, baskets full of corn, and 2,500 balls of rubber.

The villagers refused—they could never come up with such riches. That's when Malumba signaled to his guards. The soldiers lifted their rifles—guns shipped from Antwerp factories—and opened fire.

Bullets flew. People screamed and fell. Others scattered toward the walls, scratching at the wood, trying to shimmy up slick poles, to wedge themselves through gaps. Under their weight, a section of the wall collapsed. Some of the terrified people managed to jump through the hole.

The man with the mangled hand had been one of the lucky ones who made it through the broken fence. As for the others, he could say not what had happened to them.

Armed with this information, Sheppard pressed on in the direction of the Zappo-Zap stockade. When nightfall came, he and his men set up a camp in one of the deserted villages; in the forest around them, howls and crying voices echoed.

In the morning, when Sheppard's party marched again, it was as if they had passed from one circle of hell into a deeper one. Here, the villages were decorated with corpses; a woman's body was propped up against a hut with the meat carefully carved off her bones. Turning a corner in the road, they found themselves only yards away from a squad of Zappo-Zaps who had been patrolling the area, shooting survivors.

"At a curve in the forest we met face-to-face with sixteen Zappo-Zaps, who, with lightning speed, cocked their guns and took aim," Sheppard wrote. "I jumped forward, threw up my hands and cried in a loud voice, 'Don't shoot, I am Sheppard!' The man in the lead recognized me. I had met him many times at Luebo. His name is Chebamba.

[The Zappo-Zaps] let down their guns, turned them towards the bush and lowered the hammers. Chebamba walked up and caught my hand with a hearty good morning."

Sheppard's usual luck had held. The Zappo-Zap crew regarded him as an old friend, and volunteered to help him any way they could. Sheppard requested that one of the men guide him to the stockade. Chebamba agreed. The rest of the Zappo-Zaps resumed their duties, which were, Sheppard noted tersely, "hunting food and people."

"We had gone half an hour when Chebamba called my attention to smoke behind us. It was some near village which these [Zappo-Zap] men had reached and burned." With flames dancing in the trees behind them, they left the forest and stepped out onto a plain, the seared land that stretched, flat as a drumhead, all around the stockade.

It was the African equivalent of a castle, made of high, woven fences. A tiny door in one of the fences popped open, and a stream of warriors emerged one by one. They came at Sheppard yipping, shooting in the air, contorting their red-painted faces. Then Malumba, their leader, emerged from the trapdoor. He shushed his men and called out greetings. As Sheppard approached the stockade, he must have seen the corpses half concealed all around in the grass. They lay about in crumpled mounds buzzing with flies, heads cut off, flesh stripped from the legs, hands gone.

In the midst of the carnage, Malumba seemed perfectly at ease, like a host emerging from his front door to welcome a dinner-party guest. The chief could "look at the midday sun without winking," Sheppard wrote later, trying to describe the strange effect of the man's face—the slave trader had plucked out his eyebrows and eyelashes, giving his visage the eerie formality of a Kabuki mask. The bald eyes gave no hint of what went on behind them.

"Come, come to the camp," Malumba invited, the very soul of cordiality. Escorting Sheppard to the tiny door, he stepped aside and insisted his guest precede him.

No please, the missionary replied, you first.

No, no, Malumba persisted. You are by far the more illustrious chief. You should go first.

No, you are far grander, Sheppard replied.

And so Malumba dropped to his hands and knees and crawled through; Sheppard followed him.

Inside the huge enclosure, the missionary surveyed the remains of a blood orgy. Bits and pieces of bodies lay scattered about. Fires smoldered, and over them hung bamboo poles strung with flesh—what Sheppard claimed was flayed human skin. The corpses on the ground had been cut up and played with. And above it all floated a stink that clotted up his lungs, the air smoky with death.

Malumba proceeded to show his guest around, proud of his work. He pointed out the heart of Chief N'funfu, blackened and shriveled, covered with some kind of powder. Sheppard had been friends with N'funfu. "I said very little," he wrote later. "I thought it a better policy."

Over it all, over the flyspecked blood and the greasy smoke with its smell of burning hair, high up on one of the poles, fluttered a blue banner emblazoned with a gold star: the flag of the Free State government.

Once he spotted the flag, Sheppard must have guessed the rest. The government had hired the Zappo-Zaps to act as its *Force Publique,* its local police force, and sent them out to punish the Pianga region. Perhaps the villagers had refused to cooperate with the State-affiliated rubber companies. Or perhaps they'd never been given a chance to demur. Whatever the specifics, the Belgians had decided to make an example of the Pianga people; a Free State officer had ordered Zappo-Zaps to collect a "tax" of rubber, food, and slaves. If the people could not deliver the goods, they would be mowed down. The incident was meant to send a message to the rest of the Kasai: Harvest rubber or else. There would be no labor shortage in the Congo.

The flag snapped over Sheppard's head, and the fires crackled around him. He understood now why Malumba hadn't murdered him on the spot. The Zappo-Zap leader assumed that Sheppard worked for the Free State. After all, few Africans knew how to distinguish an American missionary from an Antwerp businessman. All white men—even the black ones—struck them as pretty much the same, a horde of inscrutable foreigners conspiring together in their harsh language. Sheppard had arrived at the door of the stockade in his linens, puttees, and a pith helmet. So Malumba had assumed he was a petty Free State official, come here to check whether the Zappo-Zaps had done their job and subdued the locals.

Sheppard played his new identity for all it was worth. Pretending to work for the Belgians, he took notes, conducted interviews, and snapped photos, all the while showing a hearty enthusiasm for the murders. The ruse allowed him not only to stay alive, but also to collect the evidence Morrison wanted. Notebook in hand, he leaned over the mutilated bodies—some of them people he recognized—and scribbled away. He would have to stroll among the corpses without ever letting on how heartsick he felt. He would have to pretend to be pleased at each new corpse he discovered, would have to congratulate Malumba over each skull.

How many people could pull off that kind of acting job for an hour? Sheppard managed to fool the Zappo-Zaps for two days. Throughout his stay he kept a smile pasted on his face, even as he drank water brought to him by a man with blood-spattered hands and slept in the courtyard surrounded by five hundred slave traders.

The notes he took in the stockade (titled "Interview with Chief [Malumba] N'kusa Concerning the Zappo-Zap Raid") are different from almost any other piece of writing he composed during his lifetime. Because he handed them over to the authorities immediately, they are raw—and far more revealing than his speeches or autobiography. In the notes, we get a glimpse at the uncorrected proofs of Sheppard himself—a man whose ability to hide his own feelings was far more sophisticated than he usually let on.

Pretending to be a Belgian officer, Sheppard tricked Malumba into revealing every last detail about the Free State's military operations. At one point, he even showed off his own rifle in order to goad the Zappo-Zaps into bragging about their own weapons.

He recorded one of these interviews in detail:

> "How did the fight come up?" I asked, as if curious that the Pianga people, so good and quiet, should attack them.
>
> "I sent for all their chiefs, sub-chiefs, men and women, to come on a certain day, saying that I was going to finish all the [talk about taxes]. When they entered these small gates . . . I demanded all my pay or I would kill them, so they refused to pay me, and I ordered the fence to be closed so they couldn't run away. . . . The panels of the fence fell down, and some escaped."
>
> Oh! My heart burned, but I hid it as well as possible.
>
> "How many did you kill?" I asked.
>
> "We killed plenty. Will you see some of them?"
>
> "Oh, I don't mind," I said reluctantly, [even though] that was just what I wanted.
>
> He said, "I think we have killed between eighty and ninety, and those in the other villages, I don't know. . . ."
>
> The chief and I walked out on the plain just near the camp. There were three people with the flesh carved off from the waist down.
>
> "Why are these people carved so . . . ?" I asked.
>
> "My people ate them," he answered.

Throughout this interview, Sheppard played the part of Malumba's admirer. And he performed so cleverly that he engineered a full confession from the chief. One can only wonder about how the missionary had become so capable as a spy—had he learned his trade in America, riding in Jim Crow cars and tipping his hat to the white men who forced him off the sidewalk?

After collecting evidence, Sheppard set about rescuing the survivors left inside the stockade.

"Where are the women?" he asked Malumba, because he knew that slave traders sometimes spared women in order to extract ransom from their husbands. Malumba whisked his guest off to another part of the camp, where about sixty women huddled together in a pen.

Pretending to appraise one poor girl who'd been chained to a tree stump, he fished a strange object out of his pocket, a box that fit easily in his palm. He asked the girl to stand just so, then held the box over his face, so its single black eye replaced his own eye. And in this strange fashion he stared at her out of his false eye for a moment, unblinking.

Sheppard had brought with him one of the brand-new Kodak box cameras. A forerunner of the Instamatic, the first easy-to-use camera had debuted on the market only the year before. Sheppard clicked the button, and the image of the woman bounced onto film; now the photo curls in a folder deep in an archive. A caption scrawled on the back in the missionary's bold handwriting reads, "Rescued by Sheppard from the cannibals." The caption implies that the act of taking the woman's picture was what helped to free her people, and in one way it was. As the twentieth century dawned, images from portable cameras would appear in newspapers all over the globe. Mass media and human rights were inextricably linked, and to document the woman's plight was the first step in saving her.

Once he'd taken pictures of the hostages, the missionary asked to see the hands. He'd spotted a number of corpses with their hands sawed off, and he guessed that the Zappo-Zaps were collecting these artifacts and smoking them in fires, so they could be presented as trophies to the Belgians.

Hand-collecting had become a grisly tradition in the Congo. It started years before, for practical reasons: African soldiers preferred to use bullets for hunting food rather than for killing other human beings. So some Belgian officers required soldiers to proffer a human hand for every bullet they used, to prove that they hadn't "wasted" any ammunition. Later on, the hand collecting had less to do with bullets than with tradition, a way for African soldiers to display the bounty of their killing.

So it was only natural that Sheppard, still pretending to be a Belgian officer, should wish to see the hands, and that Malumba would have been eager to show them off. It was likely he'd brought many baskets of hands to Belgians over the years, and had been paid handsomely for his efforts.

Malumba led Sheppard to a fire, outfitted with a grill. On top of it lay eighty-one right hands. Sheppard knew the exact number because he counted them. One by one, he lifted withered fists and open-palmed hands from the flames and placed them on top of each other in a basket. And he counted. Then he jotted down the figure in his notebook. This would be an important bit of evidence.

It was only after leaving the Zappo-Zap stockade, on the trip back to Ibaanc, that Sheppard allowed himself to fall apart. In the notes he kept during his investigation, the last entry reads as follows: "Later. On the way for four hours' march. Every now and then you can smell the awful stench of the wounded one, who would make his way home, but crawled off in the bush near the road to die." The fragmented sentences hint at just how disordered Sheppard's thinking had become after two days among the corpses.

Sheppard sent his report, via fast runners, to missionaries in Luebo. Morrison carried it himself to the State headquarters. With his evidence tucked under his arm, he demanded that the Belgians stop the killings in the Pianga region immediately. For once, the Free State officers cooperated with the missionaries; they sent a delegation of Belgian soldiers to break down the walls of the stockade, free the hostages, arrest Malumba, and throw him in jail. The Free State denied all responsibility for the murders, blaming Malumba instead. Understandably confused, the chief complained to his Belgian captors, "You have sent me to do this and yet you have put me in chains!"

Morrison refused to let the Free State go unpunished. He insisted that the Belgian officer who ordered the raid, not Malumba, should also be blamed. But the Congo law courts—later to become notorious for their lack of justice—failed to find any wrongdoing among the Belgians. Instead, all blame fell on Malumba, and after a few months, even Malumba was set free. It was as if the massacre in Pianga had never happened.

William Sheppard had lived alone for more than a year in Ibaanc. But soon Lucy would return. While he was recovering in his hut from the horrors of the massacre, she was click-clacking toward New York in a Jim Crow train car. She traveled alone, no baby Wilhelmina grabbing onto her linen dress or curling against her stomach. When she reached the New York pier to catch the Africa-bound steamer, she met up with Dr. Snyder. He too was returning to his duties in the Congo. Clinging to his arm was the new Mrs. Snyder. Dr. Snyder had replaced his wife so speedily that it must have disturbed Lucy. If this new wife died, would he simply get a third Mrs. Snyder? Would there be an endless parade of wives sailing to the Congo, armed only with parasols and hatboxes?

The Snyders would move back into Luebo, which by now had become a teeming community and rather comfortable place to live. Lucy had no such luck. She would tramp through the jungle to the isolated town of Ibaanc. Here, William had set up his own Presbyterian station, little more than an outpost in the frontier.

When Lucy arrived, swaying in a hammock, and stepped down into the dusty yard of her new house, her heart must have sunk. Luebo had been Paris compared to this place. The villagers crowded around to touch the long loops of her hair and the balloon of her dress. They had never before seen a Western woman, and could not stop fingering her, gaping at her, following her.

In the weeks to come, Lucy despaired as she tried to carry out her duties with the crowd of Africans always pressing close around her. In the isolated town, she became Broadway show and freak show all rolled into one; Africans would arrive in the morning and sit down around her house, to watch her as she ironed and sewed and cooked and cleaned. In the afternoon, they would take out their lunches and eat, still transfixed. They would leave only at nightfall, when the light became too dim to follow Lucy's mysterious gestures.

Her reunion with William must have been equally unsettling. A few months before, he had witnessed enough horror to drive a man mad, and then returned to the isolated village, where he'd rattled around among the Africans, hollow-eyed, haunted. The Zappo-Zap episode would seem to leave no permanent scars on Sheppard—in a few years, he'd be back on tour in the United States, charming his audiences with as much energy as ever. But in that terrible year of 1900, he must have been unhinged.

Perhaps that's why she forgave him, or, if she didn't forgive him, why she looked the other way. While Lucy was gone, William had taken an African lover. The woman had given birth to a boy named "Shepete." The name itself says a lot: The Congolese recognized Sheppard as the father.

It's hard to know much more about the affair than that. Lucy never acknowledged it publicly. Neither did William, though he did admit to his adultery years later, when church leaders confronted him in a secret meeting. The Presbyterian Church itself kept the scandal under wraps. Little information about it has survived.

But we can imagine how deeply unhappy Lucy must have been as she ironed linen on the porch, a crowd of Kuba people squatting in her yard, watching her unabashedly. They snacked on dried peanuts or grasshoppers, and discussed the show before them, the way gawkers in St. Louis stared at imported Africans. They would have gossiped mercilessly about her, this woman who preached monogamy but could not keep her own husband from straying.

No wonder Lucy complained about being put on display. No wonder she disparaged the Kuba women, with their "hair daubed with paint, [bodies] smeared with grease and [minds] filled with sin and superstition." In the tiny town of Ibaanc, everyone knew her business; every woman posed a threat; and her husband's only son belonged to his mistress. Had she remained childless in Ibaanc, her situation might have become excruciating. But luckily, within the next year she would again feel the familiar twinges and swellings of pregnancy. She would bear her husband a son.

CHAPTER 9

To Tell the World

Morrison had been convinced that if the newspapers got hold of William Sheppard's explosive report about the Zappo-Zap raid, the world would finally wake up. Europeans and Americans would understand that the rubber in their bike tires and telegraph wires had been harvested by slave labor.

In 1899, Morrison sent the report to a friend in London, who in turn passed it on to the head of the Aborigines Protection Society—the era's equivalent of Amnesty International. Sheppard's story was discussed in an important humanitarian book, *Civilization in Congoland,* and was talked about in the Belgian Parliament.

But the report failed to do more than stir up a tiny dust storm—those who saw it would have disbelieved it. In newspapers and lectures, the public heard only of the spectacular successes in the Congo: Friendly natives eager for work! Profits as high as seven hundred percent! Railroad service speeding the accoutrements of civilization into the jungle! Opportunities for young European men with initiative! Millions of empty acres of farmland waiting to be cultivated! Naked savages now clothed in the latest French fashions! Most of these glowing stories about the Congo—these lies—had been dreamed up by King Leopold.

He had spent thousands of francs to groom public opinion, bribing journalists and publishing books he passed off as scientific. And his ploy had worked. Europeans believed in the Congo Leopold had invented, not in the atrocity stories generated by a few unknown missionaries like William Sheppard.

At just about the time Sheppard's report arrived in Europe, a group of businessmen gathered around a table at a London restaurant for a lunch. Two of the men, Dutch traders, had the gaunt and hollow-eyed look of men who'd survived tropical fever, their skin scorched by the sun. They dined across from two Englishmen with desk jobs at a shipping firm, pale hands with trimmed nails resting beside their plates, napkins tucked decorously into their starched collars.

E. D. Morel, the younger of the two Englishman, might have grown bored and dreamy as the others discussed the shipping business. Perhaps he was only half listening when one of the Belgian traders veered from the ordinary topics of schedules and taxes and began to explain the grisly details of the rubber-harvesting operation in the Congo. The traders made it clear that the Congo Free State had turned into a hell far beyond the imagining of anyone in Europe; they themselves would speak out if they dared, but it would be the end of their careers. The revelation shocked Morel to his core: The "story [was] so appalling . . . that [I tossed] in sleeplessness that night, conjuring in mental vision burning villages, and . . . men and women quivering beneath the lash, chained and bleeding."

After that haunted night, Morel's life would never be the same. He feverishly tracked down whatever he could about the story: In his own company's ledgers he found ample evidence. While enormous quantities of rubber flooded into Antwerp, almost nothing in the way of payment was being shipped to the people of the Congo. Instead, boats arrived in Africa loaded with guns.

Morel also collected atrocity stories, which were beginning to filter out of the Congo. One of the most searing pieces of evidence against the State was William Sheppard's notes on the Zappo-Zap raid.

In 1901, the Englishman quit his job to devote himself to exposing Leopold's regime; by 1904, he'd founded the Congo Reform Association, which furiously published evidence against the State. But he knew that whatever evidence he managed to type up and print out in newsletters would do only so much good. Morel needed a spokesman for the movement—a man who'd seen the holocaust with his own eyes and would risk his career and reputation to stand before a crowd and tell the tale.

By 1903, William Morrison recognized that he would never be able to sway world opinion as long as he stayed in his hut in Luebo, where the mail could take months to arrive. He decided to use his upcoming furlough to sail back to Europe and America, where he could tell audiences exactly what he had seen during the last few terrible years.

He made his debut in London's Whitehall auditorium, where he squinted out at an audience of men in wool suits who nursed top hats in their laps—a powerful group of professors, writers, and members of Parliament who had gathered to hear the missionary. Morrison did not attempt to move his listeners to tears. Instead, he appealed to them as a prosecuting lawyer would: He turned the lecture hall into a courtroom and put the Free State on trial.

"I propose tonight to take as my text an article from the General Act of the Berlin Conference. . . . The sixth article of the Berlin Act was as follows," he began, and then proceeded to quote from sections of the treaty. Morrison was a deadly dull speaker.

But whether by design or luck, he'd shown up in London just at the moment when Parliament was ready to listen to criticism of King Leopold's regime. According to E. D. Morel, "No one could look into [Morrison's] straight blue eyes or take stock of his erect and vigorous carriage without an instinctive feeling of confidence."

Morrison wore sensible suits. He spoke in legalese and thought like a file cabinet. Even his atrocity stories sounded boring. His personality was entirely the opposite of Sheppard's. And yet what he lacked in charisma, he made up for in thoroughness. He had documented every lapse of the Belgians, compiling names, dates, laws violated, lists of witnesses, and photos. His case against the Free State was airtight—indeed, it was so convincing that he managed to turn the British human rights effort around. Soon after the speech, Parliament introduced a motion to "abate the evils" in the Congo, and began its own investigation into the matter. Leopold's secret would soon be out.

Sheppard's report might be circulating around London, but the author himself avoided the political debate in Europe. It would be years before he wrote another negative word about the Belgians.

Sheppard had stayed on in Ibaanc, that remote village closed in by jungle on all sides, where newspapers arrived only after months of delay. Here, the local African scene mattered much more than European politics.

In the Kasai in the first years of the 1900s, it was possible to believe that the Kuba kingdom would endure for centuries to come. A king still sat on the throne, and the area remained largely under his control. Free State soldiers looted villages sometimes, but in most places the Kuba people continued to live with as much exuberance as they ever had. Their markets bustled with buyers chatting under elephantine trees; ladies swayed along the road with bundles tied above their rumps like backwards pregnancies; little boys glued corn husks to their chins like beards and pretended to be white men, the way American boys might have pretended to be Indians.

And the bloodier traditions also endured—human sacrifices and witch trials. More than Belgian violence, Sheppard worried about violence perpetrated by the African leaders—in the early 1900s, he regarded the Kuba aristocrats as the worst violators of human rights in the region. "Thieves, liars and witches are all tried by the poisonous draught," he reported to a Virginia newspaper in 1904. "The villages are more quickly depopulated by this cruel custom and by the King's knife than by natural death." Sheppard focused his efforts on reforming these customs.

But he lavished most of his attention on the town of Ibaanc itself. He'd imagined it as a showplace, beyond the reach of racism or international hatreds. As unofficial mayor, he would rule over a utopia of African American achievement. For the station of Ibaanc was built, staffed, designed, and supervised entirely by black people. William and Lucy had started off there alone, but during the first decade of the twentieth century several other African Americans would join the staff. One particularly exceptional resident of Ibaanc, the aforementioned Althea Brown, arrived in 1904.

Sheppard himself worried less about the achievements of the African-Americans at Ibaanc than about how the place looked. He knew that this unique settlement would be judged, first and foremost, on its appearance.

By 1902 he had designed and built a street full of houses and public buildings. Carrying on the traditions he'd begun with Lapsley, he bestowed grandiloquent names on the streets. As in Luebo, the major thoroughfares were dubbed Pennsylvania Avenue and Grand Boulevard.

In addition to being Ibaanc's city planner, Sheppard also became its ringmaster. He tamed leopards, dogs, cats, eagles, monkeys, hawks, and parrots; the pets paraded through the houses and streets, performing impromptu circus acts. "When . . . Sheppard wished the sexton to ring the church bell, he would give a peculiar whistle. The parrots learned the whistle so accurately that the poor sexton rang the church bell overtime," one resident remembered.

His most hopeful gesture in Ibaanc was to hang a snapping parade of flags in front his house: French, Belgian, the Union Jack, and the Stars and Stripes. He had outfitted his house like an embassy, and in many ways it was. Belgian inspectors, German explorers, French entomologists, English agriculture experts, Kuba royalty, Kete traders—all sorts of illustrious men came tramping through town and depended on black Americans' hospitality. As one visitor wrote, "Coming in the Mission, I stood full of wonder. Neither before, neither afterwards, did I in those countries find such a delightful luxury joined to the right kind of sociability as in the stations of the American Mission." He raved about the kindness and good taste of Althea Brown, who happened to be his hostess. (The Sheppards were probably away at the time.) At dinner the German visitor sat down with Brown and enjoyed a first-class menu of oyster soup, roast mutton, chicken pie, and tart with peaches.

At the turn of the century, such a dinner was a revolutionary act. A white man and a black woman supping together as friends—and enjoying nothing less than oyster soup and delicate tarts—would have been impossible almost anywhere else on the planet.

Sheppard had imagined Ibaanc as a model of equality and peace. The Kuba chiefs who passed through would have been astounded to notice that the Christians ruled without witch trials or slaves, while the European guests would have been impressed by a settlement where curtains hung in the windows, roses climbed the gates, and biscuits came steaming from improvised ovens—a place far more stylish than many of the villages settled by the Belgians.

In creating Ibaanc, Sheppard was inspired by Virginia as well as Africa. He seemed to be trying to capture all the charm of his home state without any of its nastiness and brutality. His motivations for doing so become most poignantly clear in a piece of writing by a man named William Phipps, who grew up in Sheppard's hometown of Waynesboro. Phipps commented on how horribly bigoted the Virginia town was; how Sheppard, for all his accomplishments, never would have dared to demand equality from the white people there:

A lady [from Waynesboro] commended Sheppard in this way: "He was such a good darky. When he returned from Africa he remembered his place and always came to the back door." [That lady's] education and accomplishments were negligible compared to Sheppard's. . . . [But] Sheppard's sense of humor enabled him to tolerate such humiliations and absurdities with grace.

It's easy to understand, then, why Sheppard would be so determined to build a new Waynesboro, one that lay within the borders of a country ruled by an African king. Here, no one went to the back door. Under the snapping flash of flags from many nations, Germans, Kuba, Belgians, and Americans met as equals.

In one photo from Ibaanc, Sheppard poses with an honor guard of warriors: He labeled the picture, and himself, "the chief of Ibaanc." In another snapshot, Sheppard presides over a picnic, complete with a ragtag marching band. Yet another photo shows the black Americans decked out in lace and linen, playing a game of croquet.

Morrison had sailed off to Europe to address parliaments and newspapermen; Sheppard stayed behind in the Congo, but in some ways he traveled just as far. Rather than battling the Free State head-on, he chose to ignore it. He attempted to create a town—and an entire reality—where hatred and racism did not exist.

Though he might avoid confrontation with racist whites, Sheppard was eager to impose his will on the Kuba. The territory under his control amounted to a separate country within the Kuba kingdom, a rebel state. He had taken control of several villages, and not surprisingly, the African aristocrats resented this. After all, the "Christian" villages once had paid *them* taxes and considered *them* the chiefs.

Sheppard further insulted the Kuba leaders by allowing Prince Maxamilange to take refuge in Ibaanc. Maxamilange had befriended Sheppard in 1892, when the explorer first found his way to the Kuba palace—both men were allies of King Kot aMweeky and his clan. In the intervening years, a different family had taken control of Kubaland and the new rulers wanted Prince Maxamilange, their rival, dead. They had accused him of witchcraft and demanded that he drink poison; without Sheppard's protection, Maxamilange would surely have been killed.

To harbor the most wanted man in Kubaland would bring trouble to Sheppard. But the missionary intended Ibaanc to be a haven for refugees and misfits, a place beyond the reach of unjust laws. Besides, Prince Maxamalinge had been a friend for more than ten years. So Sheppard brought the prince to Ibaanc and gave him a place to live. His generosity would prove to be costly indeed.

In late 1903, the Sheppards decided to return to America for a few years, not just because of the worsening situation in the Congo, but also because of their son, Max. The two-year-old boy went everywhere suited up against sun and malaria, a testament to how worried his parents were about his health. One photo shows him in an enormous pith helmet and adult-sized boots—between hat and shoes, almost nothing of Max himself was visible. According to medical wisdom of the day, the African sun was deadly, so the little boy had to wear proper headgear at all times. Another picture shows just how ensconced the tot had become in village life. In it, little Max toddles beside a bare-chested warrior. Sheppard labeled this photo, "Our baby with his big cannibal friend." Max spoke only a few English words; pampered by African nursemaids, he learned to talk in the Kuba dialect.

But the oddest thing about the baby was that he bore both an American and an African name. First he'd been christened William Lapsley, a smart political move on Sheppard's part. The Congo Presbyterians loved to name things after Lapsley—chapels, scholarships, and even their steamship, the SS *Lapsley*. Like the boat, the boy would bear the name of a Presbyterian martyr. But later, to please his African friends, Sheppard gave the boy a Kuba moniker, Maxamalinge, after the prince. For the rest of his life, the boy would be known as Max.

Lucy and William had gone to great lengths to send their daughter, Wilhelmina, back to the States, where she could grow up safe from tropical diseases. Now they wanted to do the same for their son.

Though the boy had managed to survive infancy in Africa, they knew better than to push their luck.

And so in 1903, the couple and their child made the long trip back to Staunton, Virginia, where Wilhelmina had been living with relatives. For the first time, the entire Sheppard family would be together.

The parents' reunion with Wilhelmina must have been bittersweet. They hadn't seen her since she was a toddler, and now she was a skinny six-year-old with flyaway hair. She didn't recognize her parents and she couldn't talk to her new baby brother—Wilhelmina had forgotten all her Kuba, while Max knew little else.

The family reunion must also have been brief. William would travel ceaselessly during his trip—what was supposed to be a vacation—and Lucy often accompanied him. As always, the church needed them. William's sister had agreed to raise the children as her own. In two years, when the parents returned to Africa, Max and Wilhelmina would remain in the United States.

At least the children would be able to play outside, their heads bare rather than hidden under pith helmets; they could sleep at night without mosquito netting; the fevers they caught would pass in a few days instead of burning them up. As hard as the separation would have been, such thoughts must have comforted Lucy and William.

At the beginning of 1904, Sheppard waited in a train station, surrounded by ragged people toting worn-out bags of luggage. The crowd congregated under a sign that read "Colored and Freight." Sheppard lifted the flap of his London-tailored suit and conjured up a cigar. He proceeded to minister to it with the sensual absorption of a connoisseur.

By the time the train chuffed up to the station, Sheppard had trimmed his stogie. Climbing on board, he swayed past the Colored section and went on to Smoking. There, he veiled himself in a spicy-smelling shroud.

Eighty years later, Max Sheppard would remember his father's cigar smoking as one of his defining characteristics: On a train, "The first thing he would look for would be the Smoker, so he could get comfortable—he would smoke all the rest of the way." It was, perhaps, the one way William Sheppard could restore dignity to himself in an era when blacks paid the full price for a train ticket but were forced to ride on broken seats next to pigs and goats and bags of coal. He smoked himself into his own private cloud of luxury.

This particular day, Sheppard's train click-clacked through the cold air on its way to Washington, D.C. He had dinners to attend, diplomats to charm, politicians to woo. But compared to the other lobbyists flooding into the capital, the black missionary would operate at a distinct disadvantage. He could not take a cab. He could not book a room in a decent hotel. He wouldn't dare to approach the front door of a white person's home.

When Sheppard stepped out of Union Station and squashed the remains of a cigar under his toe, he looked out on a city as squalid and grand as it is today. Only a few blocks away from the Mall, immigrants and poor blacks packed into slums with names like Swamppoodle and Murder Bay. In some cases, marble-fronted mansions stood only an alley away from TB-infested flophouses.

A few decades before, Henry Adams had complained that "there were no theatres, no restaurants, no *monde*, no *demi-monde*, no drives, no splendor, and as Mme. de Struve used to say, no *grandezza*. . . . Washington was a mere political camp, as transient and temporary as a camp-meeting for religious revival."

In the early 1900s, Washington was a camp full of Congo men. President Teddy Roosevelt entertained a swirl of activists, who argued that America should take a stand against the situation in the Belgian Colony. When Morrison called on the president in 1904, he was gratified to spy a copy of E. D. Morel's book *Red Rubber* lying open on Roosevelt's desk. Sheppard himself would meet Roosevelt in 1905.

But while the reformers crowded into Washington, Leopold's henchmen were just as busy. And what they handed out was far more tempting than copies of a humanitarian book. Free trips, prime real estate in the Congo, and cushy jobs—such perks worked wonders to bolster Leopold's reputation. Journalists wrote articles that praised the Congo government and ridiculed the human rights activists. And well-known "Africa hands" like Samuel Verner, the unstable missionary who years before enjoyed Lucy Sheppard's biscuits, gushed about the marvelous business opportunities in the Free State.

The master of this propaganda machine was the Belgian ambassador to America, a man with the imposing title of Baron Ludovic Moncheur. He'd succeeded in recruiting Verner as one of his stooges. When the ambassador learned that Sheppard had come to Washington, he decided to try to buy off the black missionary as well.

And so one night in January 1904, the baron invited his prey to a dinner party. The host would have ushered his guest into a dining room and plied him with soup and cigars, and most of all with a charm that rivaled Sheppard's own. Moncheur made it clear that he regretted any misunderstandings between the Belgians and the Presbyterians. Could he, perhaps, inquire as to why Sheppard had written those terrible accusations about the Free State? It was a shame that relations had become so tense between the Presbyterians and the Free State—couldn't they patch things up?

Sheppard confessed his frustrations. He said he regretted all those nasty letters and articles Morrison had written about the Colony. Sheppard would have preferred to pursue a more diplomatic solution to the problems in the Congo, but Morrison was his boss. He could do nothing.

"I was . . . able to ascertain that Sheppard is only a tool in the hands of Morrison," the baron wrote. He reported that Morrison affixed Sheppard's name to articles without asking his colleague's permission.

Could it be true that Morrison wrote radical statements, then signed Sheppard's name to them? Perhaps in some cases. But Sheppard's inflammatory 1899 report about the Zappo-Zap raid, while it may have been tweaked and edited by Morrison, could only have been composed by Sheppard himself. He had been the lone eyewitness to the massacre; furthermore, anyone who has read Sheppard's other work would recognize his signature turns of phrase and skillful narrative style. To put it bluntly, Morrison had no ear for a story. Had he written the Zappo-Zap report, it would have come out as a lecture. Sheppard has to have been the author.

Perhaps Sheppard called himself "Morrison's tool" because he was disturbed by his boss's sending the Zappo-Zap report to major newspapers and celebrities such as Mark Twain—probably without Sheppard's consent, or indeed, the approval of the Presbyterian Church itself.

Sheppard had been betrayed. A few years before, Morrison had ordered him to march into the Zappo-Zap stronghold and face down five hundred warriors on his own. Unbelievably, he had managed to survive that mission. And now Morrison was pushing him to become one of the world's most prominent black critics of European colonialism, again forcing him to face risks that the white man himself could not even begin to imagine. This time, Sheppard would do his best to bow out.

At the turn of the century, black leaders were focused on improving conditions in the United States rather than on the international scene. Even W. E. B. Du Bois (though he did organize the first pan-African conference in 1900) had yet to turn his attention to colonialism; he was too busy with the founding of the NAACP. And while Booker T. Washington did sign on to the Congo reform movement, the cause was hardly his passion. As the head of the Tuskegee Institute and one of the most powerful political leaders in America, his gaze was steadily fixed on his own country.

It would not be until the 1920s that the pan-African movement truly became a going concern. Marcus Garvey, wearing a military costume he'd designed himself and riding in a motorcade at the head of a parade of legionnaires and nurses, embodied nascent black nationalism more than anyone else. "Africa for the Africans at home and abroad," he declared, and set about trying to found his own country. Millions of poverty-stricken blacks clung to his dream. In 1925, he went to jail on trumped-up charges and soon after was deported to Jamaica, never again to agitate in the States.

Sheppard followed a different and very conservative road to black empowerment. He recognized that if he toned down his criticism, he could not only continue to raise money from whites that could be funneled to the Congo, but also could stay on the good side of the Belgian bureaucrats who controlled his right to travel back to Ibaanc. According to historian Walter Williams, "Sheppard and his [black] colleagues might be open to charges of 'Uncle-Tom-ism,' but as missionaries entirely dependent on white church support they had little choice but accommodation if they wished to continue their work." Sheppard knew that if he began openly attacking white colonialism, he might lose his job, his funding, his passport to Africa, and his chance to help the Congolese.

The church had hired Sheppard to raise money, not to raise hell. When he returned to the United States in late 1903, Presbyterian leaders made it clear that they expected him to work his fund-raising magic. The famous explorer could draw in hundreds of dollars in a single night. And he worked tirelessly to do what the church demanded of him. On a grueling trudge through the West and South, he gave a lecture at least every day. He zigzagged from threadbare black colleges in the Deep South to frontier churches in Wyoming, from Ivy League universities like Princeton to a student conference in Nashville where thousands came to hear him.

Invariably, he drew a sold-out crowd. Extra chairs had to be crammed in next to church pews. Doors had to be kept open so that latecomers could stand on tiptoes to get a glimpse of the intrepid Africanist. People flooded in to the lecture hall not to hear about the Congo Question, but to be entertained with fantastic adventure stories from the Dark Continent. They'd come for Sheppard himself.

It was a reprise of his fund-raising tour ten years earlier. He told the same stories he had back then, about the martyred Sam Lapsley and his journey into the forbidden kingdom of the Kuba. He displayed the same artifacts, too—knives and rugs and intricately carved cups. A poster from his 1904–1905 tour bills Sheppard as the "Black Livingstone of Africa." The tag line perfectly summed up the persona Sheppard had invented for himself—a new take on an old hero. David Livingstone had survived a childhood as distressing as Sheppard's own (at ten years of age, he worked in a sweatshop and ducked beatings from his abusive father), and his only way out had been Africa. There, he proved what he was made of—the kind of man who could wrestle a lion, dole out medicines to heal the sick, and convince Africans to trek with him to unsavory places. His adventures made him a celebrity.

Sheppard clung to this vision of heroism even as it became extinct. "His experiences have been even more thrilling than any recorded by . . . Henry M. Stanley, Baker, Speke, Grant, [or] Emin Pasha," wrote one man who'd seen Sheppard's show, comparing him to the greatest explorers of the mid-nineteenth century. Sheppard, the writer implied, was first and foremost an entertainer.

Indeed, the Black Livingstone act had something of the circus in it. At a time when P. T. Barnum exported African warriors to pounce and parry under the big top, Sheppard was also diverting his audiences with exoticism. He knew how to put on a good show.

Morrison, as the first missionary to speak out against Free State atrocities, is unquestionably a hero of the Congo crusade. However, he is not exactly the hero of Sheppard's story. A passionate idealist, Morrison had little patience for the feelings of people around him. Even his closest ally, a missionary named Lachlan Vass, called Morrison a dictator.

The two men met in 1899, when Vass first stepped off a steamship in Luebo. Photos show the five-foot-two Virginian with a patchy beard, an unbuttoned coat, and a bad case of bedhead. Vass was a messy little Napoleon of a man who had such an intense will that though he knew little about boats, he managed to rebuild the SS *Lapsley* out of parts sent in from the coast and then sail it up and down the Kasai.

Vass is important to us because of his letters—typed in frantic, run-on sentences that burn with indignation. The ship's captain with the spiked, crazy hair always seemed to be peeved at somebody, usually his friends. He was not afraid to speak candidly about matters that others wouldn't, to chase the church's secrets into daylight. His letters, more than anyone else's, give us a vivid picture of the rift that had opened up in the church.

Though Presbyterian leaders like Samuel Chester (the head of the Foreign Missions department) were happy with Sheppard's performance—especially his lucrative Black Livingstone tour—Morrison and Vass were not. They lambasted their colleague for ducking the real issues. "When Mr. Sheppard arrived [in the U.S.], things were at the top notch in the Congo agitation, the press was full of reports and people were anxious to hear," Vass wrote. "We all looked forward to Mr. Sheppard's coming as a great thing for the cause, his being a colored man laboring amongst his own race, . . . and above all things his happy and effective way of presenting a subject made us expect much aid from him." According to Vass, Sheppard bitterly disappointed the human rights activists by refusing to take a stand.

Vass wrote a scathing letter to Sheppard, accusing him of abandoning the cause. With admirable patience, Sheppard replied, "Being a colored man, I would not be understood criticizing a white government before white people." Sheppard knew far better than his colleagues just how far he could push the fat-pocketed parishioners. Only as long as he remained Black Livingstone could he hope to control their hearts and purse strings. He did not want to lose his mainstream appeal.

Had he been a less tactful man, Sheppard could have pointed out that Vass and Morrison themselves had failed to stand up for human rights. Neither of the native Virginians fought racism in their home state. Had they openly criticized Jim Crow instead of King Leopold— had they attacked their own government, their colleagues, their fellow Southerners—they would have risked losing their closest friendships and perhaps their lives. But neither man did so.

The contradiction was not lost on foreign observers. British consul E. W. P. Thurston found Sheppard's resistance to Morrison's orders to be perfectly reasonable "on account of the social hatred produced by the colour question in [America]." To the British, the United States and the

Congo were not so very different, and in either country, a man had every right to protect himself from hate.

Still, Sheppard did listen to Vass, and in 1905 he began inserting some explosive material into his speeches. He was perhaps at his most daring in a lecture he delivered in Warm Springs, Virginia, a town near enough to Waynesboro that his family and friends would have been sitting in the church. On home turf, Sheppard felt safe enough to spread the truth.

Little did he realize that Baron Moncheur, the Belgian ambassador, also sat in the audience—he'd trekked all the way from Washington to attend. The ambassador expected to hear glowing praise of the Free State; after all, the last time he'd seen Sheppard, the missionary had confided that he no longer wanted to be Morrison's tool.

Black Livingstone took the stage. The newfangled electric lights made his face glow. He swaggered toward the podium and deposited his notes there. He gazed around the packed church, letting the silence ripen. The crowd, packed hip to hip in the pews, did not dare make a sound. It was an era before TV and film, when the spectacle of a man up on stage, just a man and his voice, could transport. Sheppard was the first person most of them had ever seen who'd been to Africa and survived.

He did not disappoint. Retracing his journey through the burned-out villages and into the Zappo-Zap stockade, he described the half-gnawed bodies and the blood-soaked dirt buzzing with flies. He described the baskets full of hands and the children with stumps at the end of their arms. And he made it clear that the Belgians had been responsible.

Moncheur was furious—he'd exchanged so many polite letters with Sheppard, and now this! He left the church sputtering. A reporter was on hand to observe his outrage. Within days, a story appeared—"Account of the Atrocities in the Belgian Congo"—and was picked up by the international press.

If that was not enough to make Sheppard one of the foremost critics of the Free State, a Mark Twain book published in 1905 sealed his reputation. In *King Leopold's Soliloquy,* Twain imagines the king as a cartoon character, stomping around his castle and fuming about the "meddlesome missionaries" spoiling his plans to rape the Congo. The satirical tone of the book is chillingly undercut by the photos: children displaying stump arms for the camera, a man contemplating the cut-off foot of his daughter. Twain's polemic, based largely on the writings of Sheppard, mentions the hero by name.

Sheppard had been catapulted into the spotlight; without meaning to, he had become one of the world's most outspoken black critics of white oppression.

By 1906, the job of discrediting King Leopold had become ridiculously easy. Bloated and pasty-looking, Leopold would die of stomach cancer only three years later. The man who had once masterminded the era's most ambitious public relations campaign had begun to make mistakes. One of the most egregious had been to hire a celebrity lawyer named Henry Kowalsky as his American lobbyist.

At the height of his powers, the king would have surely recognized Kowalsky as a man who would betray him. But Leopold was now distracted by his menagerie of obsessive-compulsive tics and by a demanding ex-prostitute mistress young enough to be his granddaughter. So he failed to see through his American agent.

In 1906, Kowalsky sold his story to the Hearst newspapers, leaking every secret about Leopold's undercover operations in the United States. The ensuing media blitz changed American public opinion in a matter of weeks: "King Leopold's Amazing Attempt to Influence Our Congress Exposed," screamed a *New York American* headline. Articles told how Leopold's spies had tried to buy off politicians.

The State Department hurried to distance itself from Leopold—without, of course, promising to take any specific steps in the Congo. From now on, the Presbyterians would be able to depend on a bevy of

U.S. envoys to help cut through Belgian red tape and to defend the Congo missions from attack. The United States had no strategic interests in the area, but it would now be at pains to defend its own citizens from the Free State.

For Sheppard, that change in policy would make all the difference in the coming years.

CHAPTER 10

Rubber Harvest

While Sheppard furloughed in the States, he heard reports of terrible news from the Congo mission he'd left behind. In late 1903, the SS *Lapsley*—the Presbyterians' $25,000 ship, its most essential piece of equipment—sank, drowning one American and twenty-three Africans. An article in the *Richmond Times-Dispatch* reprinted the harrowing account of one of the survivors, who'd floated to safety in a deck chair:

> [The boat] whirled so fast [in the rapids of the Congo River] that she careened . . . and in an instant we were in the whirling waters. . . . I jumped into the water amongst the . . . crew and watched men in all stages of drowning with no power to help. Awful! Awful! One man grappled me and we sank, but his hands were loosed and I came up again. . . . I . : . watched [men] die and struggle. Just as my own strength was failing, God providentially sent me a wicker chair. I climbed on that and whirled downstream away from the steamer, which was floating bottom up.

Even more devastating news came less than a year later. Ibaanc, the paradise village Sheppard designed and built, had burned to the ground. In November 1904, a band of Kuba warriors imbibed a magic potion that they believed made bullets turn to water. Then they set off to wreak retribution on the foreigners who'd invaded their land. They attacked the most obvious target: the town inside their own country where a renegade Kuba prince who called himself Shepete had had the gall to set up his own government and shelter the evil Maxamalinge. As they saw it, revenge was overdue.

But from missionary Althea Brown's point of view the attack was vicious and unwarranted. She remembered an ordinary morning in Ibaanc, the workmen smoothing the walls of the new Lapsley Memorial Church, hunters readying for a trip into the forest, children dodging each other in the market square. "Suddenly in the distance there went up a peculiar cry, the full import of which the villagers alone understood. *It was the cry of death!*" Just then, "a man came running up and presented me with a branch dipped in blood, saying the blood was that of one of our men shot dead by a [Kuba] arrow." A town nearby had erupted in flames. The Kuba warriors who had torched it were marching toward Ibaanc.

Brown ran to the orphanage and gathered the children, but she had nowhere safe to take them. The village was surrounded by bands of warriors. While the women and children of Ibaanc huddled in Brown's yard, the men of the village did their best to hold off the attackers.

The next morning, the villagers decided to risk the march to Luebo. "There must have been five hundred of us. It was a pathetic sight. Small children four and five years old were walking and even bearing burdens. The native soldiers, fearing an attack along the road, ordered us to march at full speed."

When Brown returned to Ibaanc a few days later, she found nothing but charred house posts, soot, and dead animals. The African American city of dreams had gone up in flames, partly because of Sheppard's misjudgment in harboring Maxamalinge. He had estranged the Kuba. Never again would he be welcome in their capital.

But the sunken ship and the ruined town would come to seem like minor setbacks as horror mounted in the Kasai. A few years before, King Leopold had made an exclusive deal with a rubber firm called the Compagnie du Kasai (CK). Not only did the CK have a monopoly on the area's rubber, it also could issue its own currency, impose whatever taxes it liked, run its own police force, and turn farming into a criminal act.

When Sheppard left the Kasai in late 1903, the CK's forced-labor system had been confined to a few isolated towns. But by 1906, when Sheppard returned, the firm had subsumed almost every village, making the entire region a vast concentration camp.

Oddly, it was after King Leopold finally gave up control of the Congo that matters grew worse. In 1906, as newspapers began to report on his hand-chopping and profit-skimming, Leopold recognized that it was time to divorce himself from the Congo or the international community would snatch it away from him. By 1908 he managed to hammer out a favorable deal to sell off the colony to the Belgian government. A huge lump-sum settlement, along with many perks, would allow him to retire aboard his yacht in style.

Human rights activists like E. D. Morel hoped that when the Belgian government took over the Congo, conditions would improve for the Africans. But the system Leopold had set up was simply too profitable to be dismantled. The Belgian government itself owned more than fifty percent of rubber companies like the Compagnie du Kasai. Why would it curb its own source of revenue? And so Free State officers who'd been accused of collecting baskets full of hands still lounged at the same desks; African policemen still paraded through villages with their rifles cocked; and the rubber companies still acted as de facto governments, collecting illegal taxes and harvesting laborers.

In 1908, William Morrison eloquently described just how entrenched the terror had become:

We are not now suffering from the old forms of outrage so much—hand-cutting, slave-raiding, murdering, etc.—but I am sorry to say that I believe the sum total of suffering is much more than it was formerly. Now the people are thoroughly cowed; they know from bitter experience that there is no escaping from the State. They, therefore, submit in stoical silence. I am almost surprised at discovering, by accident, the various ways in which they are wronged. Demands are made for men and the villages send for them. . . . The outrage is taking a more refined form.

Back in 1903, Sheppard could still dream of marching into the Kuba capital and winning over the king, of turning it into an African City on the Hill, far from white influence. But when he returned to the Congo in 1906, it was clear he finally had to let go of his plan. The forbidden city that he had documented fifteen years before no longer really existed. The Free State had turned it into a company town.

Emil Torday, the ethnographer who visited Mushenge in 1908, described the place as a ruin, a slum built out of the wreckage of its once-grand history: The buildings "looked bare and ugly," he wrote. "However, now and then we came on some vestige of a past, the glory of which had departed: this ramshackle house had its doorway supported by a carved pillar of exquisite workmanship, or in front of that hovel a mat was lying, made of cane tied together with string of various colours, such delicate workmanship or such rich colouring that I had never seen in Africa."

The royal family had also suffered. In 1904, the State had hunted down the Kuba king, Kot aPe (his predecessor, Mishaape, had died of smallpox a few years before). Belgian officers arrested the king on trumped-up charges, dragged him off to jail, gave him a tour of arsenals and barracks full of soldiers, and then freed him. The message was not lost on Kot aPe. He returned to the throne humbled, and tried to convince the clan leaders under his rule to surrender; they could not win against the invaders.

Torday described the impossible situation Kot aPe had found himself in. His people—a romantic and proud lot who'd had little contact with Westerners—itched to go to war. The Belgians, for their part, would use any excuse to slaughter the Kuba. The king struggled to please both sides. Torday portrays him as a hand-wringing Pontius Pilate of a man, a collaborator with a conscience. "I am old and want peace and rest; but I want such a peace as is given to the elephant who does not want to hurt anyone, but whom nobody dares to hurt; I have no use for the peace of the worm," King Kot aPe told him. The king nonetheless chose a most wormy peace—ordering his people to gather rubber until they starved, allowing the State men to patrol his villages. At formal functions, Kot aPe sat on a European chair, a gesture that would endear him to the Belgians. At the same time, he held to Kuba tradition by propping up his feet on the back of a slave. Picture him then in that contorted posture, twisted into a tortured compromise between two cultures.

Fifteen years before, when Sheppard first entered the forbidden city, he had admired a statue that stood near the palace. Carved at least a century earlier, it portrayed one of the Kuba founders holding a game board that resembled a checkerboard. As Sheppard saw it, this was a work of art that best represented who the Kuba were as a people. Though he had bought trinkets and fabrics to take home to America, it never occurred to him to make off with the statue.

But when Emil Torday saw the treasure in 1908, he knew he had to have it. If he could take it back to Europe, it would be one of the great coups of his career. "I made up my mind that it should go to the British Museum at any cost." He hired some African henchmen to help him. "The common people never knew anything about the transaction, and the statue was brought to me in the dark of night." So, wrapped up in a

scrap of old calico, Shamba—the legendary founder of the Kuba kingdom—was carried like a corpse out of the city to begin his long journey
across the ocean. He would end up squatting in the British Museum, to
be gawked at by schoolchildren, or warehoused in a crate, forever in exile.

When the Sheppards moved back to Ibaanc in 1906, they found their
paradise turned into a huddle of slapped-together buildings among the
dust and ashes. Their fellow missionaries had erected a house for them,
and Lucy set to work tailoring curtains to the new windows, turning
their luggage into tables, and sweeping the debris out of their yard.

Ibaanc now sat in the middle of a war zone. Should the missionaries
walk for a few hours in any direction, they would witness the ravages of
the rubber trade. Kuba aristocrats who had once promenaded in high
feathered hats now wore rags around their waists and ropes tied to their
necks. Farmers spent their days wandering through the jungles with
their machetes. Sometimes they managed to keep a plot of vegetables
growing in a hidden place deep in the woods, but mostly the people ate
almost nothing and snatched only a few hours of sleep between long
days of rubber-harvesting. Guards patrolled their villages and made
sure that no one wasted time on farming, cooking, or repairing houses.

In 1908, Sheppard published an article about the situation in the Kasai.
It's not clear whether he did so under pressure from Morrison or because of his own horror at what had happened to the Kuba. Whatever
his reasons, Sheppard had finally joined the fight, adding his voice to
Morrison's protests. But that voice was tellingly different from the
white writer's.

Other human rights activists tended to portray the Africans as inter-
changeable victims with little personality or culture of their own; Sheppard, on the other hand, eulogized the Kuba's lost way of life and made
it clear that the Africans had been fit to govern themselves:

These great stalwart men and women, who have from time immemorial been free, cultivating large crops of Indian corn, tobacco, potatoes, trapping elephants for their ivory and leopards for their skins, who have always had their own king and a government not to be despised, officers of the law, established in every town of the kingdom; these magnificent people, perhaps 400,000 in number, have entered a new chapter in the history of their tribe. . . . Within the last three years how changed they are! Their farms are growing in weeds and jungle, their king is practically a slave, their houses now are mostly half-built single rooms, and are much neglected. The streets of the their towns are not clean and well-swept as they once were. Even the children cry for bread.

Why this change? You have it in a few words. There are armed sentries of chartered trading companies who force the men and women to spend most of their days and nights in the forests making rubber, and the price they receive is so meager they cannot live upon it.

The article, Sheppard's most combative ever, appeared in the *Kasai Herald*, a newsletter printed on a rickety press and sent around to a few hundred Presbyterians. Sheppard must have felt safe in speaking to such a small audience—he could get the word out to his fellow Presbyterians without calling too much attention to himself.

That same year, when a British vice-consul arrived in Ibaanc, Sheppard seized another opportunity to publicize the Kuba's story, again in a way that lent him some anonymity. Wilfred Thesiger was the first foreign diplomat to examine the Congo interior, and his opinions would help sculpt British foreign policy.

Sheppard volunteered to act as Thesiger's translator and guide. Escorting the Englishman through destroyed villages, the missionary told his Kuba friends, "You see this white man? When he returns to Europe he will tell the State officials whatever you tell him, because he is very powerful."

The vice-consul, overwhelmed by his tour of thirty villages, repeated the opinions fed to him by his guide. His report, titled "The Enslavement and Destruction of the Bakuba," simply rehashed Sheppard's article in the *Kasai Herald*. It told the same story of a fabulous city gone to ruins, a proud people enslaved, and a rubber company at fault.

There had been other, more graphic reports about the Congo situation. Thesiger did not include the blow-by-blow stories about cut-off body parts that had characterized, for instance, Roger Casement's chilling portrait of the Congo. But Thesiger's findings shocked the public for other reasons. Instead of blaming a mere government, Thesiger dared to condemn an even more powerful enemy: a multinational corporation. He asserted that the Compagnie du Kasai had made its profits on the back of forced labor and torture. Following the release of the report, the firm's stock prices plummeted. Other rubber companies watched anxiously to see whether business would go on as usual in the Congo.

To ensure that it would, the directors of the CK decided to sue for libel, in order to discredit the Thesiger report. Millions of francs were at stake. The directors would have liked to make an example of Thesiger himself, but he had diplomatic immunity that protected him from libel charges. So the CK cast about for another target, a man who could be destroyed so thoroughly that no activist would ever dare take on the rubber cartel again.

That's how they settled on Sheppard. In February 1909, the CK filed suit against him for "[sullying] the respectability and injuring the credit of the Company by means of certain articles published in the 'Kasai Herald.'" Morrison was also named in the suit, for a different crime. He had made public the correspondence between himself and the rubber company, including some letters that made the CK look very bad—an action that the company claimed was defamatory.

If the two men lost the trial—which seemed likely, given the nature of the Congo courts—they would pay up to 80,000 francs or spend six years in jail.

Morrison was thrilled. The trial was sure to make for excellent guerrilla theater, exposing the inner workings of the Congo government to the rest of the world, perhaps even prompting the United States to take military action against the Belgians. "Sheppard and I prefer to go to prison rather than pay the fine," Morrison asserted. Sheppard himself did not comment, and one can only wonder whether he really did prefer to rot in a Congo prison for six years.

Like Morrison, the humanitarians in London also rooted for disaster. "I hope Morrison may be put into prison if not executed, much as I desire his freedom and life to be respected," Thesiger wrote. "We want the U.S.A. to act strongly."

Arthur Conan Doyle, who'd just become a convert to the cause, also thrilled to the romantic possibilities of a humanitarian in jail: "Morrison in the dock makes a finer Statue of Liberty than Bartholdi's in the New York harbor," he wrote. Neither Thesiger nor Conan Doyle bothered to mention the other defendant in the trial. A black man, apparently, would not make such a fine Statue of Liberty.

The Free State's legal system was notorious for handing down ghastly decisions. In 1908, missionaries filed repeated complaints against a Belgian officer who had reaped enormous rubber profits by murdering and starving local Africans. The Free State reluctantly put this villain on trial. While agreeing that he had killed more than sixty people, and that he should be condemned to death, the judge nonetheless handed down a much lighter sentence, reasoning that the defendent hadn't been fully responsible for his actions. "Long residence amongst the natives must have deprived him of all sentiments of humanity," the court decided. In other words, the Belgian officer had been infected by the Africans' "barbarity"; it was their fault, not his, that he'd gone on a killing spree.

So even though the case against Morrison and Sheppard bordered on the absurd—after all, how could an article in the tiny *Kasai Herald* have caused any damage to one of the most profitable corporations in the world?—the two men did not expect to win. Once the suit entered the Free State courts, logic would no longer matter. The State would wreak its revenge on the missionaries.

Morrison greeted the prospect with glee. If the Free State behaved as badly as usual, the world might finally notice. As for Sheppard, it's hard to say what he felt about the trial. He wrote next to nothing about it, but his silence indicates that he did not share Morrison's enthusiasm for a showdown.

The first sign of trouble was the court date. The Free State judge set the trial for May in Leopoldville. He might as well have demanded that the missionaries appear on Mars in the year 3000. As the judge would have known very well, Morrison and Sheppard could not leave Luebo in the spring. No steamship captain would dare to make the trip during the dry season; rocks protruded above the water, sandbanks swelled up to tear the bellies of ships. If the missionaries attempted to sail the Kasai River in May, they would be likely to die.

Morrison planned to sail down to Leopoldville anyway, to risk his life and those of Sheppard and the crew to get to the trial on time. But in the end, he didn't have to go to such dramatic lengths. Under pressure from the U.S. government, the Free State judge agreed to postpone the trial to July 30.

The delay gave Morrison time to come up with another plan for navigating the dry river. He decided that he himself would travel by canoe past the worst rapids of the Kasai; then he would catch a State steamship, which would take him the rest of the way.

Meanwhile, he ordered Sheppard to follow another route to Leopoldville. As usual, the black missionary got stuck with the most thankless and dangerous work. He would have to trek through Kuba-land on foot, trying to gather African witnesses to testify at the trial.

Then he would have to convince the witnesses to follow him through miles of jungle to meet the State steamer halfway down the Kasai River. It was a Herculean task, and if Sheppard met with any trouble, he would be likely to miss his own trial.

That summer, Sheppard parted with Lucy, leaving her to take charge of the orphanage, school, and medical center at Ibaanc. Then he trudged off into the jungle and toward an uncertain fate. The trip might have reminded him of his bachelor days in Africa, once again camping in villages and following the winding trails made by antelope and elephant. He didn't leave any record of how he managed to gather Kuba witnesses and convince them to travel to a city hundred of miles distant. But with characteristic dazzle, he pulled the feat off, arriving at the riverside to meet the steamship, and Morrison, with twenty warriors marching behind him.

As he hiked through Kubaland, Sheppard didn't know what awaited him in Leopoldville—humiliation, bankruptcy, prison? Perhaps he comforted himself in a lover's embrace, in the sweet sins that have often been the solace of missionaries. In the backwoods of the Kasai, he imagined his secrets would be safe.

CHAPTER 11

The Trial

In early August 1908, a steamship chugged into the port at Leopoldville. Morrison and Sheppard climbed off it, followed by their twenty African witnesses, men dressed in the kilts and brass anklets of the Kuba aristocracy, their shaved chests shining, the muscles of their backs fanning like wings.

They filed through town and into the mission run by Dr. Sims, the same place Sheppard had stayed almost two decades before when he bagged his first hippo. Dr. Sims's compound had swelled over the years—he'd added a brick-making factory, botanical gardens, and a school. It was here that the missionaries and their witnesses would stay before the trial.

They had almost two months to wait. The date had once again been moved back, this time to late September. "I am living up in the upper end room of Dr. Sims' old house, taking in the sights with the twenty [Kuba] witnesses" to entertain them, Morrison wrote. He also kept himself busy by firing off letters of protest to newspapers, and updates to his friends in London.

So much had changed in eighteen years. In Sheppard's youth, Leopoldville had been a frontier town, distinguished only by a few box-like buildings on the hillside and a boat or two bobbing in the port. But now it had become the terminus for the famous Congo railroad. Ships crowded into the dock; men carried bundles to and fro with antlike determination; train cars rattled into the station; expatriates enjoyed shooting parties on the weekends; prostitutes paraded about in a melange of European clothing; workers filed into the brick-making factory; hammer blows rang in the air.

Beyond all this bustle, the waters of Stanley Pool stretched like a sheet on a hotel bed, unmussed and starched. Squinting out his window at that lakelike expanse, Sheppard must have remembered himself as a young man—how he'd gazed at that same limpid horizon, beyond which lay the mysteries of darkest Africa, those spaces on the map that no one had yet filled in. He had been about to step off the edge of the world into a limitless freedom such as few men ever experienced.

But freedom had proved elusive. Like most other Western men, Sheppard risked his life in search of that nameless something that hovered in the mist above the deadly cataracts, where water melted into sky. You went to Africa to escape your last name, your poverty, or your skin color—to make yourself into a myth.

And whether you admitted it to yourself or not, you also went because of the women. They worked the fields with their breasts bare; they begged to touch you under your clothes, to see if you were real. Short and muscular, tall and splendid, scarified, beaded, pomaded, braided, robed, naked—a man could find whatever he craved here. Back home, the women cushioned themselves under hoop skirts and corsets; you could go mad with frustration. But here, you could indulge your slightest craving. And if you were discreet, no one would ever know.

Samuel Verner, the onetime Presbyterian missionary, had taken a Congolese mistress and fathered a child. Henry Hawkins, the church's transport agent, whom Sheppard had recruited in 1894, had done the same. (The church hadn't allowed Hawkins to bring his wife with him, effectively breaking up the marriage; Hawkins may have considered his African mistress to be his new wife.) Belgian traders routinely supported one or more mistresses. Some, like Ernest Stache, Sheppard's long-ago traveling companion, fell in love with Congolese women and married them; others had affairs; still others came to Africa as sex tourists. Even the most devout missionaries, isolated from wives or "suitable" women for years on end, found themselves succumbing to illicit lusts.

It must have been partly erotic curiosity that induced two young men, Sheppard and Lapsley, to follow the Kuba—those people known for their eye-catching loveliness. In one of the only moments in his diary where Lapsley admits to feeling something like lust, it is for a Kuba woman. He describes a night in a remote village, a hut lit by candlelight. In the soft, licking light, he catches sight of "a really beautiful woman, with pretty small mouth . . . and eyes like a gazelle, a modest and womanly and charming expression withal." She had been equally fascinated with him, that stranger with the pale eyes and skin. "She got her husband to hold [my hand] for her to examine. Then, bolder, she felt it curiously, up to the elbow, indeed. Every little while she would edge up to examine the wonder again."

It is a scene of unintended erotic power. In the light of a candle, this shy woman explores along Lapsley's arm with her fingertips, fascinated by the skin that glows the color of the moon.

Sheppard, for his part, did not write about the women. It is only from a few notes hidden deep in church files that we find evidence of his secret life.

The only certain facts are these: In the early 1900s, he fathered a son named Shepete with a Kuba woman. And in the years leading up to the trial in Leopoldville, he indulged in affairs with several other African women.

Imagine him ducking out of the sun into the cool and dark of a hut. A woman shifts, gets up. She comes toward him with a bowl of water. They exchange a few words in her language, the language of watery sounds. She sits him down on a mat, takes off his shoes, lays out plates before him. Perhaps she calls him "chief"—for he has become the head man in Ibaanc, and like any Kuba prince, has many women.

Perhaps it did not seem like a sin at the time. He had traveled such a long road to arrive in secret lands, hushed clearings striped with quivering shadows from the moon. He might have imagined that this long road stretched on, ever farther into the wilderness, into desire and its satisfaction.

He did not realize then that his road was circular, that it would lead him back to where he started from, a room in Dr. Sims's house with a view of that heartbreakingly blue lake that had once been his horizon, Morrison down the hall.

Even then, as they waited for the trial to begin, Morrison probably had all the evidence he needed to end Sheppard's career in Africa: He must have heard rumors about the affairs, the bastard son. But he was determined to keep the whole mess under wraps. The Congo crusade still needed Sheppard, and it needed him squeaky clean.

As Sheppard paced in front of his window, listening to the scritch of Morrison's pen in the next room, he must have wondered what the man was writing, and whether it concerned him.

The walls of the courtroom had been painted a sickening shade of green; paint chips blistered off the sweaty plaster and onto the filthy floor. Seats had been improvised out of piles of bricks covered with old boards. The windowpanes had fallen out, and noise from Leopoldville pressed in—birdcalls, gunshots, railroad whistles, market hubbub, and also the jabber of the curiosity seekers who had gathered outside to watch the proceedings through the broken windows and open doorway. If ever a courtroom exuded the moldering atmosphere of justice gone wrong—of files lost and people disappeared, of a complicit smile under the cruel curve of a mustache—this was it.

Sheppard escorted the Kuba witnesses into the building, charming them with a few jokes in their own language as they took their places along a wall—for he hid his nervousness well. In the white suit and Panama hat he wore that day, he towered over not only the warriors but nearly everyone else in that room. The onlookers would have whispered about him in French and English. "He appears very proud now," they might have said, "but just wait until he's carted off in chains."

And Sheppard, what did he think about as he took his seat on that rickety bench and composed his face so that he'd appear calm as he waited for his fate to be decided? Perhaps he thought of the poison cup. For two decades, his most vigorous human rights work had been in defense of the victims of witch trials, with whom he strongly identified. Years before, he'd gone weak in the knees after seeing one of these spectacles for the first time: "To my horror as I drew near [the villagers] were slowly driving a woman to whom they had given the poison. She ran about fifty yards, staggered, reeled, and fell with a thud." Later, he would invite Prince Maxamalinge to come live with him, risking his own life in order to protect his friend from a similar poison trial.

Most horrifying for Sheppard was not the poison itself, but the idea of being at the mercy of a mad judge against whom he couldn't argue, being tried in a court of law in which "the twitching of the eye, the itching of the hand, [and] the flying of a crow across one's house" could be used as evidence against him. For Sheppard, the witch trials represented the worst evil that people could inflict on each other—a torture not only of the body but of the spirit. He may have feared that he would one day become the victim of some kind of witch trial; but he probably never guessed the legal system that accused him would be European.

A few weeks before the trial, the case had seemed hopeless. Then, at the last minute, a trio of powerful men had shown up in Leopoldville to throw their support behind Morrison and Sheppard. The presence of these men would change everything. It signaled that this trial had become a case of international concern.

Two of the men, Americans, strode into the courtroom that day, exuding an air of importance, dressed in creamy suits more appropriate for a seaside holiday than the African frontier. With them a breeze seemed to sweep through the building, the fresh air of a world beyond the sweaty Congo interior. It was clear that they refused to be menaced by the moldy walls or the expats who crowded around the door or the portrait of King Leopold hanging askew on the wall. They approached Sheppard and Morrison, wished them luck, shook hands all around, and offered assurances. The two diplomats, consul William Handley and his assistant, had come thousands of miles to observe the trial, doing so under orders from President Howard Taft, who had issued a statement that the United States would follow the events with "no little concern." In other words, the U.S. government would not tolerate a crooked judge or a fixed trial.

It was a preemptive move that Morrison had not planned on—he had expected the State Department to intervene only after he and Sheppard had been slapped in jail. And though he hoped to martyr himself to gain world attention, he must have been relieved at the arrival of the diplomats.

The third celebrity to saunter through the door would have set all the Belgians to pointing and whispering. He wore a rumpled suit on his bearlike body and a triangular beard on his plump face, so that he resembled some kind of cross between Vladimir Lenin and Santa Claus. This apparition was none other than Emile Vandervelde, the leader of the Belgian Socialist Party. Vandervelde had marched at the head of an army of workers when they stormed Brussels and had been chased through the streets by soldiers and police. Elected to the parliament on the Socialist ticket, he'd been one of the few members of his party opposed to King Leopold's rule in the Congo. And when he learned about the trial against Sheppard and Morrison, he'd sailed all the way to the Congo to defend them—for free.

For months it had looked as if the missionaries would have no attorney at all, until Vandervelde, who held a law degree, had volunteered at the last moment. The atheist and the two devout Christians made an unlikely team. Vandervelde distrusted missionaries, believing them to be "tools in the hands of stronger and more evil men." And these two colonial tools also happened to be Americans, which made Vandervelde's alliance with them all the more difficult. When he announced he'd defend the foreigners, many of his countrymen vilified him as a traitor, a man who had turned against his own people. In fact, Vandervelde acted on his own peculiar sense of patriotism—he hoped that the trial would finally awaken the Belgian conscience about the Congo.

Once Vandervelde and the diplomats took their places on the benches, the mood in the room shifted. This tin-roofed dump of a court would have to pull itself to attention; the judge would have to operate according to the standards of international law. The whole world was watching.

The proceedings began with a surprise announcement from the judge. A clerk had mishandled the paperwork, lumping Morrison in with the *Kasai Herald* libel disagreement, rather than setting up separate charges against him. Reluctant to once again reschedule the trial, the judge had decided to drop the charges against Morrison. Sheppard would be the sole defendant.

Morrison must have reeled at the news. For more than a decade, he'd dedicated himself to destroying the Belgians. Before the arrival of Vandervelde, he had planned to act as his own lawyer, had compiled extensive notes and coached the witnesses, had imagined an outraged European press reacting to the words he would thunder in the courtroom. He'd been prepared—eager even—to go to jail for the sake of justice.

But now, in one arbitrary swoop, the case against him had been dismissed. Sheppard would be the star. Morrison must have been livid. Who was Sheppard anyway? A washed-up explorer, an antique left over from the early days of the mission, a stuffed trophy the people back home rolled out when they needed to raise money. Stubborn old Sheppard, who'd refused even to mention the crimes of King Leopold. This entirely dismissable relic of a man would now become far more famous than Morrison himself, would be *the* voice of the Congo Reform movement. It must have galled Morrison beyond words.

Sheppard, too, would have been disheartened at the turn of the events. When he'd written his article for the *Kasai Herald*, he never imagined that it would land him here, before a white judge in the courtroom of one of the most racist countries on the planet. If the two men could have traded places, they surely would have.

Vandervelde had no trouble flicking away the libel charges against Sheppard. These had always been flimsy, and with several diplomats looking on, the Compagnie du Kasai's gripes against the *Kasai Herald* appeared more ridiculous than ever.

Following this first victory, Vandervelde gleefully turned his attention to some of the more frivolous complaints. For instance, the CK's lawyer contended that Sheppard and his colleagues had made overtures of friendship to the Belgians with the intent to spy on them and find out their secrets. He presented evidence of the evil plot: Mrs. Sheppard and Mrs. Morrison had sent dinner invitations, thank-you notes, and candy to Belgian traders.

It was an argument that was bound to backfire. The prosecutor should have known better than to attack the friendly ministrations of female missionaries. His behavior could not have been less gallant.

Vandervelde jumped right in. He asked the courtroom what kind of cad would try to ruin the reputation of Christian ladies? The Belgians had been rude to bring their letters into court. "If I had . . . received letters from ladies thanking me for gifts, it would never have occurred to me to collect these thank you notes to be used as evidence," he noted. "But in this regard, everyone has his own value system." The Belgians might look down on the English, Vandervelde quipped, but at least the English knew better than to humiliate ladies in the courtroom.

In between such lighter moments, Vandervelde reminded his audience of the seriousness of the trial, its true meaning. "This lawsuit is actually not between the Company Kasai and Mr. Sheppard, but between the Company Kasai and the natives." It was, he made it clear, a question of human rights.

Vandervelde, the trained speaker and charismatic political figure, transformed the trial into his own show. "His speech was a marvel of eloquence, invincible logic, burning sarcasm and pathetic appeal for justice to be done in this case, not only for us missionaries, but especially for the native people," Morrison wrote. "He held the audience in the court room spellbound for over two hours."

According to Sheppard, everyone in the room had been so moved by Vandervelde's words that even the Catholic missionaries dabbed their eyes with hankies. The Kuba witnesses—whom the judge barred from testifying—also were touched by Vandervelde's support. They lined up at the end of the trial to thank the Socialist for his help.

Judge Gianpetri must have been under incredible strain: On one side of the room, U.S. envoys scribbled down notes to take back to the State Department; on the other, well-connected Belgian businessmen scrutinized his every word. The decision he handed down would have to be a dutiful bit of compromise.

In the end, he let everyone off the hook. Sheppard was cleared of the libel charges. For its part, the CK would pay a few francs to cover the costs of the trial, but no other damages; nor would it be held accountable for its treatment of the natives.

Activists like E. D. Morel had hoped that the trial would topple the Belgian system. That did not happen. But it did help lead to the breakup of the CK's monopoly in the Kasai. Following the trial, the Belgian government allowed competing rubber companies to operate in the area. Once several firms began vying for workers, conditions did improve for the Congolese, for a few years. Small as this victory was, it would be one of the few bright spots in the decades-long Belgian tyranny in the region.

Morrison was jubilant. "Throw up your hat! Sheppard & I acquitted," he wrote to Morel, as if he and his colleague had shared equal billing in the trial.

But that was not how it played in the international press. "American Negro Hero of Congo, Was First to Inform World of Congo Abuses," screamed a headline in the *Boston Herald*. Calling Sheppard "one of the most famous Americans of his race," the article gushed about his swashbuckling history in Africa: "President Roosevelt has had no such hunting adventures as befell [Sheppard and his partner Lapsley]. . . . They killed thirty-six hippopotami, two elephants and many crocodiles. Five times they were nearly captured by savages on the first journey." Sheppard was hailed for the American spirit and love of liberty that had prompted him to intervene in Congo politics. Once the Black Livingstone, he had been refurbished as a thoroughly twentieth-century hero. He had become a black Teddy Roosevelt—a frontiersman who embodied all that was most muscular and aggressive about his home country. The United States had just won the Spanish-American War and acquired the Philippines. It was celebrating the beginning of its century as a superpower. Sheppard was an ideal hero of the new, expansionist age.

Morrison was hardly mentioned in the article. He had not been a defendant in the trial, nor did he have the eye-catching résumé of his colleague. He had probably never bagged a single hippo, let alone thirty-six of them. Instead, he'd been holed up in his hut, drafting letters to kings and MPs, the kind of unglamorous activity that made him a difficult person to transform into a media darling.

Perhaps the men burst into Dr. Sims's parlor that evening after the trial. Perhaps they enjoyed some sips of sherry, precious golden liquid sent all the way from London; perhaps they pulled their chairs up to a long table to enjoy a celebration dinner, served to them by African ladies in fresh-laundered cottons. As they toasted each other, the men would have laughed and cheered in the cautious way of professional religionists, the party mood broken now and then for a prayer.

Morrison and Sheppard might have posed together in the center of the room for formal photographs, clinked glasses, and embraced. With the swirl of voices around them, the blur of white suits, the flash of camera bulbs, and the smell of cigar smoke, did they lock eyes? Did Morrison's public smile waver then? Just for a second, did Sheppard watch that bearded, beetle-browed face turn hard, and those electric blue eyes burn through him? He would have known that angry expression well. Those eyes had seared through the cautious orders from Samuel Chester composed on church stationery, through the stiff blue uniforms of the Belgian officers; Morrison's gaze burned away all that stood in his way. And now those eyes drilled into Sheppard.

CHAPTER 12

The Children's Friend

In the days after the trial, somewhere in the depths of Dr. Sims's compound, a door closed with a discreet snick of lock on latch. A trusted servant was called into a room, where voices buzzed in the parched heat of afternoon. The watery expanse of Stanley Pool shimmered outside the window. There was the sound of someone sobbing.

With the trial over, Sheppard was of no use to Morrison—the explorer was, if anything, a liability. If the press found out that Sheppard, the hero of the Congo, had fathered an African son, the movement would be discredited. All that Morrison had worked for might be destroyed. And so Morrison arranged to have his colleague whisked away.

The details of Sheppard's dismissal from Africa are hazy. Officially, he would be leaving the Congo forever because of poor health. The scandal was so carefully hidden that even Stanley Shalloff's 1970 book *Reform in Leopold's Congo*—the best and most thorough account of the Presbyterian human rights movement—does not mention it. The book says only that Sheppard retired from the Congo.

But letters and documents buried in the Presbyterian archives hint at another explanation. Shortly after Sheppard won his case against the rubber company, he was subjected to another trial. This one took place in secret and involved only a few men. Who exactly attended and what they said is not clear, the details obscured by years of cover stories and throat clearing. We do know that the men in the room included Sheppard, Morrison, and James Reavis, the codirector of the Foreign Missions department, who happened to be in Leopoldville at the time. Also present was M'peya, an African who had probably worked as Sheppard's butler, called in to offer testimony about the clandestine comings and goings in his employer's bedroom. It's unclear whether M'peya had come forward on his own or whether Morrison had sought him out.

However he ended up in that room, M'peya had a lot to say. He constructed a picture of Sheppard that must have made Morrison and Reavis look away with embarrassment: Here was their friend and colleague exposed as a compulsive adulterer. According to the servant, Sheppard had taken up with a woman during his first years in Ibaanc; then, upon returning to Africa after his furlough in 1906, he had seduced several more.

Later Sheppard would own up to these charges in a formal confession that he filed with the church. Here is his own, sketchy description of the misconduct: "Sometime in the years 1898–1899, while my wife was home and I was alone in my work, I fell under the temptation to which I was subjected in my relations with one of the native women at Ibanj Station and was guilty of the sin of adultery. My wife was away from me for about two years, and during this time, the action was repeated twice with the same person," he wrote. And he also admitted that "during the last four years spent in Africa I fell into sin with three different women."

Sheppard had been hired by the Presbyterians to model Christian values for the Africans. It's easy to understand why Morrison would want to expel from a religious community a man with several lovers.

And yet a provocative series of events suggests that Sheppard's fall had to do with racial politics. During the same period when Morrison dismissed Sheppard, he also forced two other black male missionaries to leave the Congo mission. He accused all three of the men of the same crime: sexual misconduct.

Henry Hawkins had served as the church's transport agent for fifteen years. He had performed his job with considerable skill, managing to cut deals even with racist suppliers who refused to dine at the same table with him. After many years in the Congo, Hawkins took an African lover—whom he may have regarded as a wife—and fathered a baby.

The evidence against Joseph Phipps was sketchy, but he too was asked to leave on suspicion of sexual improprieties. Years later, the church would reinstate him.

Thus in one swoop, Morrison cleared the mission of its black leaders—all of them men who had served in the Congo longer than he himself.

Sheppard's town of Ibaanc had always been a rival to Luebo, a black mission that ran according to its own rules and over which Morrison had only tenuous control. For a man as given to episodes of paranoia as Morrison, the independence of Ibaanc must have seemed dangerous. There, a group of talented black Americans—along with thousands of Africans—followed Sheppard's lead. Morrison must have been biding his time, waiting until he could take over the station.

In the decade after Sheppard left, Ibaanc was integrated, and though still staffed by blacks, was run by white missionaries. It continued to provide schooling and support for poor Africans, but it lost its unique character. Without William Sheppard, Ibaanc could not survive as a visionary city, built and decorated and ruled by African Americans. The experiment had come to an end.

Sheppard sailed from the Congo in the spring of 1910. Not everyone was pleased with the discreet way he was ushered out of Africa. In June 1910, Lachlan Vass handed in his resignation. He had been outraged by what he viewed as the coddling of Sheppard:

Things have been hushed up too much in our Congo mission along certain lines. I was talking with Dr. Snyder only last week and he in long years gone by has had complaints from the natives of Sheppard's not being straight. . . . I am sorry you feel that I have talked too freely concerning . . . Sheppard in particular. But I found scores of the thinking men of our church and thinking women who were sure as soon as they saw the [announcement] of his leaving that [they] knew there was something more serious than health back of this matter. . . . I don't expect to deceive to save Sheppard's most undeserved exalted position.

Vass made it clear that he wouldn't lie on Sheppard's behalf—that he would, in fact, do whatever he could to discredit the church's most famous missionary. Still, Sheppard's sexual habits remained a secret. Though the Presbyterians would subject him to another hearing in the United States, they took care to protect their hero's reputation.

In the fall of 1910, Sheppard's train pulled into a station in North Carolina, in a tiny cup of a town in the Blue Ridge Mountains. He would have been met by a carriage that clip-clopped along a dirt road past burbling creeks and forests of rhododendron, past a lake with a single swan cruising like a pleasure boat, and into the folds of Lookout Mountain. Here and there could be glimpsed the vacation cabins of the Presbyterian elite, their porches cluttered with fishing rods, snowshoes, and bicycles. Sheppard's carriage climbed a steep driveway to the front entrance of a hotel, a place built out of rough stone, with the expensively rustic air of a hunting lodge. Inside, he climbed the stairs past deer antlers and trophies and other outdoor paraphernalia. The dank, sad smell of vacation's end—wood smoke and rotten leaves—filled the place.

After more than twenty years, Sheppard had finally been allowed to enter Montreat, the mountain camp where white Presbyterians spent their summers. Sheppard had been summoned by Chester and Reavis, who now shared the job of directing the Foreign Missions department. The two men would have been waiting for him in a meeting room, wearing crisp wool suits and sitting erect in their chairs, legs crossed in a parody of ease. Sheppard would have sauntered through the door, inhabiting his body with the grace of someone who has survived in the outdoors for years. He would have seemed cheerful, in command of his surroundings—so is he invariably described by those who observed him even at the worst of times. Reavis and Chester, on the other hand, might have fidgeted, flicked their gazes around, avoiding each other's eyes and certainly not wanting to settle too long on the face of their old friend. They greeted him a bit too warmly, offered a chair. A clock on the wall ticked loudly in the sudden silence, as if it were clucking at them, tsk-tsk-tsking the time away.

Reavis opened the meeting, reading back to Sheppard the charges made against him at Leopoldville. "I went over all his evidence fully," he wrote later. "We advised him that the best thing was to make a full confession of the whole truth."

Folding himself into the chair, Sheppard listened to Reavis enumerate his sins—the adulteries that had been observed by African servants, and no doubt whispered about for years by his colleagues in Luebo. He must have experienced one of those moments of realization that we all dread: when we see ourselves without the flattering lens of our illusions. Sheppard had been cut down from hero of the Congo to compulsive fornicator.

"He broke down and confessed," Reavis wrote. Sheppard's sobs tore at the hearts of the other two men. "We were all in tears. I feel so sorry for him. Still . . . the confession will bring peace I believe. . . . Only a few need to know about the trouble at all. My heart goes out to him. I am devoted to him."

The three middle-aged men huddled in the room and wept—not just over Sheppard's dilemma, but over the era that was coming to an end. Within the year, all three of them would be pushed out of their Foreign Mission jobs. Holdovers from the nineteenth century, they had their own vision of what it meant to save the Africans, a quest that had little to do with international law or politics, but came down to chivalry. Rightly or wrongly, they had wanted to civilize Africans whom they imagined as thirsting for God. Part of their modest aims had been to establish a Congo mission in which black and white Americans would become coworkers and friends, would be paid the same, and would treat each other with respect. By 1920 the Foreign Missions board had changed its policies, and now discouraged blacks from applying for jobs in Africa. This was partly because, with the advent of Marcus Garvey and his radical movement that called for African self-rule and an end to colonialism, Americans of color could no longer travel to the Congo whenever they wished. Only a few decades before, black missionaries had seemed to be politically irrelevant; now many whites regarded them as revolutionaries. The Belgians barred most black Americans from entering the Congo.

Sheppard would never again return to Africa. Even if he had been able to acquire the necessary papers—which would have been difficult—the Congo he loved had disappeared. The blank map had been filled in with European names; the hidden kingdoms had been transformed into company towns; the hippos had been chased from the rivers. And Black Livingstone had become an impossible being.

Sheppard was put on probation, during which time he was forbidden to hold a position as a minister. He and Lucy eked out a living in Staunton, Virginia, and then in the slums of Louisville, Kentucky. As Lucy remembered it, "we . . . had a little home in a crowded neighborhood. . . . The noises and unkept condition of the streets and the poorly lighted and inadequately ventilated rooms were hard to accept."

In the dank quarters where the Sheppards and their children jammed together, William must have thought back to his brief stay at Montreat—trees turning golden, soil spangled with fragile sunlight, the lake with its single swan, the pock of a ball on a tennis racquet somewhere far away, laughter floating off the mountain. The paradise he would never gain entry to. A forbidden city more impenetrable than the Kuba kingdom had been.

Long ago in Luebo, he and Lapsley had called their dirt roads Pennsylvania Avenue and Boulevard de Paris, as if the grand names themselves had the power to transform, like magic spells. And now, in a similar fit of longing, he named the hovel where he and his family lived "Montreat."

In the years that followed, Sheppard picked up where he had left off in the United States, working as a speaker and freelance preacher. One offer came from John Little, a white man who headed up the "colored missions" in Louisville.

It's not clear what Little knew about Sheppard's troubles or when he learned that the missionary needed to find a job in the States. But after he'd seen Sheppard sweep into a classroom and electrify the students, Little knew he must hire this exceptional man. By the summer of 1912 the two preachers had worked out a deal: Sheppard would become pastor of Grace Church in Louisville, where his fame would attract new members to the struggling black parish. Within his first year there, the congregation swelled by fifty percent. As an old man, Max Sheppard still remembered that during one sermon his father "had them crying" and that he was "very emotional, but not one of those shouting preachers."

In addition to his duties at Grace Church, Sheppard ran a mission in an embattled neighborhood that was so down-and-out it had been nicknamed Smoketown. He and Lucy directed programs that provided cooking and sewing classes, recreation, medical services, and child care to the poor. The Sheppards were well suited to this work, since they had already created an ambitious set of services in Ibaanc.

The extreme poverty of his parishioners meant that William Sheppard had to build social change from the ground up. As in Africa, the classes he organized had nowhere to meet and the children had nowhere to play. Saving souls had become twinned in his mind with architecture; faith was a meeting hall, a palace, a square, a long road lined with banana trees. In Louisville, his efforts to provide recreation facilities for the poor eventually spurred the city to create a park, later called William Sheppard Park. A housing project would also bear his name.

Though Sheppard rooted himself in Louisville, he never ceased to see himself as a traveling speaker—or perhaps it was his larger public that never grew tired of him. According to Max, "Father wore three hats—he was a lecturer, a minister and an orator." Sheppard often took to the road to entertain and uplift with stories of Africa. In 1911, the YMCA hired him to tour the South and drum up volunteers; and Hampton Institute, his alma mater, frequently asked him to adorn its ceremonies. During one tour, he shared the stage with Booker T. Washington.

In his public appearances, he rarely mentioned Louisville or his mission work there; it was Africa the crowds wanted to hear about, cannibals, hippos, and secret palaces. And though his speeches echoed those from earlier tours, there was a difference: Then he'd been a man vigorously caught up in events unfolding in the Congo; now he was retired from the field, and the only way he would return to Africa was in memory.

What stood out in his memory—what he most often touched on in his public presentations—were the early adventures with Lapsley and his first contact with the Kuba people. In his fifties, when he wrote up his autobiography for the Presbyterian press, he stopped at age twenty-seven, the momentous year when he found his way into the forbidden city and marched out again with proof of Africa's genius. It was as if all that had happened afterward—his marriage, Morrison, the Belgian holocaust, the trial—did not exist.

Perhaps he chose to ignore the second half of his life so he could end with an upbeat finale, a hero sailing home into the sunset. As a popular entertainer and humorist, he did not know what to do with the horrific events that followed his early success. His autobiography was less a work of literature than a piece of publicity that he hoped might benefit his beloved Congo mission. So too were the other writings he left behind—speeches, manuscripts, tracts. He rarely mentions the trial. Nor does he make much of his role in the international human rights crusade.

It's easy to see why he would downplay his more radical activities. As a black man who had challenged one of the most profitable companies in the world—and triumphed—his very existence in the Jim Crow South was heresy. In the America of the 1910s and 1920s, the Ku Klux Klan reached the peak of its popularity, with about four million members, and black people—never mind famous black men who could outwit the white establishment—lived in fear for their lives.

Sheppard lived under apartheid in Louisville. There, even his white colleagues treated him like a pariah. Dr. John Little had hired Sheppard and worked closely with him, but, according to Max Sheppard, the Little family refused to socialize with the Sheppards.

Even when white admirers tried to praise him, they usually managed to insult him instead. A Louisville newspaper wondered how "a little pickaninny" could have grown into a famous explorer. And an Atlanta paper gushed that he was "probably the greatest Negro of his generation," but then added that "he is as simple and humble as a little child."

Once a virile Livingstone, Sheppard found it necessary to repackage himself as a humble Sunday school teacher. He penned books for children, producing a series based on his adventures in Africa. In these books he displayed a great love for the Congolese people whom he'd never see again—and also strange notions about what, exactly, constituted a children's story. His book *The Girl Who Ate Her Mother* is particularly odd. It tells the tale of little N'tumba, the six-year-old girl who was captured by Zappo-Zap slave traders and forced to eat the flesh of her mother. The story ends "happily" when Lapsley buys N'tumba and frees her, and the little girl converts to Christianity. It was as if Sheppard hoped to sneak in as much negative information as he could about the way Africans had been mistreated and enslaved. By putting his critiques in children's books, he disarmed the white adults who might otherwise have been threatened.

But the role of "children's friend" must have been a straitjacket for a man who had once been so powerful. In a publicity photo from 1911 or 1912, Sheppard seems to be trying hard to cast off his explorer image and recast himself as a family man. He's seated in the picture; his face has grown plump and sleek and he wears a trimmed mustache with only a hint of the handlebar in it. One flap of his beautiful coat is open to reveal the silk lining and his medal. Beside him stand Max and Wilhemina dressed in white, the little girl with a white bow that balances above her corkscrew curls; they wear the grave expressions of children forced to pose with politicians. To the far right, Lucy eyes the camera sidelong; in a billowing white shirt, she has grown monumental, queenly.

The photo indicates that there were advantages to a bourgeois existence in Louisville: The Sheppards wear lavish clothing and the children—if overly serious—appear pampered. Simply to be gathered in one room was a kind of triumph. Lucy and William had endured long periods of separation from their children; now, for the first time in his life, William Sheppard could be a full-time father. And if he took the name "children's friend" in his publicity materials, it might have been partly in celebration of the joy he took in his family.

Moreover, the family had achieved the middle-class existence that Lucy—and perhaps William also—had always dreamed about. After the first awkward years in the States, William pulled in enough money to move the family to a four-bedroom brick house on a comfortable street, East Breckenridge, with a doctor next door. Finally, Lucy had her *Ladies' Home Journal* house.

In 1979 and 1980, a team of interviewers collected family stories from Max Sheppard and his cousin Arthur Ware. Both of the men remembered less about the purported topic of the interview, William Sheppard, than they did about that house on East Breckenridge and the indomitable lady who had presided over it. Their memories—typical of the quirky, snapshot-like shards with which old people reconstruct their youth—give us tantalizing glimpses of what the Sheppards' later years must have been like.

Years of being waited on by African servants had apparently made Lucy an imperious ruler of the children. "A habit she never got out of was being waited on," Arthur Ware remembered. Once when he was ten years old playing outside the house, she called to him from upstairs. He found her seated, with some sewing on her lap. "Arthur, come here," she said, without getting up. "Hand me that spool of thread." She would not walk across the room to get it herself.

Lucy ruled over her husband in those final years, too. Ware remembers how William, an enthusiastic bargain hunter, once brought home a wagon full of soap dishes. Lucy wouldn't allow them in the house. He was "tall and portly, and she was short and stout," according to Ware, suggesting how the two had begun to grow inseparable as salt and pepper shakers. In those last years, William began to melt away, while Lucy rallied, ever more imposing in her Victorian ruffles and drapery. Africa had been his métier; the solid brick house on East Breckenridge was hers.

In 1926, when he was sixty-one, a stroke paralyzed William, and he lingered on as an invalid for a year before he died. It's tempting to make a metaphor out of his paralysis. Once, he'd controlled several towns, commanded hawks and leopards, walked with a gun slung over his shoulder. But in the United States, this outsized man had to tamp himself down. Racism had paralyzed him as surely as any stroke, robbed him of speech, deadened his arms and legs, stilled everything but his mind.

The truth is, though, that his illness was not a metaphor. Rather, it resulted from the dozens of malaria attacks and fevers he'd endured. Other veterans of Africa suffered similar fates, most notably Henry Morton Stanley. A survivor of over two hundred bouts of fever, he had succumbed to a paralyzing stroke at sixty-two, the same condition that would hit Sheppard, and at nearly the same age.

Stanley had died in a mansion, surrounded by forests and streams.

Though a rich man, he was considered in some circles to be without morals. The British press vilified him for the way he had stormed across Africa, shooting down native people, and whipping and chaining his own servants. Sheppard passed away in a modest house, and, according to his son Max, "he probably didn't have a quarter when he died." But almost everyone remembered him as a man with a heavenly sense of humor and a flamboyant generosity. According to Max, his father "always had candy for the kids; he always took bags of fruit with him to visit the sick at the hospital." In twenty years of wandering the African frontier, he had never shot at anyone, not even warriors who threatened to kill him.

Stanley and Sheppard couldn't have been more different from one another, but malaria did not recognize the moral shadings between newspaperman and missionary, did not care about one man's cruelty and the other's kindness. Nor did it observe any color lines. Death carried them away in the same slow locomotive, a train like the one that wound vertiginously along the Congo River, its narrow track surrounded by a litter of bones and teeth.

More than a thousand people had attended Sheppard's funeral in 1927. Telegrams from all over the country offered condolences to Lucy and the family.

Still, Sheppard's fame would fade almost as quickly as the sprays of camellias that perfumed the air beside his grave. It was an era when history books only recorded the doings of white men, when mainstream newspapers ignored or reviled people of color, when black American culture happened in the margins and on the sidelines. And so Sheppard fell into obscurity. Aside from manuscripts published by the Presbyterian Church, he did not begin to appear in history books until the 1960s.

But his legacy did survive among the people who'd loved him and in the places he'd visited—and Sheppard himself would have approved of the way his identity became intertwined with that of the Kuba. His alma mater, Hampton Institute, treasured the hundreds of pieces of African art that he had donated, a collection that became famous as one of the three great repositories of early Kuba artifacts in the world. Meanwhile, the Kuba themselves put Sheppard into their own version of a museum—the oral history they passed down from one generation to the next. As late as 1989, the Kuba could recite stories about how "Shepete" came to their country and made a pact with them. His legend endures in a country that, after years of strife and foreign rule, has changed its name back to Congo.

Epilogue

When William died in 1927, Lucy expanded into the empty space he'd left behind. She had held a job as a social worker since World War I, and she continued to make her rounds until she was almost seventy years old, employed by the government's Interdepartmental Social Hygiene Service as a caseworker. "It was my duty to keep young people off the streets at night, to visit dance halls and other places of amusement where conduct was apt to be questionable." Her way of speaking gives a sense of the starched, proper old woman she must have been.

And yet she remained compassionate. Her son, Max, remembered her as big-hearted—sometimes too big-hearted. After the Louisville flood of 1937, Lucy let ten or more people come to live in the brick house. Their chickens, too, were welcome.

By then, the widow of the famous explorer had become a celebrity in her own right. She'd made social calls to lonely prisoners and dragged sick people off the street and into City Hospital, brought food to the starving, and fixed up the homes of the poor. Her efforts earned her fame as a grand dame of Southern social work. She served on the board of the Colored Red Cross Hospital, became a sought-after speaker, and was the first black woman ever voted into the Presbyterian Kentucky Synod.

But Lucy considered her crowning achievement the house on East Breckenridge Street. Decades before, she and her mother, Eliza, had eked out a living in a hovel; Eliza had scrimped and starved to turn her daughter into a proper lady, or at least help her escape grinding poverty. And Lucy *had* escaped, but in the process had been forced to leave her mother alone in the United States, a woman in failing health who struggled to make a living as a maid. The guilt must have tortured Lucy.

And so she dreamed of installing her mother in a comfortable house, with family all around gathering for meals of steaming hot soup and biscuits, and doctors who'd come in the middle of the night.

"I had always longed to be able to make a home for my mother to re-pay her, in some measure, for her many sacrifices for me," Lucy wrote. On East Breckenridge Street, that dream came true. Eliza spent her last years there, presumably doted on by the daughter who adored her. It's not clear when she died.

The circumstances of Lucy's own passing have become hazy; rarely do any of the brief accounts of her life include a death date. The *Biographical Dictionary of Christian Missions* does give the date 1940, but follows it with a question mark.

Max Sheppard, the boy who'd been named for a Kuba prince, traveled through life with an unmistakable royal flair. The young man enrolled in the prestigious Art Institute of Chicago to study metalwork, though as an old man he confessed, "I didn't pursue my art as I should have—girls, you know. I was 19 years old." Still, his professors praised his work, and Max proved to be talented enough to make his living as a designer of jewelry and silverware. It was, perhaps, an unconscious echo of a Kuba tradition: Just as English princes would be trained to hunt foxes, Kuba princes were taught to become master blacksmiths and metalworkers.

Wilhelmina moved to California with her husband. In interviews, her family chose not to supply any more information about her than that.

Neither Max nor Wilhelmina had children, and so William Sheppard left no direct descendants in the United States. But he may very well have some in the Congo, because of Shepete. William Sheppard's illegitimate child grew up to carry on his father's work, at least in part, taking charge of the Presbyterian printing press in the Congo. The press itself was similar to the one on which Sheppard had published his famous article for the *Kasai Herald*. If Shepete has any direct descendants, they may still live in the vicinity of Luebo; they would have watched their country freed from Belgian rule, only to sink under the dictatorship of Sese Seko Mobutu; and, finally, to throw off that tyranny and struggle toward independence.

ACKNOWLEDGMENTS

I owe my greatest thanks to the friend who launched me on this expedition. Harvey Blume, my neighbor in Cambridge, wrote the book that inspired this one. In the beginning months of my research, Harvey loaned me papers that fueled my fascination with Sheppard. When I decided to write this book, he acted as my mentor, lavishing me with a graduate education in historiography.

I also owe a great debt to the archivists who helped dig through boxes full of Sheppard-nalia. At Hampton, Donzella Maupin guided me to obscure letters and manuscripts that filled in the blank spaces of this story. Diana Sanderson at the Presbyterian archive provided never-before-published photos. Tom Owen, at the University of Louisville, dropped all his work one afternoon to attend to my phone-called requests.

The Mesa Refuge artists colony generously provided two weeks of quiet and organic food. I am grateful for their support.

And as always, my tribe of friends supplied provocative conversation, manuscript editing, homegrown lettuce, a view of Mount Toby, rock-climbing gear, and lots of coffee. Thanks to Jon Bernhardt, Nadine Boughton, Scott Campbell, Liz Canner, Annie Harrison, Dennis Lombardi, Karen Propp, Lauren Slater, Sprax, and Karen Werner. My fabulously sweet mom never wavers in her support.

Thanks to the editors who pulled the manuscript into shape, Laurie Walsh and Sarah Manges. My agent, Kim Witherspoon, helped me transform a passion into a book proposal.

NOTES

INTRODUCTION

page

xiii   **"We saw a rain-maker"** William H. Sheppard, *Presbyterian Pioneers in Congo* (Richmond, Va.: Presbyterian Committee of Publication, 1917), p. 73.

xiii   **"Here is a history"** W. E. B. Du Bois, *The World and Africa: An Inquiry into the Part Which Africa Has Played in World History* (New York: International Publishers, 1965), p. viii.

xvii   **"The Edmistons were warmly welcomed"** Mary Dabney, *Light in Darkness* (Knoxville, Tenn.: [self-published], 1971), p. 2.

xviii   **he insisted African babies were born white** Sheppard, *Pioneers*, p. 124.

CHAPTER 1: "WHEN I GROW UP I SHALL GO *THERE*"

page

3   **"I felt as I never had"** Samuel N. Lapsley, *Life and Letters*, ed. J. W. Lapsley (Richmond, Va.: Whittet & Shepperson Printers, 1893), p. 25.

3   **"Judge Lapsley and his wife"** Sheppard, *Pioneers*, p. 19.

Notes

4 **had opposed the hiring** Stanley Shalloff, *Reform in King Leopold's Congo* (Richmond, Va.: John Knox Press, 1970), p. 18.

4 **"improbable years"** Lerone Bennett Jr., *Before the Mayflower: A History of Black America* (New York: Penguin, 1988), p. 216.

6 **Richmond mourned** *New York Times*, July 5, 1869, p. 5.

6 **The black delegates** Virginia Writers Project, *The Negro in Virginia* (New York: Arno Press and The New York Times, 1969), p. 230.

7 **a few had managed to rise out of poverty** Virginia Writers Project, p. 298.

7 **"I was afraid of him"** Arthur Ware, "Interview with Mr. Arthur Ware," interview by Dr. Larryetta Schall and Julia Vodicka, April 19, 1979, n.p.; Hampton University Archives, Hampton, Virginia.

7 **Few of his clients knew** Arthur Ware interview.

8 **"twenty-six years of age"** Register of Free Blacks, Augusta County, Va., 1810–1864.

8 **"never turned anyone from her door"** Sheppard, *Pioneers*, p. 15.

8 **"In a wee wooden schoolhouse"** W. E. B. Du Bois, *The Souls of Black Folk* (New York: Random House, 1994), p. 4.

9 **"always very kind to us"** Sheppard, *Pioneers*, p. 15.

10 **"In a back room"** Sheppard, *Pioneers*, p. 16.

10 **Booker T. Washington** Booker T. Washington, *Up from Slavery* (Boston: Western Islands, 1965), p. 54.

10 **"The first year I worked on the farm"** Sheppard, *Pioneers*, pp. 16–17.

11 **"One Sabbath afternoon"** Sheppard, *Pioneers*, p. 17.

11 **"I well remember"** William Sheppard, "Reminiscences of My Early Days at Stillman Institute," n.d.; Hampton University Archives.

12 **"He continued working"** Education Department, Executive Committee of Foreign Missions, Presbyterian Church, *William H. Sheppard: Pioneer Missionary to the Congo* (Nashville, Tenn., 1942), pamphlet, p. 8.

12 **"If you are called upon . . . ?"** Sheppard, *Pioneers*, p. 18.

13 **"I knew a few things"** Sheppard, *Pioneers*, p. 19.

13 **"evil gray eyes"** Michael McCarthy, *Dark Continent: Africa as Seen by Americans* (Westport, Conn.: Greenwood, 1983), p. 44.

13 **"It was in 1868"** Frank McLynn, *Hearts of Darkness: The European Exploration of Africa* (New York: Carroll & Graf, 1992), p. 148.

14 **"we and they must . . . deal"** Shalloff, *Reform in King Leopold's Congo*, p. 25.

14 **"One day [the young boy] was playing"** Education Department pamphlet, n.p.

Notes

15 **described such a tavern** James Weldon Johnson, *The Autobiography of an Ex-Colored Man* (New York: Dover, 1995), p. 26.

15 **By 1892, many blacks had fled** Shalloff, p. 14.

15 **He received only polite refusals** Sheppard, *Pioneers*, p. 18.

16 **"I like the black folks"** Lapsley, *Life and Letters*, p. 201.

16 **At first, he shook with stage fright** Lapsley, p. 13.

16 **"a Russian . . . captain"** Lapsley, p. 83. It is Adam Hochschild, in *King Leopold's Ghost*, who suggests that the Russian steamship captain mentioned in Lapsley's diary is probably Conrad.

17 **In his early twenties** Lapsley, pp. 18–19.

CHAPTER 2: THE SILK TOP HAT

page

19 **"If a man acts the gentleman"** Lapsley, *Life and Letters*, p. 27.

19 **"It is strange"** Lapsley, p. 27.

20 **"They spared no pains"** Sheppard, *Pioneers*, 20.

20 **"As to Sheppard"** Lapsley, p. 34.

20 **"Sheppard, Dr. Matthews and I"** Lapsley, p. 38.

20 **"He took a jaunt"** Lapsley, p. 34.

20 **"He is very modest"** Lapsley, p. 34.

22 **"[Sheppard] intentionally refrained"** Julia Lake Kellersburger, *Lucy Gantt Sheppard: Shepherdess of His Sheep on Two Continents* (Atlanta: PCUA Committee on Women's Work, n.d.), p. 9.

24 **Lapsley had landed an interview** Lapsley, p. 42.

24 **"If you go to the king"** Lapsley, p. 45.

24 **regretted that he could not complete the outfit** Lapsley, p. 45.

24 **Sanford lost his job** Joseph A. Fry, *Henry S. Sanford: Diplomacy and Business in Nineteenth Century America* (Reno: University of Nevada Press, 1982), pp. 15–16.

24 **"a close-buttoned swallowtail [coat]"** Fry, pp. 67–68.

25 **"Gus Hall's shoes"** Lapsley, p. 45.

25 **a friendly voice** Lapsley, p. 43.

26 **"I quite forgot"** Lapsley, p. 44.

26 **Lapsley marveled** Lapsley, p. 42.

27 **King Leopold II** Adam Hochschild, *King Leopold's Ghost: A Story of Greed, Terror, and Heroism in Colonial Africa* (Boston: Houghton Mifflin, 1998).

27 the "African cake" . . . seemed the most luscious Hochschild, *King Leopold's Ghost*, p. 58.

28 the king hosted a Geographical Conference Hochschild, *King Leopold's Ghost*, pp. 44–45.

28 stations popped up Hochschild, *King Leopolds's Ghost*, pp. 65–66.

28 At the Berlin Conference of 1884–85 Thomas Parkman, *The Scramble for Africa: The White Man's Conquest of the Dark Continent from 1876 to 1912* New York: Random House, 1991), p. 239.

28 Prince Bismarck Parkman, p. 241.

29 He now controlled Phillips Verner Bradford and Harvey Blume, *Ota Benga: The Pygmy in the Zoo* (New York: Dell, 1992), p. 34.

29 At midnight, the ship anchored Lapsley, p. 52.

30 "half-clad Africans" Lapsley, pp. 52–53.

30 "Mr. Lapsley called" Sheppard, *Pioneers*, p. 21.

30 he'd seen officers Fry, p. 169; and John Hope Franklin, *George Washington Williams: A Biography* (Chicago: University of Chicago Press, 1985), p. 194.

CHAPTER 3: THIRTY-SIX HIPPOS

page

33 "Women are imported" Franklin, *George Washington Williams*, pp. 248, 251.

33 Leopold was famous for humanitarian efforts Franklin, p. 216.

34 "Who is Mr. Williams?" Franklin, pp. 211–12.

34 even the white press had to acknowledge Franklin, pp. 116, 117.

34 "eat their rice" Franklin, p. 247.

35 To rule the Congo Franklin, p. 194.

35 "Thinking this was all" Sheppard, *Pioneers*, p. 22.

36 "When you are waked" Lapsley, *Life and Letters*, pp. 56–57.

36 "I came upon a boiler" Joseph Conrad, *Heart of Darkness*, critical edition, ed. Robert Kimbrough (New York: W. W. Norton, 1988), p. 19.

36 "Black shapes crouched" Conrad, pp. 20–21.

37 Estimates for the death toll Hochschild, *King Leopold's Ghost*, p. 171.

37 "These imported workmen" Lapsley, p. 58.

37 "Sheppard preached" Lapsley, p. 58.

38 they heard a chilling story Sheppard, *Pioneers*, p. 60.

38 "Emaciated by deadly fevers" Sheppard, *Pioneers*, p. 61.

38 **shared a room with Roger Casement** Hochschild, *King Leopold's Ghost*, p. 196.

38 **"Today fell into a muddy puddle"** Conrad, p. 162.

39 **they began their journey** Lapsley, p. 65.

40 **"He explained with much excitement"** Sheppard, *Pioneers*, p. 32.

40 **Williams . . . had little appreciation** Conrad, p. 94.

40 **"it was . . . their mode of mourning"** Sheppard, *Pioneers*, p. 33.

40 **"make frights of themselves"** Lapsley, p. 87.

41 **"the evil lives of white men"** Lapsley, p. 92.

42 **"he was an accomplished physician"** Samuel Verner, *Pioneering in Central Africa* (Richmond, Va.: Presbyterian Committee of Publication, 1903), p. 70.

42 **He ran his mission** Lapsley, p. 83. Hochschild is the one who suggested that the Russian steamship captain mentioned in Lapsley's diary is probably Conrad.

42 **Sims . . . seems to have been a great favorite** Lapsley, p. 76.

42 **"I was delighted"** Sheppard, *Pioneers*, p. 35.

43 **"I raised my rifle"** Sheppard, *Pioneers*, pp. 35–36.

44 **"You men are too timid"** Sheppard, *Pioneers*, p. 38.

44 **"We enjoyed a hearty supper"** Sheppard, *Pioneers*, p. 39.

44 **taught him to have deep respect** Sheppard, *Pioneers*, p. 39.

44 **Sheppard squeezed off a shot** Sheppard, *Pioneers*, p. 41.

45 **George Grenfell's station in Bolobo** Lapsley, p. 78.

45 **"We can kill you all when we like"** Lapsley, p. 81.

45 **"bold, free, good as anybody"** Lapsley, p. 76.

46 **"I wonder what [Williams] would say"** Franklin, p. 194.

46 **"It seems as if"** Lapsley, p. 82.

46 **"the Bateke think"** Lapsley, p. 83.

CHAPTER 4: UNRAVELING RIVERS

page

47 **"as cream and strawberry juice"** Lapsley, *Life and Letters*, p. 113.

48 **"Sheppard is a most handy fellow"** Lapsley, p. 94.

48 **"[It's a] bad habit"** Lapsley, p. 120.

48 **"I think of the dreadful fire"** Lapsley, p. 99.

48   they met Queen N'gankabe Lapsley, p. 100.

49   "A big storm came that night" Lapsley, p. 101.

49   Sheppard . . . bagged a hippo Lapsley, p. 101.

49   Hippo meat was currency here Lapsley, p. 104.

50   "Gentlemen" Lapsley, pp. 112–13.

50   "finding shelter on Sheppard's shoulder" Lapsley, p. 96.

50   "such a hubbub!" Lapsley, p. 109.

51   "These people" Lapsley, p. 110.

51   two emaciated men Sheppard, *Pioneers*, p. 48.

51   "[It's] Friday today" Lapsley, p. 116.

52   "I can see the pillars of smoke" Lapsley, p. 124.

52   "We told [him] that we had come back" Lapsley, p. 125.

53   this brush-off was a terrible disappointment Lapsley, p. 125.

53   "Who are these Mundele . . . ?" Lapsley, p. 126.

53   saw more evidence of destruction Lapsley, p. 127.

54   "a hurricane which passed through the countryside" Adam Hochschild, "Mr. Kurtz, I Presume," *New Yorker*, April 14, 1997, p. 41.

54   We'll only have a small allowance for luggage Lapsley, p. 136.

55   found himself humming a snatch of a hymn Lapsley, p. 137.

55   "The captain called me to the wheel house" Sheppard, *Pioneers*, p. 53.

56   "Chicot is a strip of hippo hide" Lapsley, p. 143.

57   "I shall go mad" Lapsley, p. 144.

57   "having lost all control of his temper" Lapsley, pp. 156–57.

58   "The whole country was filled with palm trees" Sheppard, *Pioneers*, p. 61.

59   surrounded by people and yet alone Sheppard, *Pioneers*, p. 62.

CHAPTER 5: CHOOSING THE KUBA

page

61   "Mr. Lapsley's gold watch" Sheppard, *Pioneers*, p. 77.

62   "There must be something in the appearance" McLynn, *Hearts of Darkness*, p. 321.

63   their own ideas about the universe Sheppard, *Pioneers*, p. 77.

63   Sheppard mixed easily with the Kete Sheppard, *Pioneers*, p. 67.

63   they excelled Sheppard, *Pioneers*, p. 72.

63   "The people had their judges" Sheppard, *Pioneers*, p. 72.

Notes

64 **Photos show him** From photos at the Hampton University Archives and the Presbyterian Historical Society, Montreat, North Carolina. Most were undated, and many may be from later periods, but probably give the sense of what Sheppard was like during his first years in Africa.

64 **"In the early morning"** Lapsley, *Life and Letters*, p. 184.

64 **"the moon and star light"** Sheppard, *Pioneers*, p. 63.

64 **a letter to Dr. Henkel** The letter is in the Hampton University Archives.

65 **"[Their] dances"** Lapsley, p. 187.

65 **"We had hoped to find"** Robert Bennedetto, ed., *Presbyterian Reformers in Central Africa: A Documentary Account of the American Presbyterian Congo Mission and the Human Rights Struggle in the Congo, 1890–1918* (Leiden: E. J. Brill, 1996), p. 101.

66 **"I haven't been able"** Lapsley, p. 198.

66 **"As for castor oil"** Sheppard, *Pioneers*, p. 67.

67 **The mother refused** Lapsley, p. 175.

68 **"The two ex-cannibals"** Lapsley, p. 117.

68 **"So fond of her sweetheart"** Lapsley, p. 180.

68 **it pleased him** Lapsley, p. 176.

68 **"the finest people about"** Lapsley, p. 173.

69 **Sheppard tells the grisly tale in full** Sheppard, *Pioneers*, p. 65.

69 **"In this awful hot-bed of corruption"** Lapsley, p. 183.

70 **towered over the other Africans** Lapsley, p. 193.

70 **"Very proud, don't take insults"** Lapsley, p. 192.

70 **had tried to reach the kingdom and had failed** William Sheppard, "Into the Heart of Africa," *Southern Workman*, Dec. 1893, pp. 182–87.

70 **their language included a word** Jan Vansina, *The Children of Woot: A History of the Kuba Peoples* (Madison: University of Wisconsin Press, 1978), p. 168.

71 **"strange and strong people"** Sheppard, *Pioneers*, p. 74.

71 **"a lake was discovered"** Sheppard, *Pioneers*, p. 74.

71 **"The isolation from Christian influences"** Lapsley, p. 203.

71 **Lapsley was elated** Lapsley, p. 191.

72 **"growing quite wild"** Lapsley, p. 192.

72 **"the two white men"** Lapsley, p. 192.

72 **started out as pale as fly grubs** Sheppard, *Pioneers*, p. 70.

72 **"While he was away"** William Sheppard, "Founders Day Speech," n.p.; Hampton University Archives.

73 **dined on roasted bees** Lapsley, p. 213.

Notes

73   "beaten with rods" Lapsley, p. 212.

73   "You are my children now" Lapsley, p. 215.

74   "All along the route" Sheppard, *Pioneers*, p. 80.

74   "Sheppard, how are you?" Sheppard, *Pioneers*, p. 80.

74   "I could not refrain" Sheppard, *Pioneers*, p. 80.

74   "seventeen men" Lapsley, p. 216.

75   ex-slaves and refugees began to show up Sheppard, *Pioneers*, p. 81.

75   "Goodbye, Sheppard" Sheppard, *Pioneers*, p. 86.

76   "I come down to my seat" Lapsley, p. 218.

76   "a poor soldier" Lapsley, p. 221.

77   "The twitching of the eye" Sheppard, *Pioneers*, p. 83.

78   "They were not hard to entertain" Sheppard, "Into the Heart of Africa," p. 183.

78   "Where is Mr. Lapsley?" Sheppard, "Into the Heart of Africa," p. 183.

78   "My heart became giddy" Sheppard, *Pioneers*, p. 84.

78   "N'tomenjila will come no more" Sheppard, "Into the Heart of Africa," p. 183.

79   "I had good hopes of his recovery" Winifred K. Vass and Lachlan C. Vass, *The Lapsley Saga* (Franklin, Tenn.: Providence House, 1977), p. 51.

79   "to pour out my soul's great grief" Sheppard, *Pioneers*, p. 84.

79   "Dear Mrs. Lapsley" Sheppard, *Pioneers*, pp. 85–86.

CHAPTER 6: BECOMING BOPE MEKABE

page

81   "If one behaves as a gentleman" Ruth Slade, *King Leopold's Congo* (London: Oxford University Press, 1962), p. 22.

83   he and his men packed up and headed . . . into the jungle Sheppard, "Into the Heart of Africa." Some of the time sequences and details in this account differ from the version of the story Sheppard wrote up twenty years later in his autobiography. Whenever the accounts disagreed, I have favored the earlier version.

84   "I slipped out of the village quietly" Sheppard, "Into the Heart of Africa," p. 184.

84   "I knew we couldn't dispose of all that food" Sheppard, "Into the Heart of Africa," p. 184.

85   "Day after day" Sheppard, "Into the Heart of Africa," p. 184.

85 **Once, Sheppard had to gobble thirty** William E. Phipps, *The Sheppards and Lapsley: Pioneer Presbyterians in the Congo* (Louisville, Ky.: Presbyterian Church, 1991), p. 43.

85 **"I was delighted"** Sheppard, *Pioneers*, p. 90.

85 **carrying a spear and wearing a loincloth** Sheppard, *Pioneers*, p. 95.

86 **"Follow those men's tracks"** Sheppard, *Pioneers*, p. 95.

86 **"If the king hears"** Sheppard, "Into the Heart of Africa," p. 184.

87 **"Now hear the words of [the king]"** Sheppard, *Pioneers*, p. 99.

87 **"The chief of this village"** Sheppard, *Pioneers*, p. 100.

88 **"You are a foreigner . . . ?"** Sheppard, "Into the Heart of Africa," p. 185.

89 **"All men wore the kilt"** Emil Torday, *On the Trail of the Bashongo: An Account of a Remarkable & Hitherto Unknown African People, Their Origin, Art, High Social & Political Organization & Culture, Derived from the Author's Personal Experience Amongst Them* (New York: Negro Universities Press, 1969), pp. 111–12.

89 **"You need not try"** Sheppard, "Into the Heart of Africa," p. 185.

90 **"Festoons of moss"** Sheppard, *Pioneers*, p. 102

90 **"Stepping out of a lovely grove"** Torday, *On the Trail of the Bashongo*, pp. 80–81.

91 **"A comparison with Japan"** Torday, pp. 118–19.

92 **Sheppard . . . bowed and clapped** Sheppard, *Pioneers*, p. 107.

92 **"the king leaned over"** Sheppard, *Pioneers*, pp. 107–8.

92 **"They knew me better than I knew myself"** Sheppard, *Pioneers*, p. 101.

93 **"I was rather careful"** Sheppard, "Into the Heart of Africa," p. 187.

94 **"their knowledge . . . was the highest"** Sheppard, *Pioneers*, p. 137.

94 **"Lord Mountmorres states"** H. H. Johnston, *George Grenfell and the Congo* (London: Hutchinson, 1908), p. 507.

94 **These accoutrements spoke volumes** Vansina, *Children of Woot*, pp. 132–33.

95 **"Isambula N'Genga did not look down"** Torday, p. 82.

95 **the Kuba learned to carve** Vansina, p. 183.

95 **a game . . . that resembled a checkerboard** Sheppard, *Pioneers*, p. 112.

95 **the entire town went dark** Sheppard, *Pioneers*, p. 117.

96 **"A young man sees a girl"** Sheppard, *Pioneers*, p. 123.

96 **He praised the Kuba** Sheppard, *Pioneers*, p. 124.

96 **"[A man named] Nnyminym"** Sheppard, *Pioneers*, pp. 135–36.

97 **"A child died suddenly in the town"** Sheppard, "Into the Heart of Africa," p. 186.

98 **Sheppard confronted the king** Sheppard, *Pioneers*, p. 131.

Notes

99   **"It is true, King"** Sheppard, *Pioneers*, p. 129.

99   **"it is the only one I have"** Sheppard, "Into the Heart of Africa," p. 186.

100   **he asked the king point-blank** Sheppard, "Into the Heart of Africa," p. 186.

100   **"I told [the king]"** Sheppard, *Pioneers*, p. 140.

101   **He carried so many artifacts** Sheppard, *Pioneers*, p. 138.

101   **"The parting with King Lukenga was touching"** Sheppard, *Pioneers*, p. 140.

101   **"When I tried to tell them"** Sheppard, *Pioneers*, pp. 142–43.

CHAPTER 7: THE WEDDING DRESS IN THE COFFIN

page

105   **"The long fingers"** Kellersberger, *Lucy Gantt Sheppard*, p. 6.

106   **"Was it not enough . . . ?"** National Portrait Gallery, *David Livingstone and the Victorian Encounter with Africa* (London: National Portrait Gallery Publications, 1996), p. 183.

106   **"There are regrets"** National Portrait Gallery, p. 50.

107   **"[I] very much desired"** Lucy Sheppard, "A Daughter of the Morning," interview by Lucien V. Rule, 1941, n.p.; Hampton University Archives.

107   **She performed at graduation every year** Kellersberger, *Lucy Gantt Sheppard*, p. 7.

110   **"Perhaps they got their civilization"** Sheppard, "Into the Heart of Africa," p. 187.

110   **"The victim's hands and feet are bound"** Sheppard, "Into the Heart of Africa," p. 184.

111   **"He will remove his robe"** Bernth Lindfors, ed., *Africans on Stage: Studies in Ethnological Show Business* (Bloomington: Indiana University Press), p. 149.

112   **"The man who did these things"** Kellersberger, *Lucy Gantt Sheppard*, p. 10.

112   **Mr. Adamson bought supplies with a bad check** Shalloff, *Reform in King Leopold's Congo*, pp. 37–38.

112   **He picked Africa** Bennedetto, *Presbyterian Reformers*, p. 137.

113   **"Her feminine instincts"** Kellersberger, *Lucy Gantt Sheppard*, p. 11.

115   **"It forces me to be overseer"** Bennedetto, p. 102.

116   **"Mrs. Snyder often said"** From a letter in the Lucy Sheppard file, Presbyterian Historical Society.

116   **"I called it the *Ladies Home Journal* house"** Kellersberger, *Lucy Gantt Sheppard*, pp. 18–19.

Notes

117 **"We did have two pretty little leopards"** Julia Lake Kellersberger, *A Life for the Congo: The Story of Althea Brown Edmiston* (New York: Fleming H. Revell Co., 1957), p. 60.

119 **"Africa became as familiar to me"** Verner, *Pioneering in Central Africa*, p. 6.

120 **"The land which all the nations of history"** Verner, p. 3.

120 **"second-class missionaries"** John R. Crawford, "The Instructive Missionary Career of S. P. Verner," n.d., p. 16; Hampton University Archives.

120 **"Sheppati!"** This spelling of Sheppard's name (as he was called by the Africans) is quoted from Verner's papers. The usual spelling is "Sheppate."

120 **"A large, well-built man"** Verner, p. 95.

121 **"a long house"** Verner, p. 95.

121 **"It was wonderful"** Verner, p. 119.

122 **"walks down the street"** Bradford and Blume, *Ota Benga*, p. 76.

122 **"It was the historic Fourth of July"** Verner, p. 209.

123 **did not sleep a wink that night** Verner, p. 213.

123 **The next day** Verner, p. 216.

123 **"We approached a small low sandy island"** Verner, p. 219.

124 **"My faith was surely needing"** Verner, p. 224.

CHAPTER 8: A BASKET OF HANDS

page

126 **"He is so much like dear Mr. Lapsley"** Kellersberger, *Lucy Gantt Sheppard*, p. 20.

127 **"a nasty piggish lot of fellows"** Bennedetto, *Presbyterian Reformers*, p. 108.

127 **"We sailed from Antwerp"** Bennedetto, p. 105.

132 **"The Zappo-Zaps, the cannibals"** William Sheppard, "Light in Darkest Africa," *Southern Workman*, April 1905, p. 220.

132 **"take a rope and . . . hang myself"** William Sheppard, "Light in Darkest Africa," p. 220.

133 **Morrison ordered him** William Sheppard, "Light in Darkest Africa," p. 220.

134 **Fromont planned** Bennedetto, p. 152.

134 **"I told [Fromont]"** Bennedetto, pp. 152–53.

134 **"When [the officer] saw that I was in earnest"** Bennedetto, p. 153.

135 **"These were orders"** Sheppard, "Light in Darkest Africa," p. 221.

Notes

136   **"Everybody had gone!"** Sheppard, "Light in Darkest Africa," p. 221.

136   **a man stumbled out of the forest** William Sheppard diary, Sept. 14, 1899, p. 1; Hampton University Archives.

137   **"At a curve in the forest"** William Sheppard diary, p. 3.

138   **They came at Sheppard** Bennedetto, p. 121.

139   **"I said very little"** Sheppard, "Light in Darkest Africa," p. 224.

141'   **He recorded one of these interviews** Bennedetto, pp. 122–23.

143   **the last entry** Bennedetto, p. 124.

143   **"You have sent me"** Sheppard, "Light in Darkest Africa," p. 225.

145   **"hair daubed with paint"** Kellersberger, *Lucy Gantt Sheppard*, p. 24.

CHAPTER 9: TO TELL THE WORLD

page

148   **"story [was] so appalling"** E. D. Morel, *History of the Congo Reform Movement*, ed. Roger William Louis and Jean Stengers (Oxford: Clarendon, 1968), p. 29.

149   **"I propose tonight"** Bennedetto, *Presbyterian Reformers*, p. 158.

149   **"No one could look"** Morel, pp. 125–26.

150   **"Thieves, liars and witches"** "Ordered the King to Stop," *Richmond (Va.) Times-Dispatch*, Feb. 19, 1904.

151   **"When . . . Sheppard wished"** Kellersberger, *A Life for the Congo*, p. 57.

152   **"Coming in the Mission"** Kellersberger, *A Life for the Congo*, pp. 58–59.

152   **"A lady [from Waynesboro]"** Phipps, *The Sheppards and Lapsley*, p. 2.

154   **One photo shows him** The photos are in the Hampton University Archives.

155   **"The first thing he would look for"** Max Sheppard, "Max Sheppard Interview," interview by Dr. Larryetta Schall and Julia Vodicka, May 13, 1980, p. 4.

156   **"there were no theatres"** Henry Adams, *The Education of Henry Adams* (New York: Modern Library, 1931), p. 256.

157   **"I was . . . able to ascertain"** Bennedetto, p. 197.

159   **"Sheppard and his [black] colleagues"** Walter L. Williams, *Black Americans and the Evangelization of Africa 1877–1900* (Madison: University of Wisconsin Press, 1982), p. 28.

160   **"His experiences have been even more thrilling"** "Interested Audience Heard Rev. Dr. Sheppard at First Presbyterian Church Sunday," *Charlotte (W. Va.) Daily Mail*, Feb. 12, 1906; Hampton University Archives.

Notes

161 **"Being a colored man"** Lachlan Vass to Henry Hawkins, June 21, 1905: Presbyterian Historical Society.

161 **"on account of the social hatred"** Shalloff, *Reform in King Leopold's Congo*, p. 111.

163 **The ensuing media blitz** Hochschild, *King Leopold's Ghost*, p. 248.

CHAPTER 10: RUBBER HARVEST

page

165 **"[The boat] whirled so fast"** "Down Congo in a Chair," *Richmond (Va.) Times-Dispatch*, Feb. 25, 1904; Hampton University Archives.

166 **"Suddenly in the distance"** Kellersberger, *A Life for the Congo*, p. 69.

166 **"There must have been five hundred of us"** Kellersberger, *A Life for the Congo*, p. 70.

168 **"We are not now suffering"** Thomas Vinson, *William McCutchan Morrison: Twenty Years in Central Africa* (Richmond, Va.: Presbyterian Committee of Publication, 1921), pp. 75–76.

168 **"looked bare and ugly"** Torday, *On the Trail of the Bashongo*, p. 111.

169 **"I am old"** Torday, pp. 161–62.

169 **"I made up my mind"** Torday, p. 148.

169 **"The common people"** Torday, p. 150.

171 **"These great stalwart men and women"** Bennedetto, *Presbyterian Reformers*, pp. 281–82.

171 **"You see this white man?"** Hochschild, *King Leopold's Ghost*, p. 262.

172 **"[sullying] the respectability"** Shalloff, p. 115.

173 **"Sheppard and I prefer"** Bennedetto, p. 383.

173 **"I hope Morrison may be put into prison,"** Shalloff, p. 129.

173 **"Morrison in the dock"** Shalloff, p. 180.

173 **"Long residence amongst the natives"** Emile Vandervelde, "Belgium and the Reforms on the Congo," *Contemporary Review*, Vol. XCVI, Dec. 1909, p. 653.

CHAPTER 11: THE TRIAL

page

177 **"I am living up in the upper end room"** Bennedetto, *Presbyterian Reformers*, p. 379.

179   "She got her husband" Lapsley, *Life and Letters*, p. 179.

181   "To my horror" Sheppard, *Pioneers*, p. 92.

181   "the twitching of the eye" Sheppard, *Pioneers*, p. 83.

182   "no little concern" Shalloff, *Reform in King Leopold's Congo*, p. 119.

183   "tools in the hands of . . . evil men" Janet Polasky, *The Democratic Socialism of Emile Vandervelde* (Oxford: Berg, 1995), p. 76.

185   "This lawsuit" Bennedetto, p. 388.

185   "His speech was a marvel of eloquence" Bennedetto, p. 405.

186   "Throw up your hat!" Bennedetto, p. 417.

186   a headline in the Boston Herald "American Negro Hero of Congo," *Boston Herald*, date and page not recorded on clipping; Hampton University Archives.

CHAPTER 12: THE CHILDREN'S FRIEND

page

190   "Sometime in the years 1898–1899" Bennedetto, pp. 424–25.

192   "Things have been hushed up too much" Lachlan Vass to Samuel Chester, June 1, 1910; Presbyterian Historical Society.

193   "He broke down and confessed" Bennedetto, p. 424.

194   "we . . . had a little home" Kellersberger, *Lucy Gantt Sheppard*, p. 27.

195   Within his first year there Phipps, *The Sheppards and Lapsley*, p. 119.

195   "had them crying" Max Sheppard, "Max Sheppard Interview," interview by Dr. Larryetta Schall and Julia Vodicka, May 13, 1980, p. 3.

196   "Father wore three hats" Max Sheppard interview, p. 3.

197   "a little pickaninny" Phipps, p. 121.

197   "probably the greatest Negro of his generation" *Atlanta News*, March 4, 1905; Hampton University Archives.

199   "A habit she never got out of" Arthur Ware, "Interview with Arthur Ware," interview by Dr. Larryetta Schall and Julia Vodicka, April 19, 1979, p. 2.

199   "tall and portly" Arthur Ware interview, p. 2.

200   "always had candy for the kids" Max Sheppard interview, p. 3.

201   the Kuba could recite stories Phipps, p. 69.

Notes

EPILOGUE

page

203   "It was my duty" Kellersberger, *Lucy Gantt Sheppard*, p. 27.

203   **Her son, Max, remembered her as big-hearted** Max Sheppard interview, p. 1.

204   "I had always longed" Kellersberger, *Lucy Gantt Sheppard*, p. 27.

204   "I didn't pursue my art as I should have" Max Sheppard interview, p. 4.

BIBLIOGRAPHY

Bedinger, Robert Dabney. *Triumphs of the Gospel in the Belgian Congo*. Richmond: Presbyterian Committee of Publication, 1920.

Bennedetto, Robert, ed. *Presbyterian Reformers in Central Africa: A Documentary Account of the American Presbyterian Congo Mission and the Human Rights Struggle in the Congo, 1890–1918*. Leiden: E. J. Brill, 1996.

Bennett, Lerone, Jr. *Before the Mayflower: A History of Black America*. New York: Penguin, 1988.

Bradford, Phillips Verner, and Harvey Blume. *Ota Benga: The Pygmy in the Zoo*. New York: Dell, 1992.

Conrad, Joseph. *Heart of Darkness*. Critical edition. Edited by Robert Kimbrough. New York: W. W. Norton, 1988.

Dabney, Mary. *Light in Darkness*. Knoxville, Tenn.: [self-published], 1971.

Du Bois, W. E. B. *The Souls of Black Folk*. New York: Random House, 1994.

———. *The World and Africa: An Inquiry into the Part Which Africa Has Played in World History*. New York: International Publishers, 1965.

Franklin, John Hope. *George Washington Williams: A Biography*. Chicago: University of Chicago Press, 1985.

Fry, Joseph A. *Henry S. Sanford: Diplomacy and Business in Nineteenth Century America*. Reno: University of Nevada Press, 1982.

Hochschild, Adam. *King Leopold's Ghost: A Story of Greed, Terrorism, and Heroism in Colonial Africa*. Boston: Houghton Mifflin, 1998.

Bibliography

———. "Mr. Kurtz, I Presume." *New Yorker,* April 14, 1997.

Johnson, James Weldon. *The Autobiography of an Ex-Colored Man.* New York: Dover, 1995.

Johnston, H. H. *George Grenfell and the Congo.* London: Hutchinson, 1908.

Kellersberger, Julia Lake. *A Life for the Congo: The Story of Althea Brown Edmiston.* New York: Fleming H. Revell Co., 1957.

———. *Lucy Gantt Sheppard: Shepherdess of His Sheep on Two Continents.* Atlanta: PCUA Committee on Women's Work, n.d.

Lapsley, Samuel N. *Life and Letters.* Edited by J. W. Lapsley. Richmond, Va.: Whittet & Sheperson Printers, 1893.

Lindfors, Bernth, et al. *Africans on Stage: Studies in Ethnological Show Business.* Bloomington: Indiana Univeristy Press, 1999.

McCarthy, Michael. *Dark Continent: Africa as Seen by Americans.* Westport, Conn.: Greenwood, 1983.

McLynn, Frank. *Hearts of Darkness: The European Exploration of Africa.* New York: Carroll & Graf, 1983.

Morel, E. D. *History of the Congo Reform Movement.* Edited by Roger William Louis and Jean Stengers. Oxford: Clarendon, 1968.

National Portrait Gallery. *David Livingstone and the Victorian Encounter with Africa.* London: National Portrait Gallery Publications, 1996.

Parkman, Thomas. *The Scramble for Africa: The White Man's Conquest of the Dark Continent from 1876 to 1912.* New York: Random House, 1991.

Phipps, William E. *The Sheppards and Lapsley: Pioneer Presbyterians in the Congo.* Louisville, Ky.: Presbyterian Church, 1991.

Polasky, Janet. *The Democratic Socialism of Emile Vandervelde.* Oxford: Berg, 1995.

Shalloff, Stanley. *Reform in King Leopold's Congo.* Richmond, Va.: John Knox Press, 1970.

Sheppard, William H. *Presbyterian Pioneers in Congo.* Richmond, Va.: Presbyterian Committtee of Publication, 1917.

———. "Light in Darkest Africa." *Southern Workman,* April 1905.

———. "Into the Heart of Africa." *Southern Workman,* Dec. 1893.

Slade, Ruth. *King Leopold's Congo.* London: Oxford University Press, 1962.

Torday, Emil. *On the Trail of the Bashongo: An Account of a Remarkable & Hitherto Unknown African People, Their Origin, Art, High Social & Political Organiza- tion & Culture, Derived from the Author's Personal Experience Amongst Them.* New York: Negro Universities Press, 1969.

Vandervelde, Emile. "Belgium and the Reforms on the Congo." *Contemporary Re- view,* Vol. XCVI, Dec. 1909.

Bibliography

Vansina, Jan. *The Children of Woot: A History of the Kuba Peoples.* Madison: University of Wisconsin Press, 1978.

Vass, Winifred K. and Lachlan C. Vass. *The Lapsley Saga.* Franklin, Tenn.: Providence House Publishers, 1977.

Verner, Samuel. *Pioneering in Central Africa.* Richmond, Va.: Presbyterian Committee of Publication, 1903.

Vinson, Thomas. *William McCutchan Morrison: Twenty Years in Central Africa.* Richmond, Va.: Presbyterian Committee of Publication, 1921.

Virginia Writers Project. *The Negro in Virginia.* New York: Arno Press and The New York Times, 1969.

Washington, Booker T. *Up from Slavery.* Boston: Western Islands, 1965.

Williams, Walter L. *Black Americans and the Evangelization of Africa 1877–1900.* Madison: University of Wisconsin Press, 1982.

ARCHIVES

Hampton University Archives, Hampton, Virginia

Hampton has an extensive collection of photographs, correspondence, and clippings related to William Sheppard. Many of the obscure newspaper articles referred to in *Black Livingstone* were drawn from the collection. In addition, Hampton provided the interviews with Lucy Sheppard, Max Sheppard, and Arthur Ware.

Presbyterian Historical Society, Montreat, North Carolina

This archive supplied most of the photographs for this book, many of which were drawn from the Sheppard family album. In addition, the archive houses extensive correspondence between missionaries and Presbyterian leaders in the United States.

University of Louisville Archive, Louisville, Kentucky

This archive contains an unpublished memoir by John Little.

INDEX

Index

Index

Index

Index

Index

Index

Index

FOR THE BEST IN PAPERBACKS, LOOK FOR THE

In every corner of the world, on every subject under the sun, Penguin represents quality and variety—the very best in publishing today.

For complete information about books available from Penguin—including Penguin Classics, Penguin Compass, and Puffins—and how to order them, write to us at the appropriate address below. Please note that for copyright reasons the selection of books varies from country to country.

In the United States: Please write to *Penguin Putnam Inc., P.O. Box 12289 Dept. B, Newark, New Jersey 07101-5289* or call 1-800-788-6262.

In the United Kingdom: Please write to *Dept. EP, Penguin Books Ltd, Bath Road, Harmondsworth, West Drayton, Middlesex UB7 0DA.*

In Canada: Please write to *Penguin Books Canada Ltd, 10 Alcorn Avenue, Suite 300, Toronto, Ontario M4V 3B2.*

In Australia: Please write to *Penguin Books Australia Ltd, P.O. Box 257, Ringwood, Victoria 3134.*

In New Zealand: Please write to *Penguin Books (NZ) Ltd, Private Bag 102902, North Shore Mail Centre, Auckland 10.*

In India: Please write to *Penguin Books India Pvt Ltd, 11 Panchsheel Shopping Centre, Panchsheel Park, New Delhi 110 017.*

In the Netherlands: Please write to *Penguin Books Netherlands bv, Postbus 3507, NL-1001 AH Amsterdam.*

In Germany: Please write to *Penguin Books Deutschland GmbH, Metzlerstrasse 26, 60594 Frankfurt am Main.*

In Spain: Please write to *Penguin Books S. A., Bravo Murillo 19, 1° B, 28015 Madrid.*

In Italy: Please write to *Penguin Italia s.r.l., Via Benedetto Croce 2, 20094 Corsico, Milano.*

In France: Please write to *Penguin France, Le Carré Wilson, 62 rue Benjamin Baillaud, 31500 Toulouse.*

In Japan: Please write to *Penguin Books Japan Ltd, Kaneko Building, 2-3-25 Koraku, Bunkyo-Ku, Tokyo 112.*

In South Africa: Please write to *Penguin Books South Africa (Pty) Ltd, Private Bag X14, Parkview, 2122 Johannesburg.*